MADHYAMAKA SCHOOLS IN INDIA

MADHYAMAKA SCHOOLS IN INDIA

A Study of the Madhyamaka Philosophy and of the Division of the System into the Prāsaṅgika and Svātantrika Schools

PETER DELLA SANTINA

MOTILAL BANARSIDASS PUBLISHERS
PRIVATE LIMITED • DELHI

First Edition: Delhi, 1986
Reprint: Delhi, 1995

ISBN: 81-208-0153-9

Also available at:

MOTILAL BANARSIDASS

41 U.A. Bungalow Road, Jawahar Nagar, Delhi 110 007
120 Royapettah High Road, Mylapore, Madras 600 004
16 St. Mark's Road, Bangalore 560 001
Ashok Rajpath, Patna 800 004
Chowk, Varanasi 221 001

PRINTED IN INDIA

BY JAINENDRA PRAKASH JAIN AT SHRI JAINENDRA PRESS,
A-45 NARAINA, PHASE I, NEW DELHI 110 028
AND PUBLISHED BY NARENDRA PRAKASH JAIN FOR
MOTILAL BANARSIDASS PUBLISHERS PRIVATE LIMITED,
BUNGALOW ROAD, DELHI 110 007

TO

the late Prof. LAL MANI JOSHI

who laboured tirelessly to shed a brighter light
on the vast and profound Buddhist Tradition
and to reveal it in its rightful role as one
of the great pillars of Indian Culture

CONTENTS

FOREWORD

This book is a welcome addition to the growing literature in English on the history and philosophy of the most famous school of Buddhist thinkers known as the Madhyamaka. For a thousand years (100 to 1000 A.D.) this school held aloft the banner of Buddhist soteriology and gnosiology in India and produced a series of technical treatises (*śāstras*) in Sanskrit. Most of these treatises were destroyed by anti-Buddhist fanaticism and vandalism carried on first by the Brahmanical Hindus and then by invading Muslims. Only a small number of Buddhist texts in their original form has survived not in India but in the neighbouring Buddhist lands.

Recently Professor David Seyfort Ruegg has published a short but excellent account of the literature of this school (*The Literature of the Madhyamaka School of Philosophy in India*, Wiesbaden: Otto Harrassowitz, 1981). This book for the first time presents a systematic history of the Madhyamaka literature in India. Although a history of the Madhyamaka School of Buddhist Philosophy is still a desideratum, a number of able scholars have over the years contributed significantly to our knowledge of several aspects of the Madhyamaka thought. Since the original works of the philosophers of this school are preserved in their Tibetan translations, most of the modern scholars interested in the study of the Madhyamaka doctrines and dialectics are making use of Tibetan sources. Two recent doctoral dissertations in this area based on Tibetan materials are still unpublished: *Language and Existence in Mādhyamika Buddhist Philosophy*, Oxford University D. Phil. Thesis (1978), pp. 390 by Dr. Paul Martin Williams, and *A Question of Nihilism: Bhāvaviveka's Response to the Fundamental Problems of Mādhyamika Philosophy*, Harvard University Ph.D. Thesis (1980), pp. 482 by Dr. Malcolm David Eckel. An important and valuable work, also a doctoral thesis, based on both the Sanskrit and Tibetan sources has been recently published. This is called *Reason and Emptiness : A Study of Logic and Mysticism* by Dr. Shotaro Iida (Tokyo : The

Hokuseido Press, 1980). Japanese Buddhist scholars have been publishing their valuable researches in the area of the Madhyamaka thought and literature mostly in Japanese language, and a large number of students of the subject are not able to read their publications.

Dr. Peter Della Santina's *Madhyamaka Schools in India: A Study of the Madhyamaka Philosophy and of the Division of the System into the Prāsaṅgika and Svātantrika Schools* is based on the Tibetan sources. He has made use also of Nāgārjuna's *Mūlamadhyamakakārikā* with Candrakīrti's *Prasannapadānāmamadhyamakavṛtti*. In his treatment of the philosophical problems which became the centre of controversies between the Prāsaṅgikas and the Svātantrikas, he largely follows the outlines found in the *dBu ma spyi ston* of bSod nams Seṅ ge.

The work is well planned and well executed. In earlier chapters the author sets forth early history and basic doctrines of the Madhyamaka School. Here he also discusses elements of Indian formal logic which appear in the sources employed in subsequent chapters. In a series of four chapters we are then presented with a detailed picture of the rise and growth of controversy between the two groups of the Mādhyamika thinkers. In another series of subsequent four chapters, we have a brilliant discussion of the trenchant critique of the theory of origination of entities offered by the great masters like Nāgārjuna, Buddhapālita, Bhāvaviveka, and Candrakīrti. In course of this discussion the reader will find the differences between different sets of arguments against the same theory advanced by the philosophers of the two schools. This section also brings to light Bhāvaviveka's criticism of the views of the Prāsaṅgikas and Candrakīrti's polemics against Bhāvaviveka. The last chapter attempts a kind of summing of the entire work.

The book of Dr. Santina is substantially based on his doctoral dissertation approved by the University of Delhi. It is the result of several years of his devoted study and patient intellectual labour. In spite of his serious physical disabilities, he studied Buddhist thought, mastered Tibetan language to a remarkable degree, and has set an inspiring example of a heroic struggle for conquest of ignorance and possession of the proverbial 'wisdom eye.' I have no doubt that his book will earn for him a place of honour in the assembly of Buddhist scholars in general, and Tibetologists in particular. Students of India's philosophical history will find this a source of much needed knowledge about the subtle and profound teachings bearing on the crucial conceptions of *śūnya* and *śūnyatva*. Here they will find, in readable language and lucid style, an account of the ideas of those ancient Buddhist sages and philosophers who sought to clear the forest of speculative opinions by rationally examining the structure of language and logical reasoning. As a philosophy of philosophies, the Madhyamaka System has stood the test of time and advancement of modern thought, and is likely to become a long lasting source of intellectual challenge to all thinking minds. I hope this book will contribute to a better understanding of the Madhyamaka thought and promote further studies into the niceties of and differences between absolute negation (*prasajya-pratiṣedha*) and relative negation (*paryudāsapratiṣedha*) of any theoretical proposition.

L. M. Joshi

15 *January* 1983
Haverford College

Margaret Gest Visiting Professor in the Cross-Cultural Study of Religion

INTRODUCTION

The Madhyamaka system of philosophy, as it evolved in India and Tibet, has not until relatively recent times received much attention from modern Indian and Occidental scholars. The study of the Madhyamaka, indeed, lagged far behind the study of the Vedānta or even of Theravāda Buddhism. This is, perhaps, not surprising, inasmuch as the Madhyamaka virtually disappeared from the land of its origin centuries ago. Though it continued to flourish in Tibet and Mongolia, these lands were all but inaccessible to most modern scholars. Hence, it was not until relatively late in the history of modern Buddhist scholarship, that the existence of a vast quantity of Mahāyāna Buddhist literature in Sanskrit, Tibetan and Mongolian was even discovered.

The modern study of the Madhyamaka philosophy can therefore be said to have actually commenced only a scant sixty or seventy years ago. Two great Occidental Indologists, one French and one Russian, must be credited with initiating the serious study of the Madhyamaka among modern scholars.[1] Both these pre-eminent figures, La Vallee Poussin and Theodor Stcherbatsky, turned their attention to the works of Nāgārjuna and Candrakīrti. Stcherbatsky's *The Conception of Buddhist Nirvāṇa*[2] remains even today a valuable aid to students of the Madhyamaka philosophy.

Thereafter, the modern study of the Madhyamaka again fell into a period of relative neglect, and it was not until the last two decades that the Madhyamaka again began to receive the attention of Indian and Occidental scholars. Among these recent contributions to the study of the Madhyamaka philosophy, Professor T. R. V. Murti's *The Central Philosophy of Buddhism*[3] stands out as a remarkably comprehensive exposition of the Madhyamaka philosophy on the basis of authoritative texts. Recent years have also seen the publication of two English translations of the *Mūlamadhyamakakārikā* of Nāgārjuna, the fundamental treatise of the Madhyamaka system, one by Doctor Frederick

Streng[4] and the other by Dr. Kenneth K. Inada.[5] Dr. K. V. Ramanan[6] and Dr. R. H. Robinson[7] have also contributed valuable studies of the Madhyamaka based primarily upon Chinese sources.

Nonetheless, the state of our knowledge of the Madhyamaka philosophy is still far from satisfactory. Although as we noted, the *Mūlamadhyamakakārikā* has recently been twice translated into English, we still have no complete translation into English of Candrakīrti's commentary on this work, the *Prasannapadā*. This is a serious deficiency because the kārikā is extremely cryptic and tends to be unintelligible without the aid of an authoritative commentary. Again, the *Śūnyatāsaptati* and *Yuktiṣaṣṭikā* of Nāgārjuna, which are important treatises of the Madhyamaka system, have thus far not been translated into any modern European language. As for the works of the other principal exponents of the Madhyamaka like Buddhapālita, Bhāvaviveka, Candrakīrti, Śāntideva, Śāntarakṣita and Kamalaśīla, only three—the *Śikṣāsamuccaya*[8] and *Bodhicaryāvatāra*[9] of Śāntideva and the *Tattva-Saṁgraha*[10] of Śāntarakṣita have been translated into English while another, the *Madhyamakāvatāra* of Candrakīrti has been partly translated into French.[11] The *Karatalaratna* of Bhāvaviveka has also been translated into French.[12] Thus, it is evident that our knowledge of the Madhyamaka philosophy is still fragmentary, inasmuch as a comprehensive picture of the Madhyamaka is not readily available to scholars and students.

This is perhaps why, even today, the Madhyamaka philosophy is often misunderstood by those who are only superficially acquainted with it. The most conspicuous example of this kind of misunderstanding is the interpretation of the Madhyamaka, which is popular in some circles, as nihilism. This interpretation, however, does not withstand comparison with the actual doctrine of the Madhyamaka as it is presented in the original texts of the system. In this connection, it must be noted that the publication of Professor Murti's work has gone a long way toward correcting this facile misunderstanding.

Given the still rather inadequate state of our knowledge of the Madhyamaka philosophy, it seems that modern scholars and students who turn their attention to the study of this system would do well to see themselves as explorers seeking to uncover new areas of knowledge, rather than as arbiters attempting to settle conclusively the philosophical problems which they study. This is, in fact, the attitude which we have adopted in carrying out this present research.

If, as we have tried to indicate, the state of our knowledge of the Madhyamaka philosophy as such is far from complete, it must be said, in all candour, that our knowledge of the division of the system into the Prāsaṅgika and Svātantrika schools is all but non-existent. There has thus far been not even a single volume published devoted to this problem. We have in fact seen only two articles written by two Japanese scholars and published in *The Nava-Nālandā Mahāvihāra Research Publication.*, Volume I[13] and in *Two Truths in Buddhism and Vedānta*[14] which take up the question. Professor Guenther's *Buddhist Philosophy in Theory and Practice* also includes some material on the two Madhyamaka Schools.[15] Professor Jeffrey Hopkins' doctoral thesis, done at the University of Wisconsin, apparently contains quite a lot of material regarding the philosophy of the Prāsaṅgika school and Professor David Eckles's doctoral thesis completed at Harvard University is a study of the philosophy of Bhāvaviveka, the founder of the Svātantrika school. These recent studies will undoubtedly contribute much to our knowledge of the division of the Madhyamaka system into the two schools, when and if, they become available to the general public. We have unfortunately not had the opportunity to consult these manuscripts.

It may be asked why the question of the division of the Madhyamaka system into the two schools has received so little attention from modern scholars. We may suggest that the answer to this question is twofold. In the first place, the philosophical problem involved in the division is an extremely difficult one, as is universally acknowledged by both classical and modern scholars. In the second place, the original texts of the Svātantrika school, with only two exceptions, the *Madhyamakahṛdayakārikā*, and *Tarkajvālā*[16] of Bhāvaviveka, have been lost in the Sanskrit and are preserved only in Tibetan translations. An additional difficulty is presented by the fact that the Svātantrikamadhyamaka philosophy is, in fact, today virtually extinct even among Tibetans.

Although the Svātantrika philosophy was taken up and preserved by a number of notable early Tibetan Madhyamaka scholars, it steadily lost ground over the centuries in Tibet and was eventually replaced by the Prāsaṅgika philosophy which became the orthodox philosophy of the four major sects of the Tibetan Buddhist scholastic tradition.

This situation has in large part determined our own approach to the study of the division of the Madhyamaka system into the two schools. Indeed, it was our original intention to undertake a comparative study of some of the principal texts, authored by the foremost Indian exponents of the two schools, like the *Prajñāpradīpa* of Bhāvaviveka and *Prasannapadā* of Candrakīrti. It, however, became immediately apparent that if we were to attempt a direct study of texts like the *Prajñāpradīpa* and *Prasannapadā*, it would be extremely difficult to ascertain the actual nature of the division into the two schools. Such texts are, properly speaking, general expositions of the Madhyamaka philosophy, hence, the passages contained in them which have a direct bearing on the problem we had undertaken to study are necessarily few and far between. The attempt to extract the relevant portions from lengthy treatises like the two cited above would therefore obviously be most time consuming and laborious. Moreover, texts like the *Prajñāpradīpa*, although preserved only in Tibetan translation, have not been actively studied by Tibetans for many years. Thus, the search for someone able to competently elucidate their meaning to us seemed little short of hopeless.

Given these considerations, we concluded that we would do better by making use of a recognised and authoritative indigenous Tibetan exposition of the origin, nature and development of the division between the two schools. This, it seemed clear, would enable us to approach the philosophical problem which we had undertaken to study more efficiently and with more satisfactory results.

The use of an indigenous Tibetan exposition for the purpose of studying the division of the Madhyamaka system into the Prāsaṅgika and Svātantrika schools is easily justifiable, since the controversy between the two schools which had begun in India, was actively pursued in Tibet over the course of several centuries. The Tibetan Madhyamakas were therefore without doubt fully conversant with the principal issues involved in the dispute. We selected, for the purpose of our study, the exposition of the division of the Madhyamaka system into the two schools given by the master bSod-nams Sen-ge in the work entitled, *The General*

Meaning of Madhyamaka (*dBu-ma Spyi-ston*).[17] bSod-nams Sen-ge, who lived in the fifteenth century, was not too far removed from the era during which the dispute between the Prāsaṅgikas and Svātantrikas was pursued with intensity on Tibetan soil. bSod-nams Sen-ge is, moreover, widely recognised by Tibetans as a peerless expositor of Buddhist doctrine and his explanation of the origin, nature and development of the division between the two schools is accepted by a not inconsiderable portion of the Tibetan scholastic tradition.

We have not, however, confined ourselves to merely presenting bSod-nams Sen-ge's exposition of the problem at hand. We have sought to supplement his exposition through a careful consideration of some of the original Indian texts of the Madhyamaka system which have direct relevance to the issues involved in the dispute between the two schools. Inasmuch as an acquaintance with the nature of the Madhyamaka philosophy as such is essential for a correct comprehension of the limited philosophical problem of the division between the two schools, we have considered some of the important works of the founder of the system, Nāgārjuna. These include the *Mūlamadhyamakakārikā*,[18] the *Śūnyatāsaptati*,[19] the *Vigrahavyāvartanī*,[20] and the *Ratnāvalī*.[21] In addition, we have made use of Candrakīrti's commentary to the *Mūlamadhyamakakārikā*, the *Prasannapadā*,[22] which takes up in the first chapter the questions raised by Bhāvaviveka's criticism of the approach of the Prāsaṅgika.

We have developed our interpretation of the division of the Madhyamaka system into the Prāsaṅgika and Svātantrika schools along the lines suggested by bSod-nams Sen-ge. bSod-nams Sen-ge maintains that the principal issue which divided the two schools is an epistemological or pedagogical one. According to him, the Prāsaṅgikas and Svātantrikas differed over the question of the character of the arguments which were to be employed by the Madhyamaka, in order to bring about an understanding of the doctrine of the Madhyamaka, on the part of opposing philosophers. bSod-nams Sen-ge holds that there are no very great ontological or philosophical differences between the two Madhyamaka schools. What distinguishes them is the character of the arguments which they employed in order to convince their opponents of the truth of the philosophy which they mutually shared.

It must here be mentioned that there does exist another interpretation of the nature of the division between the two schools; the foremost exponent of which is the Venerable Tsoṅ-Kha-pa, the father of the dGe-lugs-pa order of Tibetan Buddhists. According to him, the issue which divided the two schools is not that of the character of the arguments to be employed against opponents of the Madhyamaka, but rather a philosophical difference involving the acceptance of a particular kind of real existence of entities on the part of the Svātantrikas. According to his interpretation, the Svātantrikas accepted the existence of entities by virtue of their characteristic marks.[23] This existence of entities by virtue of their characteristic marks, Tsoṅ-Kha-pa holds, is not at all accepted by Prāsaṅgikas, and this constitutes the principal difference between the two schools. It is clear that this interpretation given by Tsoṅ-Kha-pa emphasises ontological or philosophical difference between the two schools. It is equally clear that Tsoṅ-Kha-pa's interpretation is at variance with that offered by bSod-nams Sen-ge.

For our part, we have not attempted to deal with the interpretation of the division between the two schools given by Tsoṅ-Kha-pa. To do so, would have required the vast expansion of this present study; an expansion which was precluded by temporal limitations. Moreover, Tsoṅ-Kha-pa's interpretation of the division between the two schools has already, to a very limited extent, been brought to the attention of modern scholars and students while bSod-nams Sen-ge has not. It, therefore, seemed better to devote ourselves to bringing out an interpretation of the division which has at least an equal claim to legitimacy and which has thus far escaped the notice of modern Indian and Occidental scholars.[24]

Our study of the Madhyamaka philosophy and of the division of the system into the two schools is roughly divided into three parts, the first, introductory, the second, general and the third, specific. In chapters one through four, we have examined the origins and fundamental conceptions of the Madhyamaka philosophy. The principles of Indian formal logic, which are to figure prominently in our subsequent discussion of the arguments employed by the Prāsaṅgika and Svātantrika schools, are introduced.

Chapters five through nine deal with the origin and development of the controversy between the two Madhyamaka schools in India and in Tibet. We have tried to focus upon and discuss some of the principal issues around which the controversy between the two schools centred. Our discussion of the philosophical problem at hand in this and in the last part of the text by and large follows the outlines suggested by bSod-nams Sen-ge in the *dBu-ma spyi-ston.*

Chapters ten through sixteen are devoted to the examination of the arguments advanced by the Madhyamakas against the concept of origination or causality. The arguments advanced by Nāgārjuna, Buddhapālita, Bhāvaviveka and Candrakīrti against the concept of origination are presented and discussed in detail. Through the consideration of the arguments advanced by the principal Indian exponents of the two Madhyamaka schools against the concept of origination, the characteristic difference in the arguments employed by the Prāsaṅgikas and Svātantrikas becomes apparent. The polemics advanced by Bhāvaviveka and Candrakīrti against the arguments employed by the Prāsaṅgikas and Svātantrikas respectively are examined.

The final chapter of our study falls somewhat outside the tripartite division suggested above. This is because in it we have attempted to recapitulate the essential points made throughout the course of the text and to present some additional information regarding a number of the secondary differences between the two Madhyamaka schools. bSod-nams Sen-ge's exposition of the method of argument advocated by the Prāsaṅgikas is also summarised in the final chapter.

It must be stressed that we do not in the least pretend to have offered a comprehensive study of the Madhyamaka philosophy and of the division between the Prāsaṅgikas and Svātantrikas. Our approach has been selective and we have not attempted to examine directly the voluminous texts of the Svātantrikas preserved in Tibetan translations. Neither can our study claim to be altogether impartial, since we have been guided throughout by the interpretation given by bSod-nams Sen-ge who was himself a Prāsaṅgika. Again, no attempt has been made to settle finally the question of the relative merits of the doctrines of the Prāsaṅgika and Svātantrika schools. Given the present state of our knowledge of the Madhyamaka and of the philosophies of the two schools, any such attempt would certainly be premature.

Nonetheless, we do venture to hope that this present study does contribute in some degree, however small, to our knowledge of the Madhyamaka philosophy and of the division of the system into the Prāsaṅgika and Svātantrika schools which has so far remained an enigma to modern scholars and students. A viable interpretation, based upon an authoritative original text, of the principal difference which divided the two Madhyamaka schools has been presented, perhaps for the first time. In the process some light has been thrown upon the development of Madhyamaka philosophy and logic in India, particularly over the period extending from the second to the sixth centuries C.E. It may also be added that despite the reservations expressed above regarding the impartiality of our study, we believe that the picture of the Svātantrika doctrine which emerges from these pages is not a distorted one.

Mention must also be made of another problem which inevitably faces any writer who seeks to express the concepst of ancient Indian philosophy in a modern European language. It is the problem of terminology. The selection of terms capable of expressing adequately the concepts of Buddhist philosophy has in the past, and continues even today, to occasion considerable controversy among modern scholars of the subject. Indeed, another fifty or one hundred years may easily be required before an acceptable and standardised modern lexicon is evolved capable of satisfactorily translating the concepts of Buddhist philosophy into English and other European languages.

Since this present study is occupied with the discussion of the Madhyamaka philosophy, and to a lesser extent with that of Indian formal logic both of which contain numerous technical concepts, we have had to employ a very large number of technical terms throughout the course of the text. In the choice of English terms for translating the concepts of the Madhyamaka philosophy and logic, we have been guided by two principal considerations: linguistic and functional. Thus it has been our attempt to conform insofar as possible, in our English rendering of Sanskrit or Tibetan technical terms to the original linguistic signification of the terms. We have, however, resorted to functional translations in cases where the literal rendering of the original terms seemed unduly awkward in English and where the functional equivalence of the original terms with the English terms was sufficiently clear. This was particularly found to be desirable in the case of the translation of a number of technical terms used to express logical concepts.

In all this, however, one point must be stressed. The use of a technical vocabulary of any sort presupposes a certain familiarity on the part of the reader with the universe of discourse in which the terms are being used. Keeping this in mind, we have tried to indicate the philosophical context in which the terms we have employed operate. Thus, it is hoped that our use of a technical vocabulary which was, given the nature of our subject, inevitable, will not present an insuperable obstacle to the comprehension of the ideas we have tried to convey. Moreover, for the benefit of those conversant with Sanskrit and Tibetan, we have supplied the equivalents in those languages of the technical terms used throughout the text.

Finally, it must be admitted that we have had no training in formal Occidental logic. We have, therefore, not attempted to correlate our description of the logical problems taken up in this study with any system of formal Occidental logic. Whether or not the picture of Indian and Madhyamaka logic which emerges from our treatment is wholly or partly comparable with any existing system of formal Occidental logic is a question which others may feel free to attempt to answer.

We are deeply indebted to a great many individuals for the completion of this present study. First, and foremost, we should like to give our very special thanks to H. H. Sakya Trizin without whose help this study would never have been even begun. Very special thanks are due to the Venerable Khenpo Appey Rinpoche, Principal of the Sakya Institute of Tibetan Buddhist Philosophy, Dehra Dun, India and to the Venerable Lobsang Dakpa and Venerable Migmar Tsering also of the Sakya Institute for the extensive instruction and assistance which they provided us in the study of our principal original text, the dBu-ma-spyi-ston of bSod-nams Sen-ge. We must thank our eminent and able advisors from the Department of Buddhist Studies of the University of Delhi, Dr. K. K. Mittal and Geshe G. Gyatso for their invaluable advice and encouragement.

We should also like to thank Shri Harsh Kumar of St. Stephens' College and the Department of Sanskrit of the University of Delhi for his gracious help in the study of the Sanskrit texts of the *Vigrahavyāvartanī* and the *Prasannapadā*. Thanks are also due to T. C. Dhongthog Rinpoche, former librarian of Tibet House, New Delhi, for his indispensable aid in the preparation of an English translation of the biography of bSod-nams Sen-ge. We also owe our thanks to Mr. Sonam, Lecturer in Tibetan, School of Foreign Languages, Ministry of Defence, New Delhi, for his help in the preparation of the English, Sanskrit and Tibetan glossary found at the end of this text. I am deeply indebted to Professor L. M. Joshi, for his constant encouragement and valuable suggestions and for his contribution of the Foreword to this volume. Thanks are also due to Venerable Lozang Jamspal, Venerable Ngawang Samten Chophel and Mr. Indu Dharan for their generous help. Last, but certainly not least, I should like to express my deepest appreciation to my wife Krishna for the immeasurable effort, dedication and patience which she devoted to the preparation of this manuscript.

References

1. Poussin La Vallee, '*Re'flexions*', '*Buddhica*', *Harvard Journal of Asian Studies*, 1937. Poussin. La Vallee, '*Madhyamaka*' in Hastings *Encyclopaedia of Religion and Ethics* in 1915; Stcherbatsky Th. *Nirvāṇa, Die drei Richtungen in der Philosophie des Buddhismus*, Rocznik Orjentalistyczny X. 1934, pp. 3-37.

2. Stcherbatsky. Th. *The Conception of Buddhist Nirvāṇa*. 1927.

3. Murti, T. R. V., *The Central Philosophy of Buddhism*, London, 1955.

4. Streng, Frederick J, *Emptiness—A Study in Religious Meaning*. New York, 1967.

5. Inada, Kenneth K., *Nāgārjuna: A translation of his Mūlamādhyamika-kārikā with an Introductory Essay*. Tokyo, 1970.

6. Ramanan, K. V., *Nāgārjuna's Philosophy*. Varanasi, 1970.

7. Robinson, Richard H., *Early Mādhyamika in India and China*. London, 1967.

8. Bendall, Cecil and Rouse, W. H. D. (Tr.), *Śikṣā-samuccaya*. Motilal Banarsidass, Delhi, 1971.

9. Matics, Marion L. (Tr.), *Bodhicaryāvatāra*, New York, 1970.

10. Jha, Ganganath (Tr.) *Tattvasaṁgraha*. 2 Vols. Gaekwad Oriental Series, Nos. LXXX and LXXXII, 1937, 1939.

11. Poussin, La Vallee, *Le Museon*, 1907, 1910, 1911.

12. Translated by Poussin, La Vallee as *Mahāyānatālaratna Śāstra* (*Le Joyau dans la Main*) in MCB ii (1932-1933).

13. Kajiyama, Y. *Bhāvaviveka and the Prāsaṅgika School*. Mookerjee, Satkari (ed.). The Nava-Nālandā-Mahāvihāra Research Publication. Vol. I, Patna, 1957, pp. 289-331.

14. Iida, Shotara, *The Nature of Samvṛti and the Relationship of Paramārtha to it in Svātantrika-Madhyamika*. Sprung M. (Ed.), *Two truths in Buddhism and Vedānta*. Dordrecht-Holland. 1973, pp. 64-77.

15. Guenther, H. V., *Buddhist Philosophy in Theory and Practice*. London. 1976.

16. Murti, T. R. V., *The Central Philosophy of Buddhism*. p. 98.

17. *dBu-ma-spyi-ston*, published by Sakya College, Mussoorie, 1975.

18. English translations of Kārikās from the *Mūlamādhyamikakārikā*, found in the text, are based upon a comparative study of Dr. K. Inada's translation and the original Sanskrit text. Vaidya, P. L. (ed.) *Mādhyamakasāstra* of Nāgārjuna. Buddhist Sanskrit Texts—No. 10. Published by The Mithila Institute. Darbhaṅga, 1960. pp. 1-259.

19. A thus far, unpublished English translation of the *Śūnyatāsaptati* alongwith its autocommentary was made by the Venerable L. Jamspal and the author from the Tibetan translation preserved in the bsTan-'gyur (mDo. XVII. 4) in Delhi. 1973-74.

20. English translations from the *Vigrahavyāvartanī* and its autocommentary are based upon a comparative study of Satkari Mookereje's English rendering of the work, published in The Nava-Nalanda Mahavihara Research Publication. Vol 1. Patna, 1957 (*The Absolutist's Standpoint in Logic*. pp. 1-175) and the original Sanskrit text edited by Vaidya, P. L. Op. cit. pp. 277-295.

21. Translated and edited by Hopkins, Jeffrey and Lati, Rimpoche with Klein, Anne entitled *The Precious Garland and the Songs of the Four Mindfulness* (The wisdom of Tibet Series—2). George Allen and Unwin Ltd. London, 1975.

22. References to this text are based upon a comparative study of Professor Stcherbatsky's translation. *The Conception of Buddhist Nirvāṇa* and the original Sanskrit text edited by Vaidya P. L., Op.cit. pp. 1-259.

23. [illegible]

24. The works which nave thus far been published on the question seem to suggest an acquaintance familiarity with Tsoṅ-Kha-pa.

CHAPTER I

THE ORIGINS OF THE MADHYAMAKA PHILOSOPHY

While the Madhyamaka as a systematic philosophy arose only in the second century C. E. with the figure of the great scholar and saint ācārya Nāgārjuna, the essentials of the Madhyamaka were anticipated by the earlier Buddhist tradition, as it developed out of the teachings of the Buddha Śākyamuni. We may say right at the outset that we do not subscribe to the interpretation, offered by some, according to which the Mahāyāna in general, including the Madhyamaka system, is regarded as an incongruous development within Buddhist philosophy. On the contrary, we maintain that the Madhyamaka represents a legitimate interpretation of the original teaching of the Buddha. This contention is supported by substantial canonical evidence of quite an early date. Our interpretation is also fully supported by certain modern scholars, such as Professor T. R. V. Murti who goes so far as to endorse the Madhyamaka's claim to represent the quintessence of the teaching of the Buddha.[1] Due credit must be given to Professor Murti for providing a lucid description of the Madhyamaka system which does justice to the importance of this central philosophy of Buddhism.

The essentials of the Madhyamaka system were anticipated by the Buddha, as is evident even from the Pāli sources. The tetralemma (Catuṣkoṭi), which is so characteristic of the Madhyamaka, is met with at numerous places within the Pāli canon, as is the concept of the void or emptiness (śūnyatā). It should also be recalled that the Law of interdependent origination (pratītyasamutpāda) is universally acknowledged by all the Buddhist schools, including the Madhyamaka, to be the essence of the teaching of the Buddha. Moreover, the characteristic interpretation of the law of interdependent origination in the Madhyamaka philosophy is possible in complete agreement with the utterances of the Buddha, even as they are recorded in the Pāli dialogues. This will be shown through relevant citations.

In addition, the direct precursors of the Madhyamaka philosophy were the Prajñāpāramitā Sūtras. The close affinity between the Madhyamaka, as a systematic philosophy, and the philosophy of the Prajñāpāramitā literature has perhaps not escaped anyone who has turned his attention to these matters. We shall attempt to illustrate this affinity with the help of a number of specific citations later in this chapter. The fact that the Madhyamaka system is obviously indebted to the Prajñāpāramitā Sūtras for much of its philosophical content, also attests, in part, to the antiquity of its origins. Indeed, it is now accepted that at least one of the Prajñāpāramitā Sūtras is of a quite early date.

The dialectical analysis employed by the Madhyamaka is evident in the presentation of the fourteen inexpressibles (avyākṛta) found in the Pāli canon. These fourteen alternatives, which the Buddha refused to assent to, are met with at a number of places within the Pāli dialogues.[2] The fourteen propositions which the Buddha Śākyamuni refused to assent to are as follows: 1. that the world is eternal, 2. that the world is not eternal, 3. that the world is both eternal and not eternal, 4. that the world is neither eternal nor not eternal, 5. that the world is finite, 6. that the world is not finite, 7. that the world is both finite and not finite, 8. that the world is neither finite nor not finite, 9. that the Tathāgata exists after death, 10. that the Tathāgata does not exist after death, 11. that the Tathāgata both exists and does not exist after death, 12. that the Tathāgata neither exists nor does not exist after death, 13. that the self is identical with the body, 14. that the self is different from the body. The Buddha refused to agree to any of the above propositions when they were put to him by the wanderer Vacchagotta.

The structure of the presentation of the fourteen inexpressibles is dialectic. The primary alternatives are the eternalist and the nihilist. The former affirms the existence of a transcendental ground of phenomena, while the latter denies the existence of any such ground. It is quite likely that the Buddha could have had before him the eternal matter (prakṛti) of the Sāṅkhya and the materialist's denial of the non-emperical, as examples of the two primary alternatives.

The first two sets of four alternatives seek to determine whether the world is limited in time and in space. The eternalist affirms that the world is eternal and unlimited, while the nihilist maintains that it has temporal and spatial limits.

The propositions regarding the existence or non-existence of the Tathāgata after death refer to the reality or unreality of an unconditioned mode of being. The phrase 'after death' (paramaraṇāt) signifies an existence apart from all phenomena. The former alternative affirms the reality of unconditioned existence, while the latter denies the possibility of such existence.

The two primary alternatives, the eternalist and the nihilist, are also reflected in the last two propositions mentioned in the fourteen. In this case, the eternalist affirms the existence of a transcendental principle, i.e., the self or soul, independent of the psycho-physical states, while the nihilist or materialist maintains that there exists nothing apart from the psycho-physical states. The latter view was in fact advocated, in the Buddha's own day, by the materialist Ajita Kesa Kambalin.

The fourteen propositions enumerated in the avyākṛta constitute mere conceptual constructions which are superimposed upon the nature of reality. They are intellectual falsifications which only obscure and bifurcate the real (tattvam). They purport to provide accurate descriptions of reality when, in fact, they simply distort it. The fourteen propositions are, therefore, fit to be rejected as the useless fabrications of speculative philosophers.

The Buddha discarded all theories in the *Brahmajāla-Sutta* of the *Dīgha Nikāya*, as dogmatism (diṭṭhivāda), and refused to be drawn into the net (jāla).[3] The wanderer Vacchagotta asked the Lord : why he did not answer the fourteen questions presented in the avyākṛta definitely while other philosophers did so and whether he had any theory of his own. The Lord answered in the *Majjhima Nikāya* 1, discourse no. 72, "The Tathāgata, O Vaccha, is free from all theories...Therefore the Tathāgata has attained deliverance and is free from attachment, inasmuch as all imaginings, all agitation, all false notions, concerning an Ego or anything pertaining to an Ego, have perished, have faded away, have ceased, have been given up and relinquished."[4] The Lord said, "To hold that the world is eternal or to hold that it is not, or to agree to any other of the propositions you adduce, Vaccha, is the jungle of theorising, the wilderness of theorising, the tangle of theorising, the bondage and the shakles of theorising, attended by ill, distress, perturbation, and fever; it conduces not to detachment, passionlessness, tranquility, peace, to knowledge and wisdom of Nirvāṇa."[5]

Māluṅkyāputta reflected, "...that the Tathāgata exists after death, that the Tathāgata does not exist after death, that the Tathāgata both exists and does not exist after death, that the Tathāgata neither exists nor does not exist after death—these the Blessed one does not explain to me."[6] Again Vacchagotta asked the Lord, "Gotama, where is the monk reborn whose mind is thus freed? (The Lord replied)—Vaccha, it is not true to say that he is reborn.—Then, Gotama, he is not reborn. Vaccha, it is not true to say that he is not reborn. —Then, Gotama, he is both reborn and not reborn. —Vaccha, it is not true to say that he is both reborn and not reborn. —Then, Gotama, he is neither reborn, nor not reborn. —Vaccha, it is not true to say that he is neither reborn nor not reborn."[7]

The Buddha was aware that the fourteen propositions, presented in the avyākṛta, reflect the primary alternatives of eternalism and nihilism. He explains the reason for his silence to Ānanda, after Vacchagotta had departed. "If, Ānanda, when asked by the Wanderer: 'Is there a self?' I had replied to him: 'There is a self', then Ānanda, that would be siding with the recluses and Brahmins who are eternalists. But if, Ānanda, when asked 'Is there not a self?' I had replied that it does not exist, that, Ānanda, would be siding with those recluses and Brahmins who are annihilationists."[8]

The structure as well as the content of the fourteen inexpressibles of the Pāli canon is exactly paralleled in the *Mūlamadhyamakakārikā* and other works of Nāgārjuna. Thus, he writes, "If the world has limits, how could there be another world? Again, if the world has no limits, how could there be another world? The continuity of the function of the aggregates (skandhas) is like the continuity of a flame, and so it is not possible to speak of limits and non-limits."[9] Again, in the *Ratnāvalī* Nāgārjuna writes, "Sights, sounds and so forth were said by the conqueror neither to be true nor false. ...Thus ultimately this world is beyond truth and falsehood. Therefore, he does not assert that it really exists or does not. These in all ways do not exist, how could the omniscient-one say they have limits or no limits, or have both or neither."[10] Again, in the *Mūlamadhyamakakārikā* it is stated, "Since all entities are of the nature of emptiness (śūnyatā), where, by whom and in what manner could such false views on eternity etc. arise."[11]

Regarding the status of the Tathāgata after death, Nāgārjuna writes, "It cannot be said that the Blessed one exists after Nirvāṇa or not or both or neither."[12] Indeed, Sāriputta had questioned Yamaka whether the true self of the Tathāgata is his material form and had received a negative reply. Yamaka replied in a similar manner to the questions whether the Tathāgata is in the material form, or it in him, or different from it and so on with respect to the four other aggregates which make up the empirical individual. Yamaka admitted that the Tathāgata is not in the five aggregates collectively, nor is he without the five aggregates. Sāriputta then confronted his interlocutor with the conclusion that even in life Yamaka cannot comprehend an essence, the Tathāgata. Even in life Yamaka cannot demonstrate that the Tathāgata really exists.[13] Nāgārjuna writes, "It cannot be said the Blessed one exists in life, or not, or both, or neither."[14]

Regarding the questions concerning the identity or difference of the self and the psycho-physical states, Nāgārjuna writes that the self is neither identical with nor different from the body, nor both nor neither.[15]

The Buddha, indeed, taught that there are two primary views, eternalism (bhavadiṭṭhi) and nihilism (vibhavadiṭṭhi). No one adhering to either of these views can hope to be free of the world. Those who realise the origin, nature and contradiction of these two views can be free from the grip of existence (saṁsāra). The lord said, the world is used to rely upon duality, it is and it is not, but for one who sees, in accord with truth and wisdom, how phenomena arise and perish, for him there is no is or is not. That everything exists, is Kātyāyana, one alternative. That it does not is another alternative. Not accepting either of the alternatives, the Tathāgata proclaims the truth from the middle position.[16]

Nāgārjuna has expounded essentially the same idea. "The Lord" he states, "has taught the abandonment of the conceptions of existence and non-existence."[17] "One who conceives of the mirage-like world that it does or does not exist is consequently ignorant. When there is ignorance, one is not liberated."[18] "Ask the worldly ones, the Sāṅkhyas, Vaiśeṣikas and the Nirgranthas, the proponents of a person and aggregates, if they propound what passes beyond existence and non-existence. Hence know that the nectar of the Buddha's teaching is called the profound, an uncommon doctrine passing far beyond existence and non-existence."[19] Nāgārjuna makes specific reference to the instructions given by the Buddha to Kātyāyana in the following stanza. "According to the instructions of Kātyāyana, the two views of the world in terms of existence and non-existence were criticised by the Buddha for similarly admitting the bifurcation of entities into existence and non-existence."[20]

We have suggested that the Madhyamaka philosophy is founded upon an interpretation of the fundamental Buddhist doctrine of interdependent origination. While the Ābhidharmika schools, the Vaibhāṣikas and the Sautrāntikas understood the doctrine of interdependent origination propounded by the Buddha Śākyamuni to mean the temporal succession of momentary and discrete existences which were in themselves real, the Madhyamaka interpreted the doctrine of interdependent origination to signify the universal relativity and unreality of all phenomena. According to the Madhyamaka, the doctrine of interdependent origination is meant to indicate the dependence of all entities upon other entities. This is equivalent to their lack of self-existence (svabhāva) and emptiness (śūnyatā).

The interpretation advocated by the Madhyamaka is in complete agreement with some of the utterances of the Buddha recorded in the Pāli canon. The following passage from the *Majjhima Nikāya* may be offered as evidence of this fact. The Buddha declared that form, feeling and the like are illusory, mere bubbles. "Dependent on the oil and the wick" (Buddha declared) "does light in the lamp burn; it is neither in the one nor in the other, nor anything in itself; phenomena are, likewise, nothing in themselves. All things are unreal, they are deceptions, Nibbāna is the only truth."[21]

In the *Śūnyatāsaptati* Nāgārjuna writes, "Since the own-being of all entities is not in (the individual) causes and conditions, nor in the aggregation of causes and conditions, nor in any entity whatsoever, i.e., not in all (of these), therefore, all entities are empty in their own being."[22] In the *Ratnāvalī* it is also stated, "when this exists that arises, like short when there is long. When this is produced, so is that, like light from a flame. When there is long there must be short; they exist not through their own nature, just as without a flame light too does not arise."[23] Again Nāgārjuna points out that the Buddha declared that elements are deceptive and unreal. Therefore, he says, "The Buddha simply expounded the significance of emptiness (śūnyatā).[24] He has also said in the *Śūnyatāsaptati* that whatever originates dependently as well as that upon which it depends for its origination do not exist.[25] Nāgārjuna precisely indicates the standpoint of the Madhyamaka in the following stanza found in the *Mūlamadhyamakakārikā*. "We declare that whatever is interdependently originated is emptiness (śūnyatā). It is a conceptual designation of the relativity of existence and is indeed the middle path."[26] "No element can exist" he writes, "which does not participate in interdependence. Therefore no element which is not of the nature of emptiness can exist."[27]

Moreover, even on the evidence of the Pāli canon, the Buddha appears to have regarded the doctrine of emptiness (śūnyatā) as the real essence of his teaching. The Buddha spoke of the monks of the future period in the following way in the *Saṁyutta Nikāya*. "The monks will no longer wish to hear and learn the suttāntas proclaimed by the Tathāgata, deep, deep in meaning, reaching beyond the world, dealing with the void (suññatā-paṭisamyuttā), but will only lend their ear to the profane suttāntas proclaimed by disciples, made by poets, poetical, adorned with beautiful words and syllables."[28] This passage found in the Pāli canon clearly supports the Madhyamaka contention that the doctrine of emptiness represents the real heart of the teaching of Śākyamuni.

Although the Buddha undoubtedly formulated a doctrine of elements (dharma), it is evident that the Buddha meant it to have only provisional utility. In the *Alaguddupama Sutta,* the Buddha compares the doctrine of elements to a raft. Once the goal has been attained and the ocean of existence has been crossed, the doctrine ought to be discarded since its utility has then been exhausted.[29]

Indeed, Professor Murti has rightly indicated that while the doctrine of elements can be without difficulty subordinated to the doctrine of emptiness, the reverse is not possible.[30] The statements of the Buddha which speak of emptiness and of the unreality of all phenomena cannot be understood in any other way than as the ultimate teaching. These considerations suggest the division of the truth into the phenomenal (samvṛti) or conventional (saṁvyavahāra) and the ultimate (paramārtha) which is employed by the Madhyamaka. A similar distinction is suggested with respect to the canonical scriptures which may be divided into those of expedient import (neyārtha) and those of direct import (nītārtha).

Mention must here be made of another important element present in the teaching of the Buddha from its very inception. This is the concept of ignorance (avidyā) which is regarded as the cause of illusion and bondage. A concept closely associated with that of ignorance is that of imagination or conceptualisation (vikalpa) which according to the Buddhist view is responsible for the character of one's perception of reality. As it has been suggested, these concepts were central to Buddhist philosophy from the outset, though it must be admitted that the full extent of their significance did not become apparent until the advent of the Madhyamaka.

Even the Ābhidharmika philosophy which attempted the first systematic synthesis of the Buddha's teaching in conformity with a realistic and pluralistic ontology attributed the notions of substance, permanence, the whole and the universal to subjective conceptualisation (vikalpa). According to the Ābhidharmika philosophy, these conceptualisations are uncritically imposed by ordinary people upon what are in reality momentary and particular elements. Imagination conditioned by ignorance fashions the notions of the self and the permanent, which in turn result in attachment, aversion and delusion.

The Sautrāntika school of the Ābhidharmika philosophy was a very vigorous form of the critical attitude of early Buddhism consistent with realism and pluralism. The Sautrāntika declared many of the elements which the Vaibhāṣikas had accepted as real to be merely subjective and ideal.[31] The Madhyamaka pursued the critical attitude already evident in the doctrines of the Ābhidharmika schools to its logical conclusions. For the Madhyamaka, not only the notions of substance, permanence and so on were subjective thought constructions imposed upon reality by the mind, but also causality, existence, non-existence, motion and the like were mere conceptualisations.

The Buddha indeed, in order to indicate that existence is conditioned by imagination and is nothing in itself referred to a parable of the demon Vepacitta who was bound or freed according to the evil or good nature of his thoughts.[32] In short imagination (kalpanā) was bondage for the Buddha and the cessation of imagination and false notions was liberation. This doctrine is further elaborated in the Prajñāpāramitā literature and is one of the fundamental conceptions of the Madhyamaka philosophy.

The semicritical philosophy of the Ābhidharmika schools, the Vaibhāṣikas and the Sautrāntikas was only a preliminary step. The inadequacy of the doctrine of elements became increasingly apparent to critically minded philosophers like the Buddhists. It is, thus, not surprising that the earlier phase of Buddhist systematic philosophy should have in time led to the wholly critical philosophy of the Madhyamaka.

The following passage is contained in the *Kāśyapaparivarta* portion of the *Ratnakūṭa Sūtra,* one of the earliest texts of the Mahāyāna. "Oh Kāśyapa, substance (ātmā) is one alternative. Insubstantiality (nairātmya) is another alternative. That which is the middle path avoiding these two alternatives is formless, unperceivable, non-abiding, unapprehendable, indescribable and uncontainable. It is, Oh Kāśyapa, called the middle path."[33] Nāgārjuna expresses the same idea in the *Ratnāvalī.* He states that there is a position (pakṣa), hence there is a counterposition (pratipakṣa). Neither of them is real.[34] This conception of the inconceivable and indescribable nature of reality which transcends the categories of thought is further amplified in the Prajñāpāramitā literature.

The oldest of the *Prajñāpāramitā Sūtras* was probably the *Aṣṭasāhasrikā Prajñāpāramitā.* It is likely that the *Śatasāhasrikā Prajñāpāramitā,* the *Pañcaviṁsatisāhasrikā Prajñāpāramitā,* the *Saptaśatikā Prajñāpāramitā* and the *Prajñāpāramitāhṛdaya Sūtras,* were expansions and abridgements of the former. This is contrary to the opinion often held according to which the *Sāhasrikā Prajñāpāramitā Sūtra* is thought to have been abridged into the *Aṣṭasāhasrikā* and so on. Professor Murti however cites the evidence afforded by Haribhadra's commentary to the *Abhisamayālaṅkāra* in support of the above interpretation.

The *Aṣṭasāhasrikā Prajñāpāramitā* was translated into Chinese in 172 C.E. by Lokarakṣa. This fact leads Professor Murti to suppose that the *Aṣṭasāhasrikā* probably dates from the first century B.C. if not earlier.[35]

The predominant theme of the Prajñāpāramitā literature is that there is no change or decay, no origination, extinction, coming or going, no identity, no differentiation, no self, not-self, existence, non-existence and so on. All the above are merely imagined by the ignorant. The reality of the aggregates, elements and the like is rejected. The doctrine of interdependent origination is interpreted to mean the essential relativity of all phenomena which exist dependently. The insubstantiality of the person (pudgalanairātmya) which was central to the Ābhidharmika systems is extended to include all entities (dharmanairātmya). All phenomena, therefore, according to the Prajñāpāramitā literature, are devoid of self-existence (niḥsvabhāva) and empty (*śūnya*). The division into the two truths, conventional and ultimate is also suggested in the Prajñāpāramitā literature as is the doctrine of the non-differentiation of the phenomenal and the ultimate.

We shall now proceed to consider a number of passages from the Prajñāpāramitā literature and to compare them with some of the statements of Nāgārjuna. Inasmuch as the Prajñāpāramitā literature is admittedly voluminous, we have for our purposes chosen to consider only the verse summary of the *Aṣṭasāhasrikā Prajñāpāramitā* and the *Prajñāpāramitāhṛdaya Sūtra* which in themselves provide a reasonably comprehensive representation of the philosophical content of the Prajñāpāramitā literature as a whole.

In the verse summary of the *Aṣṭasāhasrikā Prajñāpāramitā-Sūtra* it is stated, "The Bodhisattva finds that all these dharmas are entirely empty......When the Bodhisattva does not course in form, in feeling, or perception, in will, or consciousness, but wanders without home, remaining unaware of coursing firm in wisdom, his thoughts on non-origination—then the best of all the calming trances cleaves to him."[36] In the above passage the rejection of the reality of the aggregates alluded to earlier is abundantly clear. The importance of one of the principal themes of the Madhyamaka philosophy, i.e. the negation of origination is also indicated. In the *Prajñāpāramitāhṛdaya-Sūtra* it is also stated that in emptiness neither the aggregates (skandhas), sense-spheres (āyatanas) nor elements (dhātus) exist.

Nāgārjuna indeed rejects the reality of the aggregates in the fourth chapter of the *Mūlamadhyamakakārikā* as well as in the *Śūnyatāsaptati*. His criticism in both works is directed against the notion of the reality of form (rūpa) and is intended to be applied to the remaining four aggregates. Nāgārjuna argues that form cannot exist disassociated from its material cause, i.e. the four great elements (catvārimahābhūtāni).[37] Form is therefore devoid of self-existence and is thus empty.

Also in the *Śūnyatāsaptati* Nāgārjuna writes, "If form were originated from the great elements, form would originate from an imperfect (cause)."[38] Again the four elements also do not exist, because though it may be thought that their existence is proven through their characteristic marks, their characteristic marks do not exist before the elements themselves. Therefore, inasmuch as the characteristic marks are unproven, the characterised elements are also unproven.[39] Here too the application of the logic of the equivalence of interdependence and emptiness is evident.

Again Nāgārjuna says that form does not exist, because it is altogether not apprehended.[40] Though it may be thought that the existence of form is proved by the perception of it, that perception does not exist in reality because it originates from causes and conditions. Again, whatsoever originates from causes and conditions, i.e. originates dependently, is devoid of self-existence and hence it is ultimately not existent.[41]

Nāgārjuna argues further that inasmuch as the intellect which is thought to perceive form as well as form itself are impermanent, i.e. momentary, the latter cannot be apprehended by the former.[42]

Just as form and the other aggregates which originate dependently do not exist in reality, so also all elements or entities are empty. The verse summary of the *Aṣṭasāhasrikā* states, "All elements (dharmas) are not really there, their essential original nature is empty."[43] The text further states that the Bodhisattva comprehends all elements as empty, signless, unimpeded and without any duality.[44] The fundamental contention of the Madhyamaka is indeed that all entities are essentially empty.

Again the independent reality of the four cardinal tenets of the Ābhidharmika philosophy, i.e. impermanence, suffering, notself and impurity is rejected in the Prajñāpāramitā literature. Thus, it is stated in the verse summary that impermanence and permanence, suffering and happiness, the self and notself, the pure and the impure, are of just one suchness (tathatā) in emptiness.[45]

Nāgārjuna referring to the same four doctrines makes the

following statement in the *Mūlamadhyamakakārikā*. "If ātman, purity, permanence and bliss are not to be admitted, then likewise anātman, impurity, impermanence and suffering are not to be admitted."[46] Here also inasmuch as purity, impurity, and so on are only relative concepts which originate dependent upon one another,[47] they are declared not to exist ultimately.

Furthermore the view that notions like existence and non-existence as well as all entities are mere concepts originated from the conceptualising activity of the mind is explicitly expressed in the Prajñāpāramitā literature. The verse summary contains the following statement. The foolish imagine existence and non-existence. Non-existence as well as existence they fashion. As facts, both existence and non-existence are not real.[48] Again it is stated that the fool who has admitted into himself the notion of I and mine is forced by that quite unreal notion of I to undergo birth and death again and again.[49] It is further said in the same text, "As many beings as there are in the low, middle and high (regions of the) world, they have all, so has the Sugata said, been brought about by ignorance."[50]

Nāgārjuna also argues that inasmuch as existence and non-existence are notions which are only obtained relative to each other neither are real.[51] He also writes in the *Ratnāvali*, "By him who speaks only to help beings, it was said that they all have originated from the conception of I and are enveloped with the conception of mine."[52] Again he has said, "The wheel of existence (bhavacakra) originates from the propensity for false conceptualisation."[53]

The ultimate truth as it is described in the Prajñāpāramitā literature transcends thought and is inexpressible. Thus, it is stated in the verse summary, that wisdom is free from construction and non-discriminating.[54] Again, it is said in the same text, "All words for things in use in this world must be left behind. All things originated and made must be transcended. The deathless, the supreme, incomparable gnosis is then won."[55]

Nāgārjuna writes in the *Mūlamadhyamakakārikā*, "Unconditioned, quiescent, non-conceptualised, non-discriminated and non-differentiated, these are the characteristics of reality."[56]

The division into the two truths, conventional and ultimate which is so characteristic of the Madhyamaka system is also suggested in the Prajñāpāramitā literature. As it is stated in the verse summary of the *Aṣṭasāhasrikā*, "As mere talk, the Bodhisattva cognizes all these elements which the Buddha has demonstrated, practised and revealed."[57] In the *Mūlamadhyamakakārikā* Nāgārjuna states, "The teaching of the Dharma by the various Buddhas is based on the two truths. Mainly the conventional and the ultimate. Those who do not know the distinction between the two truths, do not comprehend the profound nature of the Buddha's teaching."[58] The various statements of the Buddha are expressions of conventional reality (vyavahārasatya). They have no ultimate reality. Thus, Nāgārjuna indicates that from the ultimate standpoint not any dharma with respect to anyone at any place was ever taught by the Buddha.[59]

Nonetheless, according to the doctrine of the Prajñāpāramitā literature and the Madhyamaka phenomena and ultimate reality are essentially non-differentiated and identical. As it is stated in the verse summary, "The space-element in the eastern direction, and in the southern, and so in the western and northern direction is boundless; above and below, in the ten directions, as far as it goes there is no multiplicity, and no difference is attained. Past Suchness, future Suchness, present Suchness, the Suchness of the Arhats, the Suchness of all dharmas, the Suchness of the Jinas—all that is the Dharma-Suchness, and no difference is attained."[60] Thus, the Enlightenment of the Sugatas, is free from differentiated dharmas. In the *Prajñāpāramitāhṛdaya-Sūtra* it is also stated, form is not different from emptiness. Emptiness is not different from form.

Nāgārjuna writes in the *Mūlamadhyamakakārikā*, "Saṁsāra is nothing essentially different from Nirvāṇa. Nirvāṇa is nothing essentially different from Saṁsāra."[61] He also states, "The nature of the Tathāgata is also the nature of this worldly existence. The Tathāgata is without any self-existence (svabhāva) and this worldly existence is likewise so."[62]

Thus, it may be said that the essential teaching of the Prajñāpāramitā literature is that all entities which originate dependently are ultimately unoriginated, unextinguished and empty. This idea is precisely expressed in the following passage contained in the verse summary of the *Aṣṭasāhasrikā*, "The Bodhisattva who understands interdependent origination (pratītyasamutpāda) as non-origination and this wisdom as non-extinction, as the rays of the sun free from the covering of the clouds, so he has dispelled the covering of ignorance."[63] Nāgārjuna likewise states that interdependent origination is characterised by the negation of origination and extinction.[64] He has also declared that inasmuch as all entities are interdependently originated they are empty, and that since no entity which is not interdependently originated exists, so also no entity exists whose nature is not emptiness.[65]

Among the other canonical works which almost certainly influenced Nāgārjuna and the formulation of the Madhyamaka philosophy were the *Saddharmapuṇḍarīka Sūtra* and the *Samādhirāja Sūtra*. Nāgārjuna quotes from the former and he seems also to have been familiar with at least the gāthā portions of the latter.[66] Candrakīrti at any rate quotes very freely from the *Samādhirāja Sūtra* in the *Prasannapadā* and it was undoubtedly held in very high esteem by the exponents of the Madhyamaka system.

Another canonical work of a relatively early date which could well have influenced Nāgārjuna is the *Ratnakūṭa Sūtra*. About forty Sūtras including the *Kāśyapaparivarta*, *Pitāputrasamāgama*, *Upālipariprcchā* and so on are included in the Ratnakūṭa class in the Tibetan and Chinese collections.

Thus, it is evident from our consideration of the philosophical content of the Prajñāpāramitā literature that the doctrine of Śūnyatā which was systematically expounded by the Madhyamaka was central to it. Yet this śūnyatā should also not be thought to be anything in itself. It should not be seized upon as a position or view. The *Samādhirāja Sūtra* indicates that while emptiness is the middle path avoiding the two alternatives of existence and non-existence, the wise should also not abide in the middle.[67] The standpoint of the Madhyamaka is properly speaking not a position at all, but a philosophically critical attitude. Nāgārjuna has also declared, "The wise ones have said that emptiness is the relinquishing of all views. Yet it is said that those who adhere to the idea of emptiness are incorrigible."[68] It is also significant that among the twenty types of emptiness listed by Haribhadra in his commentary to the *Abhisamayālaṅkāra*, the fourth is the emptiness of emptiness.[69] It is, therefore, clear that the emptiness of the Prajñāpāramitā literature and of the Madhyamaka system cannot be interpreted as a philosophical position among other philosophical positions. It is qualitatively different from the doctrines advanced by dogmatic philosophers.

In this opening chapter we have attempted to indicate the philosophical origins of the Madhyamaka system and to illustrate the continuity of the philosophical development within the Buddhist tradition from the time of Śākyamuni up to that of Nāgārjuna. From the evidence we have aduced, it ought to be abundantly clear that the Madhyamaka philosophy represents a logical and perhaps inevitable development out of the earlier Buddhist teachings. Thus, the emergence of the Madhyamaka as a systematic philosophy within the Buddhist tradition is by no means inexplicable or incongruous. Indeed, there is ample evidence as we have shown to support the Madhyamaka's claim to represent the profound and essential import of Buddhist philosophy as a whole.

References

1. Murti, T. R. V., *The Central Philosophy of Buddhism*, p. 55.
2. References for avyākṛtas from the Pāli sources: *Majjhima Nikāya I* pp. 426-32 (*Sutta* 63); pp. 483 ff (*Sutta* 72); *Saṁyukta Nikāya* III, pp. 257 ff (*Vacchagotta Saṁyuttam*); *Saṁyukta Nikāya* IV, pp. 374-403 (*avyākata Saṁyuttam*); *Mahānidāna Brahmajāla Sutta* (*Dīgha Nikāya*); *Mahālisutta* (*Dīgha-Nikāya*)... *Poṭṭhapāda Sutta* (*Dīgha-Nikāya*); *Milinda Pañho*, pp. 144 ff.
3. Murti, T. R. V., *The Central Philosophy of Buddhism*, p. 40.
4. *Ibid*, p. 45.
5. *Ibid*, p. 47.
6. Robinson, R. H., *Early Mādhyamika in India and China*, p. 54, cites Majjhima Nikāya, 63.
7. Robinson, R. H. *ibid*, cites *Majjhima Nikāya*, 72.
8. *Saṁyutta Nikāya*, pp. 400-401.
9. *Mūlamadhyamakakārikā*, XXVII. 21, 22.
10. *Ratnāvalī*, II. 104-6.
11. *Mūlamadhyamakakārikā*, XXVII. 29.
12. *Ibid*. XXV. 17.
13. Murti, T. R. V., *The Central Philosophy of Buddhism*, pp. 53-54.
14. *Mūlamadhyamakakārikā*, XXV. 18.
15. *Ibid*. XXVII. 15, 16, 17 and 18.
16. *Majjhima Nikāya* I, p. 65; *Udāna*, p. 33; *Itivuttaka*, pp. 43-44; *Saṁyutta Nikāya II*, p. 16 and 61 ff.
17. *Mūlamadhyamakakārikā*, XXV. 10.
18. *Ratnāvalī*, I. 56.
19. *Ibid*., I. 61-62.
20. *Mūlamadhyamakakārikā*, XV. 7.
21. Murti, T. R. V., *The Central Philosophy of Buddhism*, p. 50.
22. *Śūnyatāsaptati*, Stanza 3
23. *Ratnāvalī* I. 48, 49.

24. *Mūlamadhyamakakārikā*, XIII. 1, 2.
25. *Śūnyatāsaptati*, 14 commentary.
26. *Op. cit.* XXIV. 18.
27. *Mūlamadhyamakakārikā*, XXIV. 19.
28. Murti, T. R. V., *The Central Philosophy of Buddhism*, p. 51.
29. *Ibid*, p. 52.
30. *Ibid.* p. 53.
31. *Ibid*, pp. 81-82.
32. *Ibid.* p. 52.
33. Quoted in the *Prasannapadā* commentary to *Mūlamadhyamakakārikā* XVIII. 6.
34. *Ratnāvalī*, II. 104.
35. Murti, T. R. V., *The Central Philosophy of Buddhism*, pp. 83-84.
36. adapted from Conze, Edward: *The Perfection of Wisdom in Eight Thousand Lines and Its Verse Summary*, Chapter I, 8-10, p. 10.
37. *Mūlamadhyamakakārikā*, IV. 1-3.
38. *Śūnyatāsaptati*, 45
39. *Ibid.* 27 and commentary, *Mūlamadhyamakakārikā*, V.
40. *Śūnyatāsaptati*, 47.
41. *Śūnyatāsaptati*, 47 commentary.
42. *Śūnyatāsaptati*, 49 and commentary.
43. adapted from Conze, Edward, *Verse Summary* I. 28, p. 12.
44. *Ibid.* XXVI. 3, p. 57.
45. *Ibid.* II. 2, p. 13.
46. *Mūlamadhyamakakārikā* XXIII. 22.
47. *Ibid.* XXIII. 10, 11.
48. Conze, Edward. *Verse Summary* I. 13, p. 10.
49. *Ibid.* XXII, 6. p. 51.
50. adapted from *Verse Summary* XXVIII. 5, p. 61.
51. *Śūnyatāsaptati* 19 and commentary;also *Mūlamadhyamakakārikā*, XV. 5,6.
52. *Ratnāvalī*, I. 27.
53. *Pratītyasamutpādahṛdayakārikāvṛtti*, Stanza, 5.
54. Conze, Edward, *Verse Summary*, X. 10, p. 28.
55. adapted from *Verse Summary* I. 27, p. 12.
56. *Mūlamadhyamakakārikā*, XVIII. 9.
57. adapted from Conze, Edward, Verse Summary, XVIII. 7, p. 42.
58. *Op. cit.* XXIV. 8, 9.
59. *Mūlamadhyamakakārikā*, XXV. 24.
60. adapted from Conze, Edward, Verse Summary, XVI. 1-2, p. 38.
61. *Op.cit.*, XXV. 19.
62. *Mūlamadhyamakakārikā*, XXII. 16.
63. adapted from Conze, Edward, *Verse Summary*, XXVIII. 7, p. 62.
64. *Op. cit.* Maṅgalācaraṇaṁ.
65. *Mūlamadhyamakakārikā*, XXIV. 18, 19.
66. Murti, T. R. V., *The Central Philosophy of Buddhism*, p. 85.
67. *Ibid.* Footnote 3 to p. 85.
68. *Mūlamadhyamakakārikā*, XIII. 8.
69. Murti, T. R. V., *The Central Philosophy of Buddhism.* Appendix, p. 352.

Chapter II

THE PRINCIPAL EXPONENTS OF THE MADHYAMAKA SYSTEM IN INDIA

As we noted at the outset of the foregoing chapter, the Madhyamaka as a systematic philosophy was initially formulated by the great Buddhist scholar and saint ācārya Nāgārjuna. A great many episodes of perhaps a legendary character have been naturally associated with the life of this outstanding religious figure. The popular and traditional accounts of the life of ācārya Nāgārjuna invariably include at least some of these legends. Nonetheless, it is beyond doubt that Nāgārjuna was an historical personality.

A number of facts about the ācārya's life can be established with relative certainty. Modern scholars have for the most part tended to believe that Nāgārjuna lived some time during the later part of the second century. This, however, does not accord with recent archeological finds which indicate that Nāgārjuna more probably lived during the last quarter of the first and first quarter of the second centuries C.E.[1]

Nāgārjuna was born in the south, in what is now Andhra and was the son of a Brahmin. He travelled to Nālandā where he received ordination from Rāhulabhadra[2] and where he apparently remained for some time. The later portion of his historical life seems to have been largely spent at Śrīparvata[3] in Andhra at the monastery built for him by his friend and patron King Gotamīputra of the Śātavāhana line of Andhra. Indeed, it was for the King Gotamīputra that Nāgārjuna wrote the *Suhṛllekha* and *Ratnāvalī*.

Among the most important and popular legends associated with the life of the great ācārya are those concerning his birth and conversion and his procurement of the Prajñāpāramitā Sūtras. It is said that at the time of Nāgārjuna's birth a prophet foretold that if the child lived he would achieve unsurpassed greatness, but that unfortunately he would not live for more than seven days. By making appropriate offerings to Brahmins and Monks, his parents succeeded in extending his life to a period of seven years. However, it was foretold that beyond that period nothing could be done to prolong his life. Thus, his parents who were unwilling to behold his eminent death sent him away from their abode along with attendants and provisions for a long journey.

It is said that eventually he came to Nālandā where he became acquainted with the great Brahmin Saraha.[4] Nāgārjuna related the prophecy concerning his impending death to Saraha[5] who advised him that his life might be saved if he renounced the world. It is said that Nāgārjuna then agreed to do so and was initiated by Saraha into the mandala of Apāramitāyus. Through reciting the dhārani of the latter, Nāgārjuna was saved from the early death which had been prophesied for him.

Nāgārjuna's evident association with the Prajñāpāramitā literature is explained through the following legend commonly associated with his life. It is said that one day while he was engaged in teaching the doctrine to an assembly of listeners, he noticed that two of the youths who had been listening to his discourse disappeared beneath the ground when he had finished. The two youths were Nāgas[6] who invited the ācārya to their kingdom where he is said to have been presented with several volumes of the Prajñāpāramitā literature.[7]

Ācārya Nāgārjuna produced works of unequalled excellence in all areas of Buddhist philosophy and religion. Even excluding those works traditionally ascribed to Nāgārjuna the authenticity of which cannot be definitely established, Nāgārjuna's literary and philosophical contribution to the Buddhist and Indian intellectual tradition was immense.

Among the works definitely authored by Nāgārjuna perhaps the most important are the *Mūlamadhyamakakārikā*,[8] the *Śūnyatāsaptati*,[9] and autocommentary, The *Yuktiṣaṣṭikā*[10] and the *Vigrahavyāvartanī*[11] and autocommentary. The first three are predominantly expositions of the Madhyamaka philosophy. In them Nāgārjuna systematically criticises the independent reality of all entities and concepts through a variety of analytical and critical arguments. Thus, he expounds the principal elements of the Madhyamaka philosophy like : interdependent origination (pratītyasamutpāda), insubstantiality (niḥsvabhāvatā), emptiness (śūnyatā) and the middle path (madhyamapratipada).

The *Vigrahavyāvartanī* is an extremely interesting and valuable work which defends the Madhyamaka philosophy against the objections advanced by realists. From it a clear picture of the standpoint of the Madhyamaka in the area of epistemology and logic emerges. Inasmuch as the *Vigrahavyāvartanī* is particularly relevant to our study, an entire chapter has been devoted to it later in the text.

In addition to these works, Nāgārjuna almost certainly wrote the *Vaidalyasūtra* and *Prakaraṇa*, the *Vyavahārasiddhi*, the *Suhṛllekha*, the *Ratnāvalī*, the *Catuḥstava* (Nirupama, Lokātīta, Cittavajra and Paramārtha Stava), the *Pratītyasamutpādahṛdayakārikā* and *Sūtrasamuccaya*. Among these works, the *Vaidalyasūtra* and *Prakaraṇa*, the *Ratnāvalī* and *Suhṛllekha*, the *Catuḥstava* and the *Sūtrasamuccaya* perhaps deserve additional mention. The *Vaidalyasūtra* and *Prakaraṇa* is devoted to the refutation of the charges levelled by the realist logicians against the Madhyamaka. The *Ratnāvalī*, *Suhṛllekha* and *Sūtrasamuccaya* are interesting in that in them Nāgārjuna devotes his attention to the exposition of the practical application of Buddhist philosophy in religious discipline. The *Catuḥstava* is composed of devotional stanzas of the highest quality which indicate that Nāgārjuna in addition to being a philosopher par excellence was also possessed of a highly developed religious temperament.

In addition to these works, the *Prajñādaṇḍa*, the *Mahāyānaviṁśaka*, the *Upāyahṛdaya*, the *Mahāprajñāpāramitāśāstra*[12] and the *Daśabhūmivibhāṣāśāstra*[13] are said to have been written by Nāgārjuna. The authenticity of all these works is hard to establish beyond doubt, however all of them could well have been composed by Nāgārjuna. The *Mahāprajñāpāramitāśāstra* is not included in the Tibetan collection, however the *Daśabhūmivibhāṣāśāstra* is included. Nāgārjuna is also traditionally believed to have authored a great many works in the areas of medicine, alchemy and Tantra.

Nāgārjuna's immediate disciple and successor was Āryadeva. He merits a place among the great classical exponents of the Madhyamaka system which is second in importance only to that accorded to Nāgārjuna. Indeed, he must be said to share with the latter the honour of having founded the Madhyamaka system.

As in the case of the life of his master Nāgārjuna, the life of Āryadeva as it is traditionally retold is embellished with a great many attractive legends. Nonetheless, in the case of Āryadeva also there is no reasonable doubt that he was an historical personality. Nor is there any reason to doubt that he studied at the feet of Nāgārjuna. Thus, it may be said with relative certainty that Āryadeva was a younger contemporary of Nāgārjuna.

We are told by both Candrakīrti[14] and Tāranātha that Āryadeva was the son of King Pañcaśṛṅga[15] of the island of Siṁhala. Āryadeva, though he ascended to the throne of the land, was strongly inclined toward religion and so was moved to renounce the world. He received his monastic vows according to Tāranātha from the abbot Hemadeva.[16] He completed the study of the entire Tripiṭaka in his native land and then travelled to India on pilgrimage to visit the holy places of the various regions.

Tāranātha says that he met Nāgārjuna shortly before the latter left for Śrīparvata from the land of King Uḍayana.[17] Then at Śrīparvata he studied under Nāgārjuna. Bu-ston says that he became proficient in all the branches of science and in all the heterodox and orthodox philosophical systems.[18]

According to Tāranātha's account,[19] after the death of Nāgārjuna, Āryadeva assumed the responsibility for preserving and furthering the doctrine. He worked for the benefit of living beings through study and meditation in the area around Śrīparvata. He constructed twentyfour monasteries and made all of them centres of the Mahāyāna.

Again, according to Tāranātha, there was at that time a Brahmin called Durdharṣakāla,[20] who lived in the city of Khortā in Nalanī in the east. This Brahmin was at that time going about engaging Buddhists in philosophical debates and contests of miraculous powers and defeating them. When he reached Nālandā, the monks there were unable to face him and so they sent for help to Āryadeva.[21]

Āryadeva, it is said, thought the time was right to meet the Brahmin in a contest of knowledge and power, and so he set out for Nālandā. On the way, according to Tāranātha's account, he came upon a woman who required his eye in order to accomplish her religious practice. It is said that Āryadeva then gave her one of his eyes.[22]

When he reached Nālandā, Āryadeva through his skill in debate and miraculous powers, defeated the Brahmin Durdharṣakāla in a public contest. Eventually, the Brahmin was converted and became a master of Buddhist teaching.

Bu-ston's account of these incidents of Āryadeva's life differs slightly from that given by Tāranātha. The name of the Brahmin for instance who Āryadeva is said to have defeated is given as Mātṛceta.[23] Also, according to Bu-ston, the monks of Nālandā sent a message to Nāgārjuna who was then residing at Śrīparvata, but it was Āryadeva who went in his place.[24]

According to Tāranātha,[25] Āryadeva then remained at Nālandā for a considerable period of time after which he again returned to the south. Tāranātha says that in Ranganātha near Kāñcī he entrusted Rāhulabhadra with the responsibility for the teaching and passed away.

Tāranātha's account mentions that it was during the reign of King Candragupta, son of King Śālacandra that Āryadeva resided at Nālandā. His account also mentions a legend which gained great popularity in Tibet according to which Āryadeva was miraculously born of a lotus in the pleasure garden of the King of the island of Siṁhala. The King, according to the legend, raised Āryadeva as his son. Tāranātha, however, rejects this story on the evidence supplied by Candrakīrti in the introductory portion of his commentary to Āryadeva's *Catuḥśataka* and other Indian historical sources.[26]

Āryadeva's most important literary production is the *Catuḥśataka*. The work expounds the doctrine of insubstantiality (niḥsvabhāvatā). It is arranged in sixteen chapters of twenty-five stanzas each. The first half of the text is concerned with the religious discipline advocated by the Madhyamaka system, while the second is devoted to the refutation of opposing philosophical doctrines. Another work, the *Śataśāstra* attributed to Āryadeva was translated into Chinese by Kumārajīva in C.E. 404. It however according to Professor Murti seems to be an abridgement and rearrangement of the contents of the *Catuḥśataka*. The *Śataśāstra* is incidentally also not found in the Tibetan collection. Among the other important works of Āryadeva according to Bu-ston are the *Hastavalaprakaraṇa*, the *Skhalitapramathanayuktihetusiddhi*, the *Jñānasārasamuccaya* and so on.

Āryadeva followed the philosophical method of Nāgārjuna. We have Candrakīrti's authority for the fact that there exists no difference in the philosophical standpoints of Nāgārjuna and Āryadeva.[27] Thus, they are considered the founders of the Madhyamaka system. Āryadeva in his works devoted more attention to the criticism of heterodox philosophical systems, especially those of the Sāṅkhya and Vaiśeṣika. Although Nāgārjuna was also certainly familiar with these systems, he criticises their doctrines less frequently in his works than he does those of the Ābhidharmika philosophy. It seems that Nāgārjuna was first concerned to establish the Madhyamaka as the ultimate essence of Buddhist philosophy. Āryadeva demonstrated that the philosophical method of the Madhyamaka could be systematically and successfully applied to the doctrines of the heterodox schools. Thus, it is certainly true to say that the Madhyamaka philosophy owes much of its stability to the contribution of Āryadeva.[28]

With the advent of the masters Buddhapālita and Bhāvaviveka the Madhyamaka system entered a new phase. It was then that the Madhyamaka system was divided into the Prāsaṅgika and Svātantrika schools. The division in fact occurred as the result of the different interpretations offered by these two ācāryas of the philosophy of Nāgārjuna and Āryadeva.

Buddhapālita is considered the founder of the Prāsaṅgika-madhyamaka school because he held that the essence of the Madhyamaka philosophy could only be revealed through arguments *ad absurdum* (prasaṅgavākya). He probably lived during the first half of the third century C.E. According to Tāranātha's[29] account, Buddhapālita was born in a place known as Hamsakrīḍa, in Tambala in the south. He renounced the world and became vastly learned in the scriptures.

Buddhapālita studied under the master Saṁgharakṣita, a disciple of Ārya Nāgamitra, and learned from him the original works of Nāgārjuna. It is said that he attained the highest knowledge through intense meditation and that he had a direct vision of Ārya Mañjuśrī.

He is said to have taught the doctrine at the Dantapurī monastery in the south. There he expounded the works of Nāgārjuna, Āryadeva, Āryasūra and others. It is said that at last Buddhapālita practised the guṭikāsiddhi and attained success.

The only work of Buddhapālita which has been recorded is the *Mūlamadhyamakavṛtti*, the commentary which he wrote on the *Mūlamadhyamaka Kārikā* of Nāgārjuna. This work although lost in the original, is preserved in Tibetan translation.[30]

The master Bhāvaviveka to whom the credit of founding the

Svātantrikamadhyamaka school belongs may well have been a younger contemporary of Buddhapālita.[31] Be that as it may, Bhāvaviveka according to Tāranātha[32] studied the works of Buddhapālita only after the latter had passed away. The master Bhāvaviveka advanced his own interpretation of the thought of Nāgārjuna and refuted the opinion expressed by Buddhapālita. He maintained that independent syllogisms could be legitimately used by the Madhyamaka to convince opponents of the truth of the philosophy of emptiness.

According to Tāranātha, Bhāvaviveka was born in a noble Kṣatriya family in Malya-ra in the south. There he renounced the world and became a scholar of the Tripiṭaka. Later, he travelled to Madhyadeśa and studied under the master Saṁgharakṣita. From the latter he learned many Mahāyāna sūtras as well as the works of the master Nāgārjuna.

It is said that when he returned to the south he had a vision of Vajrapāṇi and that he attained extraordinary meditative powers. He became the head of about fifty monasteries in the south and delivered numerous discourses on the doctrine. Finally, he too practiced guṭikasiddhi and attained success.[33]

Tāranātha adds that while Buddhapālita did not have many followers, Bhāvaviveka had thousands of disciples and monks who followed him. As a result Tāranātha says his views were spread more extensively than those of Buddhapālita.

Bhāvaviveka composed a number of works of which perhaps the most important is his commentary to Nāgārjuna's *Mūlamadhyamakakārikā* entitled the *Prajñāpradīpa*.[34] In addition, he is said to have composed the *Madhyamakāvatārapradīpa*,[35] the *Madhyamakapratītyasamutpāda*, the *Karatalaratna*, the *Madhyamakahṛdayakārikā* and its commentary the *Tarkajvālā*.[36] Bhāvaviveka was undoubtedly well versed in the contemporary philosophical systems of his day, since the *Tarkajvālā* contains detailed expositions of the doctrines of the Sāṅkhya, Vaiśeṣika and Vedānta.[37]

Another outstanding exponent of the Madhyamaka system was the master Candrakīrti. He was, indeed, the foremost exponent of the Prāsaṅgikamadhyamaka school and his rigorous formulation of the orthodox Prāsaṅgika standpoint is accepted even today by the living Buddhist traditions of Tibet and Mongolia. Candrakīrti severely criticised Bhāvaviveka and the method of argument which he advocated for the Madhyamaka. He followed the method of argument suggested by Buddhapālita in his approach to the Madhyamaka philosophy, however the quantity and quality of his literary works in time earned him a place among the classical exponents of the Madhyamaka of even greater importance than that occupied by Buddhapālita.

Candrakīrti certainly lived later than Bhāvaviveka and Diṅnāga and was probably contemporaneous with Dharmakīrti. According to Tāranātha's account, he was born in Samanta in the south. He mastered all the branches of science at an early age and was ordained in his native land. He mastered all the Piṭakas as well as the Śāstras and Upadeśas of Nāgārjuna. He studied under many disciples of Bhāvaviveka and under Kamalabuddhi, a desciple of Budhapālita.[38]

It is said that Candrakīrti became supreme among the scholars of his time and was made the abbot of Nālandā. He popularised the teaching of Buddhapālita through composing many important works.[39]

It is said in addition that he often exhibited miraculous powers. He is, for instance, said to have supplied the entire Saṅgha with milk by milking the cow portrayed in a picture. Stone pillars and walls could not obstruct the movement of his hand or body. It is said that he defeated many opponents and eventually went again to the south.

In the country called Koṅ-ku-na, he is said to have defeated many opponents of the doctrine and converted most of the Brahmins and householders to Buddhism. He established many large centres of the doctrine.

According to one account mentioned by Tāranātha, Candrakīrti again spent a long time at the Manubhaṅga hill. There it is said he strove to attain the highest siddhi and achieved success. Bu-ston's account[40] of the life of Candrakīrti is in substantial agreement with that given by Tāranātha.

Candrakīrti's contribution to the philosophical literature of the Madhyamaka system was immense. Best known of his works are the *Mūlamadhyamakavṛttiprasannapadānāma*, a commentary on the *Mūlamadhyamakakārikā* of Nāgārjuna and the *Madhyamakāvatāra* an independent work on the Madhyamaka system. He also wrote an autocommentary on the *Madhyamakāvatāra* as well as commentaries on the *Yuktiṣaṣṭikā* and *Śūnyatāsaptati* of Nāgārjuna and on the *Catuḥśataka* of Āryadeva. Candrakīrti was evidently conversant with the philosophical developments of his time for he undertakes to criticise the doctrine of the Vijñānavāda, which had no doubt gained in popularity since the time of Nāgārjuna. Candrakīrti also comments on the worth of the logical innovations introduced by Diṅnāga.[41] He is also said to have written a number of works on Tantra among which the most important is the *Pradīpa-uddyotana*[42], a commentary on the *Guhyasamājatantra*.

Another great exponent of the Prāsaṅgikamadhyamaka school was the master Śāntideva. He composed works of the highest value concerning the spiritual discipline of the Madhyamaka. He is perhaps the last of the great Indian exponents of the Prāsaṅgika school.

Śāntideva lived perhaps a half century later than Candrakīrti.[43] According to the accounts given by both Tāranātha[44] and Bu-ston Śāntideva was born as the son of the king Kalyāṅavarman of Saurāṣṭra. He was then given the name Śāntivarman. Bu-ston says that he learned the methods of propitiating Mañjuśrī, and as a result he had visions of the deity in his dreams from his early youth.[45]

When he was about to ascend to his father's throne, he had visions of Mañjuśrī and Tārā in a dream on the night before his coronation was to take place.[46] Both deities strongly advised him not to accept the kingdom and so that very night he fled.

It is said that eventually he came to a spring at the edge of a forest where he met a woman who led him to a Yogī who was residing in a cave in the forest. Śāntideva is said to have been instructed by the Yogi and to have attained extraordinary knowledge through meditation. It is said that the woman and the Yogī were emanations of Tārā and Mañjuśrī. Thereafter he continuously had visions of Mañjuśrī.[47]

According to both Tāranātha and Bu-ston, Śāntideva was ordained by the abbot Jayadeva who was the foremost of five hundred scholars residing at Nālandā in Madhyadeśa.[48] It was then that he received the name Śāntideva.

For some time he remained at Nālandā and it was there that he composed two of his most important works, the *Sūtrasamuccaya* and the *Śikṣāsamuccaya*. When he was asked by the assembled scholars to recite a sūtra, he taught the *Bodhicaryāvatāra*. When he came to the stanza at the outset of the ninth chapter of the work which runs, "When existence and non-existence cease to be present before the intellect", he rose into the sky. Though his body became invisible, his voice continued to be heard until his recitation was completed.

According to the Tibetan accounts, Śāntideva then went to the south to Śrīdakṣiṇa and remained in the city of Kaliṅga in Triliṅga. Envoys were sent there to persuade him to return to Nālandā, however the master refused. Nonetheless, he told them where copies of the *Sūtrasamuccaya* and *Śikṣāsamuccaya* could be found. The *Bodhicaryāvatāra* was preserved in a version of one thousand stanzas as it was retained in the memory of the scholars of Nālandā. It is said that he then renounced the marks of a monk and lived as naked ascetic. Among the marvellous feats attributed to him the story of his defeat of the heretics led by Śaṅkaradeva somewhere in the south of India is widely recounted.[49] It is said that an enormous maṇḍala of the god Maheśvara was constructed in the sky by the heretics. Through his miraculous powers Śāntideva called up a great blast of wind which scattered the heretics and their maṇḍala.

Śāntideva is also said to have converted five hundred ascetics who were followers of the Pāṣaṇḍika teaching through sustaining them with food and drink when they had been deprived of their livelihood. It is also said that he converted a thousand beggars by similarly supplying them with sustenance when a famine befell the region in which they were living.

As it has been said, Śāntideva's most important works are the *Bodhicaryāvatāra* and the *Śikṣāsamuccaya*. The former is a work of the highest merit which takes up, among other topics, the creation of the enlightenment thought (bodhicitta). The ninth chapter of the *Bodhicaryāvatāra* is particularly interesting for its exposition of the standpoint of the Madhyamaka philosophy. Like Candrakīrti, Śāntideva rigorously criticises the doctrine of the Vijñānavāda.

The *Śikṣāsamuccaya* is a compendium of excerpts from Mahāyāna Sūtras which illustrate the practical religious discipline of the Madhyamaka. Śāntideva supplies twenty seven stanzas which serve as the headings under which the excerpts are collected.[50] The *Sūtrasamuccaya* is an abridged exposition of the contents of the *Śikṣāsamuccaya*.

Among the other classical Indian exponents of the Madhyamaka system, the masters Śrīgupta, Jñānagarbha, Śāntarakṣita and Kamalaśīla deserve mention. All of them were followers of the Svātantrikamadhyamaka, or Yogācārasvātantrikamadhyamaka schools. Bu-ston remarks that while Buddhapālita and Candrakīrti are the two principal representatives of the Prāsaṅgikamadhyamakas, or the Lokaprasiddhivargacārimadhyamakas, the teacher Bhāvaviveka is a follower of the Sautrāntikamadhyamakasvātantrika school. According to Bu-ston Śrīgupta, Jñānagarbha, Śāntarakṣita and Kamalaśīla are adherents of the Yogācāramadhyamakasvātantrika system.[51] These various schools within the Madhyamaka system gave their own interpretations of the thought of Nāgārjuna and Āryadeva.

The Master Śrīgupta was an adherent of the Svātantrika philosophy. It is said that he was worshipped by King Vimalacandra. Śrīgupta was a disciple of Sampradūta[52] and seems to have resided in Bhaṁgala.[53] Śrīgupta composed the *Tattvāloka*,[54] a work on Madhyamaka philosophy and logic.

The master Jñānagarbha was born in Odivisa.[55] It is said that he resided in the east during the time of King Gopāla. He studied under Śrīgupta in Bhaṁgala and attained fame as a great Svātantrika scholar. It is said that Jñānagarbha defeated opponents in debate and could recite numerous sūtras from his memory. He propitiated for a long time Ārya Avalokiteśvara and at last had a vision of the deity moving the cintāmaṇicakra. Jñānagarbha composed the *Madhyamakasatyadvayakārikā* and wrote his own commentary on the work.[56]

The Madhyamaka master Śāntarakṣita is the foremost representative of the Yogācāramadhyamaka or the Yogācāramadhyamakasvātantrika school. It was he and his immediate disciple Kamalaśīla who introduced systematic Buddhist philosophy into Tibet. Śāntarakṣita apparently lived sometime between King Gopāla and King Dharamapāla.

Śāntarakṣita composed the *Tattvasaṁgraha*, a compendium of the doctrines of philosophical systems and the respective criticisms appropriate to them. He also wrote the *Madhyamakālaṅkārakārikā* on which he composed his own commentary. In addition he is credited with the composition of a number of works on Tantra and on Prajñāpāramitā.

According to Bu-ston, Śāntarakṣita belongs to the philosophical tradition which included before him : Jñānagarbha, Śrīgupta, Bhāvaviveka, Nāgārjuna, Rāhula and Śāriputra. The portraits of these were painted on the walls of the monastery of bSamyas which was established in Tibet by Śāntarakṣita.[57]

Śantarakṣita's immediate disciple was Kamalaśīla. Like his master, he too went to Tibet. He composed the *Madhyamakāloka*[58] expounding the Madhyamaka philosophy in accord with the interpretation favoured by the Svātantrikas. He also wrote the *Bhāvanākrama* as well as a commentary on the *Madhyamakālaṅkāra* of Śāntarakṣita.

Kamalaśīla met Hva-shan Mahāyāna, an exponent of the Chinese school of Buddhism in a philosophical debate in Tibet, the outcome of which largely determined the subsequent character of Tibetan Buddhism. Eventually, he met his death in Tibet at the hands of assasins.

Thus, in this chapter we have attempted to survey briefly the lives and works of some of the outstanding classical Indian Madhyamaka scholars. In addition, we have tried to indicate their respective places in the development of the Madhyamaka philosophy. Nāgārjuna, Āryadeva, Buddhapālita, Bhāvaviveka, Candrakīrti, Śāntideva, Śrīgupta, Jñānagarbha, Śāntarakṣita and Kamalaśīla were selected for discussion in this chapter either because of their overall importance to the development of the Madhyamaka philosophy, or because we shall have occasion to consider their views in greater detail in subsequent chapters.

References

1. Ramanan, V., *Nāgārjuna's Philosophy*, pp. 27-28.
2. Bu-ston, *History of Buddhism*. Translated by Obermittei, E., II, p.123.
3. *Op. cit.*, p. 25.
4. According to Tibetan tradition the Great Brahmin Sāraha and Rāhulabhadra appear to be identical.
5. Bu-ston, *History of Buddhism*, II, pp. 123.
6. Nāgas are semi-divine beings who dwell beneath the earth.
7. Bu-ston, *History of Buddhism*, II, p. 124.
8. rTsa-ba-śes-rab.
9. Stoṅ—ñid-bdun-cu-ba. *bstan-'gyur-mdo*. XVII. No. 4.
10. Rigs-pa-drug-cu-pa. *Tg. mdo*. XVII. No. 2.
11. rTod-pa-bzlog-pa. *Tg. mdo*. XVII. No. 5.
12. Chinese Tripiṭaka Nanjio, II 69.
13. *Ibid.* 1180.

14. Murti, T. R. V., *The Central Philosophy of Buddhism*, p. 92.
15. Tāranātha, *History of Buddhism*. Translated by Lama Chimpa and Chattopadhyaya, Alaka, p. 124.
16. *Ibid.*
17. *Ibid.*
18. Bu-ston, *History of Buddhism*, II, p. 130.
19. Tāranātha, *History of Buddhism*, p.124.
20. *Ibid.*
21. *Ibid.* p. 125.
22. *Ibid.* p. 126.
23. Bu-ston, *History of Buddhism*, II, p. 130.
24. *Ibid.*
25. Tāranātha, *History of Buddhism*, p. 126.
26. Tāranātha, *History of Buddhism*, pp. 123-124. Bu-ston follows the legendary account. Bu-ston, *History of Buddhism*, II. p. 130. Professor Murti also refers to the account given by Candrakīrti. Murti, T. R. V., *The Central Philosophy of Buddhism*, p. 92.
27. Murti, T. R. V., *The Central Philosophy of Buddhism*, p. 92.
28. *Ibid.*
29. Tāranātha, *History of Buddhism*, p. 186.
30. Tg. mdo. XVII. 20. Tāranātha, *History of Buddhism*, p. 186.
31. Murti, T. R. V., *The Central Philosophy of Buddhism*, p. 95.
32. Tāranātha, *History of Buddhism*, p. 186.
33. *Ibid.* pp. 186-187.
34. *Tg. mdo.* XVIII. 8.
35. *Tg. mdo.* XVII. 1.
36. *Tg. mdo.* XIX. 2.
37. Murti, T. R. V., *The Central Philosophy of Buddhism*, p. 98.
38. Tāranātha, *History of Buddhism*, p. 198.
39. *Ibid.* pp. 198-199.
40. Bu-ston, *History of Buddhism*, II, pp. 134-135.
41. Murti, T. R. V., *The Central Philosophy of Buddhism*, p. 100; Stcherbatsky, Th., *The Conception of Buddhist Nirvāṇa*, pp. 211-215.
42. *Tg. Rgyud.* XXVIII. I.
43. Murti, T. R. V., *The Central Philosophy of Buddhism*, p. 87 and footnote 6 to p. 100.
44. Tāranātha, *History of Buddhism*, p. 215.
45. Bu-ston, *History of Buddhism*, II. p. 162.
46. *Op.cit.* p. 215.
47. Tāranātha, *History of Buddhism*, p. 216.
48. *Ibid.* p. 217; Bu-ston, *History of Buddhism*, II, p. 162.
49. Bu-ston, *History of Buddhism*, II, 165; Tāranātha does not mention the name of Saṅkaradeva.
50. Murti, T. R.V., *The Central Philosophy of Buddhism*, p. 101.
51. Bu-ston, *History of Buddhism*, II, p. 135.
52. Tāranātha, *History of Buddhism*, p. 225.
53. *Ibid.* p. 253.

54. De-kho-na-nid-snaṅ-ba. quoted by bSod-nams Sen-ge in the *dBu-ma-spyi-ston*, p. 267.

55. Tāranātha, *History of Buddhism*, p. 259.

56. According to Śākya mChog-lDan Jñānagarbha visited Tibet during the reign of Khri-sroṅ-lDe-bTsan and it was there that he composed the *Madhyamakasatyadvayakārikā*. The *complete works of Sākya-mChog-lDan*, Vol. 14, p. 517.

57. Bu-ston, *History of Buddhism*, II, p. 190.

58. dBu-ma-snan-ba. According to Śākya mChog lDan the *Madhyamakāloka* was composed in Tibet. *Op.cit.* Vol. 14, p. 517.

Chapter III

THE MADHYAMAKA PHILOSOPHY

In this chapter we attempt a general introduction to the Madhyamaka philosophy as it was formulated by Nāgārjuna and some of the other principal exponents of the system. We shall attempt to indicate the fundamental philosophical orientation of the Madhyamaka and its approach to philosophical problems. The discussion therefore inevitably proceeds from the general to the particular. It is hoped that this chapter will supply an overall picture of the Madhyamaka philosophy which will facilitate an understanding of the subsequent chapters which deal with the alternative methods evolved within the Madhyamaka system of handling a specific philosophical problem.

Attention must first of all be drawn to the fact that philosophical systems in India were seldom, if ever, purely speculative or descriptive. Virtually all the great philosophical systems of India, Sāṅkhya, Advaitavedānta, Madhyamaka and so forth, were preeminently concerned with providing a means to liberation or salvation. It was a tacit assumption with these systems that if their philosophy were correctly understood and assimilated, an unconditioned state free from suffering and limitation could be achieved. Thus, it may be said that Indian philosophy in general and the Madhyamaka have a fundamentally soteriological orientation. If this fact is overlooked, as often happens as a result of the propensity engendered by formal Occidental philosophy to consider the philosophical enterprise as a purely descriptive one, the real significance of Indian and Buddhist philosophy will be missed.

If we are to appreciate the functioning of soteriology, we must first look at the initial immediate experience which impels the philosophical venture inasmuch as it is concerned with liberation or salvation. This immediate experience is that of suffering and limitation. The initial starting point for the soteriological philosophies of India is therefore the fundamentally dissatisfactory nature of existence as we ordinarily experience it. Indeed, without this immediate experience of suffering and limitation, soteriological philosophy must remain an enigma.

This immediate experience of the dissatisfactory nature of existence was termed suffering (duḥkha) by the Buddhist. Suffering and limitation is therefore the fundamental philosophical problem. Its removal is the concern of soteriological philosophy, which seeks the means appropriate and capable of removing suffering.

Since the philosophical enterprise is essentially a rational one and since causality is the fundamental principle governing rational experience, the soteriological philosopher first seeks to uncover the cause of suffering. For the Buddhist ignorance (avidyā) or craving (tṛṣṇā) is the cause of suffering. Of these ignorance is the more fundamental because it conditions craving. Thus, it may be considered the dominant cause of suffering. The Sāṅkhya and Advaitavedānta also reached somewhat similar conclusions.[1]

In counter-distinction to the immediate experience of suffering, the soteriological philosopher admits the possibility of an unconditioned state characterised by the absence of suffering and limitation. Thus unconditioned state is either experienced immediately by the enlightened or mediately by the neophyte; it is Nirvāṇa, liberation or salvation.

Once the two states, that of suffering and limitation, and the unconditioned state, have been experienced immediately and mediately, and the cause of the former determined, the soteriological philosopher then sets about formulating specific and effective means of achieving the transition from the conditioned to the unconditioned. This is the concern of practical or applied soteriology, which reveals itself in the formulation of various methods of achieving an unconditioned state.

We have said that the starting point of soteriological philosophy is the immediate experience of suffering and limitation. For the soteriological philosopher, suffering and limitation pervade the conditioned universe. For the Buddhist, therefore, suffering and limitation are present in all conditioned states whether they be relatively fortunate or miserable. Separation, distress, frustration, temporality and so on all constitute suffering. Conditioned existence which is characterised by birth, decay and death is of the nature of suffering and limitation.

The unconditioned, the attainment of which is liberation, is by implication free of all the predicates applicable to conditioned existence. The task of soteriological philosophy indeed depends upon the experience, immediate or mediate, of an unconditioned state. The Buddha declares in a celebrated *Udāna* passage that if there were not an unborn, an unconditioned, there would not be an escape from suffering and limitation.[2]

The nature of the unconditioned is beyond thought and language. It admits of no definition in terms of existence, non-existence and so forth. It is unoriginated and unextinguished, and its attainment is said to be peace and bliss; liberation from suffering and bondage.

We have said that for the Buddhists, as well as for some other Indian soteriological philosophers, ignorance is the cause of suffering and limitation. This is an immediate indication of the importance of the subjective element in Buddhist and some other soteriological philosophies of India. For these philosophical systems the transition from conditioned existence to the unconditioned is, at least in part, a subjective change involving the epistemological subject. This conception of the subjective nature of liberation is most evident in those philosophical systems which have been termed absolutist[3], like the Madhyamaka and Śaṅkara's Advaitavedānta. Nonetheless, its beginnings are also present in dualistic or pluralistic philosophies, like those of the Sāṅkhya and the Ābhidharmika. For the Pre-Madhyamaka Buddhist schools, the Vaibhāṣikas and the Sautrāntikas, subjective imagination (vikalpa) conditioned by ignorance (avidyā) is responsible for the notions of permanence, a self and so on. As a consequence attachment, aversion, and delusion exist and give rise to suffering and limitation. When the false notions of permanence, a self and so on, which originate from subjective imagination are abandoned, detachment and liberation are attained.

This conception is in complete consonance with the requisites of soteriological philosophy discussed above. It however has one major shortcoming. It fails ultimately to resolve the problem of conditioned existence. Conditioned existence is for these schools real, as real as the unconditioned. The goal of soteriological philosophy however is the attainment of an unconditioned state and escape from conditioned existence. The conception of the Ābhidharmika does not supply a completely satisfactory solution to the fundamental problem of soteriological philosophy, because the goal of soteriology, i.e. liberation, and a significant part of reality are sundered. The Sāṅkhya conception similarly fails to supply an ultimately satisfactory soteriological philosophy for essentially the same reason.[4] These two dualistic and pluralistic soteriological philosophies, the Sāṅkhya and the Ābhidharmika, were subjected to an absolutist critique which sought to identify reality completely with the goal of soteriology. This was done in the Brahmanical tradition by Śaṅkara's Advaitavedānta and in the Buddhist by the Madhyamaka.

For the absolutist soteriological philosopher, conditioned existence characterised by the experience of suffering and limitation is mere appearance, or illusion. This illusion owes its existence to the bewilderment and ignorance of the epistemological subject. For these systems, liberation and the unconditioned are reality. The suffering and limitation of conditioned existence is illusion which only appears as real to the epistemological subject so long as he remains under the influence of delusion.

As is evident the absolutist soteriological philosophies have the advantage of identifying, without residue, the whole of reality with the goal of soteriology. In addition the absolutist philosophies negation of duality annihilates the ground of the subjective illusion which is responsible for the appearance of the suffering and limitation of conditioned existence. The transition from conditioned existence to the unconditioned is subjective and is effected by the annihilation of ignorance. Conditioned existence and the unconditioned are in reality identical. The appearance of the former is only subjective illusion.

The Madhyamaka indeed paved the way for the absolutist standpoint in Indian philosophy. It was the first system to consistently employ the distinction between the two standpoints, phenomenal (saṁvṛti) and ultimate (paramārtha). This distinction is paralleled almost exactly in the Advaitavedānta.[5] The latter, which in fact represents the other principal example of the absolutist standpoint in Indian philosophy, formulated its doctrine in the light of the Madhyamaka philosophy.

Reality, for the absolutist, must be unconditioned. Phenomena exist relative to other phenomena and are conditioned by them. Hence the universe as it appears to ordinary perception is ultimately unreal. The universe of relative or subjective illusion is superseded by unconditioned reality. When the obscurations of ignorance and emotions are removed the actual state of reality, as unconditioned and inexpressible, reveals itself.

For the absolutist, phenomena are like a mirage or a dream. Phenomena, like a mirage or a dream, appear as the result of a combination of conditions. The relative existence of phenomena is thus apparitional. Despite the fact that phenomena appear, they are devoid of any substantiality. Therefore, for the absolutist phenomena are of the apparitional nature of a mirage or a dream.

The principal architect of illusion is consciousness (citta) or the intellect (buddhi). Consciousness conditioned by propensities (vāsanā) fabricates the phenomenal universe which is but the construction of imagination (prapañca)[6]. The process of fabrication is, however, instinctive and unconscious.

The Madhyamaka philosophy lays great stress on the role of intellectual functions in the fabrication of the universe. This concept, although elevated to the status of ultimate reality by the exponents of the Vijñānavāda, is of almost equal importance for the Madhyamaka. The latter, however, does not go so far as to accord ultimate reality to consciousness as does the Vijñānavādin. The importance accorded by the Madhyamaka to the role of consciousness in the fabrication of the universe is evident not only in the doctrine of the synchronistic school of Śāntarakṣita but also in the thought of Nāgārjuna and Candrakīrti.

The role of consciousness, or the intellect in the philosophy of Nagārjuna and Candrakīrti, is indeed very prominent. Nāgārjuna at several places attributes the appearance of the universe of phenomena to intellectual functions. Candrakīrti is even more specific in his opinion that intellectual functions are responsible for the appearance of phenomena, as shall be seen shortly. Indeed the synthesis of the philosophies of the Madhyamaka and Vijñānavāda advocated by Śāntarakṣita, according to which the former is accepted as valid of ultimate reality and the latter valid with respect to the phenomenal, seems to have been very much implicit in the thought of Nāgārjuna and Candrakīrti. A survey of the works of these two Madhyamaka masters will reveal that they both stressed the role played by intellectual functions in the fabrication of the phenomenal universe.

In the *Pratītyasamutpādahṛdayakārikā* Nāgarjuna suggests that causality is the work of imagination (vikalpa). He also declares, "The wheel of existence originates from the propensity for erroneous imagination (vikalpa)."[7] In the *Śūnyatāsaptati* and *Mūlamadhyamakakārikā*, Nāgārjuna states that the emotional obscuration of attachment, aversion and delusion originate from imagination (vikalpa).[8] The former are extinguished in emptiness. Thus, for Nāgārjuna intellectual functions and constructs like propensities, imagination and thought constructions are responsible for the sustenance of the phenomenal universe.

Candrakīrti echoes Nāgārjuna, but goes much further. He declares that concepts like knowledge and the object of knowledge, the verbal expression and the object expressed, the agent and action are the constructions of imgination (vikalpa). The same is true of the aggregates like form and feeling and of the notions of objects like a jug, cloth, a crown, a chariot, a man and a woman. The notions of profit, loss. happiness, notoriety, praise, blame, and so on are all nothing but the constructions of imagination. These notions originate from thought constructions (prapañca) which Candrakīrti declares are beginningless.[9] The extent of the list of notions which, according to Candrakīrti, originate from imagination leaves little doubt that for him this intellectual function is responsible for the appearance of the whole of the phenomenal universe. As it will be observed, the notions cited by Candrakīrti include those belonging to the categories of commonsense, epistemology, language, ethics, philosophy and society.

Candrakīrti parallels the thought of Nāgārjuna when he states that the knowledge of all phenomena which originate from intellectual functions as empty of self-existence (svabhāva) results in their extinction in emptiness. The foremost among the constructions of imagination is the conception that entities possess objective reality. The whole network of the constructions of imagination, which include all the notions cited above originates from this fundamental misconception. The extinction of this conception results in the dissolution of all the erroneous constructions of imagination.[10]

Thus, for the Madhyamaka, the phenomenal universe which is but the construction of thought is fabricated by imagination conditioned by propensities. It is a subjective illusion which is of the nature of an erroneous perception. The Madhyamaka likens the erroneous perception of the phenomenal universe to the perception of a snake in the place of a rope under the influence of imperfect lighting.[11] Candrakīrti likens the perception of the phenomenal universe to the perception of hair experienced by one suffering from defective vision.[12] Inasmuch as the phenomenal universe is an illusion, it has no ontological status. Thus, it cannot ultimately be said of the phenomenal universe that it exists, does not exist, originates or is extinguished, etc.[13] Just as fictitious appearances which have no objective reality appear to the deluded, so the phenomenal universe appears to the naive consciousness. In reality the nature of phenomena, like the nature of the ultimate is devoid of any substantiality, empty and inconceivable.

Nāgārjuna declares, "Just as an illusory elephant which is only a delusion of consciousness comes not from anywhere, goes not nor really stays, so this world of illusion which is just a delusion of consciousness comes not from anywhere, goes not nor really stays."[14] Conditioned phenomena for the Madhyamaka are devoid of substantiality like appartitions conjured up by a magician. Śāntideva states, "An effect also does not come from anywhere, it does not stay, nor does it go elsewhere. What difference then has this effect which originates from causes and conditions and which is held to be real by deluded people, from a magical show."[15]

The Madhyamaka, thus, expresses the view that phenomena like dreams and illusion are ultimately empty of any objective reality. The critics of the system have often confused this doctrine deliberately or otherwise with nihilism. The Madhyamaka has, thus, been assailed by its opponents as follows. If indeed the phenomenal universe is empty of any objective reality and is similar to an illusion, then the factuality of the universe as it is experienced by the vast majority of mankind must necessarily be discarded. The law of causality as well as its ethical co-relative, the law of karma, can have no place in such an illusory universe. Such a philosophy, so the argument goes, is equivalent to scepticism and nihilism.

Nāgārjuna was quite evidently aware of this possible misunderstanding of the doctrine advocated by the Madhyamaka. He declares of Śūnyatā, that this doctrine wrongly understood ruins the unwise because they sink into the filth of nihilistic views.[16] Nāgārjuna also states, "A wrongly understood emptiness ruins an unintelligent person. It is like a snake badly caught or a magical formula wrongly executed."[17]

The Madhyamaka's contention that the phenomenal universe is empty of objective reality and illusory ought not to be considered in isolation. Immediately it must be recalled that it presupposes the distinction between the two standpoints, phenomenal and ultimate. Therefore, Nāgārjuna declares that those who do not understand the distinction between the two standpoints cannot appreciate the doctrine of the Madhyamaka which is the profound truth of Buddhism.[18]

The Madhyamaka's declaration that phenomena are devoid of independent reality and therefore illusory is made from the standpoint of the ultimate truth (paramārthasatya). It does not contradict the law of causality as it operates in the phenomenal universe. Nāgārjuna is extremely specific in declaring that the law of interdependent origination (pratītyasamutpāda) and emptiness (śūnyatā) are identical in import. Their distinction depends upon the standpoint taken. Not only is emptiness in complete correspondence with the law of interdependent origination, but is in fact immediately derived from the latter. Thus, a complete and unbiased picture of the Madhyamaka philosophy must include the two indispensable elements of interdependent origination and emptiness which correspond to the two standpoints phenomenal and ultimate relied upon by the Madhyamaka. Indeed, Nāgārjuna declares several times that whatever is interdependent origination is emptiness.[19]

Causality means for the Buddhist origination dependent upon a combination of conditions. The doctrine of emptiness is not at variance with the law of phenomenal causality, however the doctrine which attributes independent reality to entities is. Independently existing phenomena do not require causality. The function of causality with respect to such phenomena is altogether incomprehensible.

Nāgārjuna elaborates the doctrine of the equivalence of interdependent origination and emptiness in the *Vigrahavyāvartanī*[20] and in the *Śūnyatāsaptati*.[21] In fact the philosophical equation usually includes three terms, interdependent origination, insubstantiality and emptiness. Phenomena are interdependently originated (pratītyasamutpanna). They are therefore devoid of independent existence (niḥsvabhāva) which equals their emptiness (śūnyatā).

Phenomena originate from a combination of conditions. They do not come into existence of themselves, nor do they appear unless the appropriate conditions are present. The existence of phenomena is therefore conditioned and relative. This quality of existing dependent upon and relative to other factors is termed the emptiness of phenomena. Thus, it is quite evident that interdependent origination and emptiness go hand in hand. The former corresponds to the phenomenal, the latter to ultimate reality.

Emptiness is not only in correspondence with the phenomenal universe governed by the law of interdependent origination, but is also completely compatible with commonsense notions regarding the pragmatic applications of the law of causality. Nāgārjuna demonstrates in the *Vigrahavyāvartanī*[22] that the ordinary utility of phenomena is consistent with emptiness. The same is true of the law of karma.

No doubt causality and the law of karma are subjective illusions constructed by imagination. Nonetheless they exercise their respective functions with infallible regularity until such time as an unconditioned state is attained through the annihilation of imagination. Only when an unconditioned state is attained is there release from the laws of causality and karma.

As we have noted for the Madhyamaka all phenomena are empty (śūnya). Emptiness annihilates the alternatives constructed by imagination like existence and non-existence. It transcends thought and expression and is declared to be the actual nature of all phenomena. This is the ultimate truth for the Madhyamaka. The attainment of knowledge of the ultimate truth effects a soteriological change in the subject. When this knowledge is of an extraordinary and immediate character, it results in liberation or salvation.

According to the Madhyamaka, the enlightened possess extraordinary and immediate knowledge of ultimate reality. The neophyte, on the contrary, must be led initially to a mediate cognition of ultimate reality by means of arguments, statements and examples. These constitute the discoursive soteriology of the Madhyamaka. These devices of discoursive soteriology which are intended to produce in the neophyte a mediate cognition of the ultimate have no objective reality for the enlightened. Such devices are pragmatic in nature and are validated merely by their effectiveness in producing the soteriological change which is wanted. The devices of discoursive soteriology are illusory no doubt, but that does not prevent them from exercising their intended function. Nāgārjuna makes this point very clearly in the *Vigrahavyāvartanī*,[23] as will be seen later. This too is in complete accord with what we have said about the compatibility of the ultimate emptiness of all phenomena with their relative reality.

Candrakīrti declares that ultimate reality does not correspond to thought or expression. The neophyte however cannot be expected to comprehend the nature of the ultimate without having it demonstrated to him. Thus, so that the neophyte may be brought to a cognition of the ultimate, conventional reality, i.e. the phenomenal is employed. Candrakīrti goes on to quote a passage from the *Catuḥśataka* of Āryadeva to the effect that without relying upon worldly conventions, one cannot approach the world.[24]

While ultimate reality is inexpressible because it is devoid of any object of consciousness, still in accord with the conventions of the world, phenomenal reality is admitted provisionally. Candrakīrti declares that through imagination various epithets of the ultimate are mentioned.[25]

The enlightened employ the devices of discoursive soteriology as a convenient means of producing a mediate cognition of the ultimate truth in the neophyte. They adduced the arguments and examples which are likely to appeal to their interlocutors and to produce the desired cognition. The enlightened thus bring about a cognition of the ultimate reality in the neophyte through arguments which the latter is capable of understanding.[26]

The arguments and examples employed by the enlightened are intended to produce a soteriological transition in the neophyte. Candrakīrti says that the neophyte whose vision is obscured by ignorance fabricates the conception that phenomena exist in reality. Phenomena, however, do not exist at all from the ultimate standpoint of the enlightened. The neophyte is therefore tormented by something which is quite unreal and which is merely imagined by him to exist. The enlightened seek to induce the neophyte to abandon the cause of his torment, i.e., the mistaken conception that phenomena exist in reality through the devices of discoursive soteriology.[27]

As we have seen for the Madhyamaka the phenomenal universe is fabricated by consciousness or the intellect through imagination. This process of fabrication is however instinctive and unconscious. The characteristic method of the discoursive soteriology of the Madhyamaka is reflective or self-conscious examination (parīkṣā). In this way the efficient power of the intellect which functions unconsciously to fabricate the phenomenal universe is used to self-consciously dismantle the constructions of imagination through rational analysis. The Madhyamaka uses a distinct kind of logic in its self-conscious examination of the constructions of imagination. It must not be confused with the ordinary empirical logic which functions within the limits of the phenomenal. The latter is concerned with securing the success of volitional action directed toward an object and presupposes to a greater or lesser extent a realistic ontology. The logic employed by the Madhyamaka, on the other hand, is concerned with revealing the nature of ultimate reality. It is not therefore coincidental that Madhyamaka scholars consistently avoided the term logic (nyāya) when speaking of the critical philosophical method of the Madhyamaka. They preferred to speak of it as reasoning (yukti) or to employ some phrase which indicates that the logic of the Madhyamaka is intended to determine the nature of ultimate reality.

This does not mean however that the logic of the Madhyamaka is irrational or even mystical as that term is usually understood. The Madhyamaka logic like the logic in use in the world employs empirical categories like existence, non-existence, identity, difference and time. However, unlike ordinary logicians, the Madhyamaka does not admit the reality of these categories. The critical arguments of the Madhyamaka function through these categories given by the structure of thought but their intention is to expose the logical impossibility of every fabrication of consciousness. This, when accomplished, results in a mediate cognition of the unconditioned nature of ultimate reality.

The phenomenal universe is commonly thought to be a collection of objects held together by relationship. The objects are empirical facts given directly in experience. The relationships are either objective or subjective concepts depending upon one's philosophical bias. It is important to remember however that for the Madhyamaka both objects and relationships are constructed by imagination. Thus, when the Madhyamaka declares that all entities, i.e. phenomena are ultimately unreal, the phrase all entities exhausts the totality of objects.

The categories of existence and non-existence, identity and difference and time sustain and structure the phenomenal universe. They do not however enable us to formulate a consistent and ultimately rational picture of reality, nor are they in themselves consistent or ultimately logically possible. When examined critically, all phenomena are ultimately relative, devoid of independent existence and empty.

The Madhyamaka critically examines an endless variety of phenomenal fabrications of consciousness through a logic of dialectic designed to reveal the unconditioned and ineffable nature of ultimate reality. In order to illustrate the philosophical method of the Madhyamaka, let us look at the system's treatment of some of the more important objects of the Madhyamaka critique. It may perhaps be convenient to begin with the criticism of what may be the most fundamental of all the constructions of imagination, the concept of existence, and then proceed to consider the system's treatment of other phenomena like causality, karma, the Self etc.

Ultimate existence cannot be attributed to phenomena. Ultimate existence would be unconditioned and independent, however as we have seen, phenomena exist relative to other factors.[28] Moreover if phenomena existed ultimately, i.e., had an independent existence, they would not be subject to extinction and destruction. They would then be eternal static verities.[29] Ultimate existence can therefore not be predicated of phenomena.

As an empty concept too, existence is ultimately impossible. It has no conceptual reality of its own, but is relative to the notion of non-existence. The concept of existence is therefore devoid of independent reality and is thus ultimately unreal.

Nor can absolute non-existence be predicated of phenomena, since phenomena do possess an apparitional nature, i.e., they appear before consciousness relative to conditions. Again as an empty concept, non-existence like existence is ultimately impossible. The concept of non-existence does not possess any independent reality, but exists relative to the notion of existence.

Non-existence is therefore ultimately unreal. Moreover, existence and non-existence are also not intelligible in terms of identity or difference. Existence and non-existence cannot exist dissociated from each other, but neither can they exist together. Thus, existence and non-existence both are ultimately unreal.

So far as causality is concerned, as we have already noted, it cannot have any function with respect to phenomena which exist ultimately. Phenomena which have an independent reality do not require causality. Alternatively, if phenomena absolutely do not exist, it cannot be thought that they can be brought into existence by causal conditions. Again the relationship between cause and effect cannot be comprehended either in terms of identity or difference. If the cause is identical with the effect, causality is impossible, if different, it is also impossible. Moreover the causality is similarly impossible whether the cause and effect be simultaneous or successive. Hence causality is logically impossible if considered from the standpoint of ultimate truth. Inasmuch as a considerable part of the latter portions of this text shall be devoted to the Madhyamaka treatment of the problem of causality, we may for the present content ourselves with this rather terse summary. The full extent of the Madhyamaka's critique of causality will become apparent as we proceed.

At this point, it is important to note that identity and difference, which have been mentioned several times, also do not possess any independent reality. Ultimate identity and ultimate difference are logically impossible. Like existence and non-existence, identity and difference cannot exist together, but dissociated from each other they are also impossible.

Again the Madhyamaka considers the notions of a characteristic and the characterised substratum, in other words attribute and substance. Nāgārjuna devotes portions of both the *Mūlamadhyamakakārikā* and *Śūnyatāsaptati* to this question.[30] The latter work also contains a rather detailed examination of the notions of a characteristic and the characterised substratum. The problem is an important one because it is upon the conception of the inherent relationship between a characteristic and the characterised substratum that the realist rests his contention that phenomena possess objective reality. The question also concerns epistemology, since the realist takes the perception of a characteristic as verification of the existence of a substratum.

Neither a charactetistic nor the charactetised substratum exist ultimately. They possess no independent reality. Through the characterised substratum a characteristic exists. Again through a characteristic the characterised substratum exists. Neither exist independently. Inasmuch as neither a characteristic nor the characterised substratum exist ultimately, they cannot ultimately establish each other. Thus, a characteristic and the characterised substratum are logically impossible if considered from the standpoint of ultimate truth. The realist's contention that the existence of a substratum is proved by its characteristic is vacuous. The notion of ultimately existing characteristics is likewise impossible.[31]

The Madhyamaka also criticises the notion of action (karma). Nāgārjuna takes up the question of karma in the seventeenth chapter of the *Mūlamadhyamakakārikā* and in the *Śūnyatāsaptati*. Karma does not exist ultimately because it does not possess independent reality. Neither karma nor the author of karma, i.e. the agent, exist independently. Karma originates from adherence to a self inasmuch as the latter is simply a construction of imagination; karma does not ultimately exist. As for the author of karma he exists only relative to karma. If action does not exist, the agent also is impossible. As is evident, this discussion also touches upon the question of substance and attribute. Again the fruit of karma cannot exist apart from an agent and action. Since the latter two are ultimately unreal, the fruit of karma is also impossible from the standpoint of ultimate truth. Since all three agent, action, and fruit are thus ultimately unreal, the experiencer of the fruit of action is also ultimately impossible. Karma as well as the concepts of an agent, an individual, a fruit and an experiencing subject which are necessarily associated with it are all devoid of independent reality. They are therefore ultimately empty and similar to a fairy city in the sky, a mirage and a dream.[32]

The Madhyamaka also examines the concept of a self (ātman). Nāgārjuna devotes the eighteenth chapter of the *Mūlamadhyamakakārikā* to a critique of the self. Oddly enough the concept receives only incidental attention from Nāgārjuna in the *Śūnyatāsaptati*.

The self too is a relative concept. It exists relative to the psychophysical constituents (upādānaskandha). Therefore the self does not possess any independent or ultimate reality. The psycho-physical constituents similarly exist relative to the notion of a self, therefore they too are devoid of independent reality. While the self and the psycho-physical constituents depend one upon the other for their existence, they are not intelligible either in terms of identity or difference. The self and the psycho-physical constituents are not identical, but neither can they exist disassociated from each other. The self and the psycho-physical constituents are therefore empty; the unreal constructions of imagination.[33] Nāgārjuna's critique of the relationship between fire and fuel contained in the tenth chapter of the *Mūlamadhyamakakārikā* is equally valid in the case of the self and the psycho-physical constituents.

The Madhyamaka also rejects the ultimate reality of concepts like time and motion. Motion is exhaustively discussed by Nāgārjuna in the second chapter of the *Mūlamadhyamakakārikā* and the concept of time is taken up in the nineteenth chapter of that work and in the *Śūnyatāsaptati*. The discussion of these two concepts, especially the former again touches upon the question of the relationship between substance and attribute.

Motion, like the other notions we have taken up does not possess independent reality. It is, therefore, ultimately impossible. The concept of motion exists relative to a subject of which it is predicated. The subject which moves and motion are, therefore, mutually dependent one upon the other for their existence. Hence motion is ultimately unreal. Moreover motion is also seen to be impossible when it is examined by means of the three moments of time—past, present and future. Motion therefore since it does not exist independently or rationally does not exist ultimately.

As for time, it too is a concept devoid of independent reality. The notion of time exists relative to phenomena. Disassociated from phenomena, time is impossible. Phenomena do not exist ultimately. Therefore, time too is unreal. Moreover, time itself is not a unitary concept but is divided into three components—past, present and future. Past, present and future time again are devoid of independent reality inasmuch as they exist only relative to each other. Hence, time too is a construction of imagination which is devoid of objective reality. It does not exist ultimately.

Thus, all phenomena are found to be devoid of independent reality when examined critically. All phenomena are therefore, ultimately only emptiness (śūnyatā). Emptiness annihilates the dialectical alternatives fabricated by consciousness. It is, for the Madhyamaka, the middle path taught by the Buddha.[34]

The erroneous doctrines of eternalism and nihilism result from the fundamental conceptual alternatives of existence, non-existence, identity and difference. Existence, non-existence, identity and difference are extinguished in emptiness which is beyond thought and ineffable. The extinction of the concepts of existence, non-existence and so on, in śūnyatā is liberation. It is an unconditioned state free from all duality. Thus, the ultimate goal of soteriological philosophy is indicated through the critical method of the Madhyamaka.

References

1. According to the Sāṅkhya, it is the mistaken association of the spirit (puruṣa) with matter (prakṛti) which is the cause of limitation and bondage. For the Advaitavedānta also it is a mistaken superimposition (adhyāsa) of differentiation upon undifferentiated reality of Brahman which engenders suffering and limitation.
2. Murti, T. R. V., *The Central Philosophy of Buddhism*, p. 48.
3. The term absolutist has been applied by modern scholars to those Indian philosophical systems which advocate ultimate non-duality (advaya or advaita). While the term absolutist which is borrowed from Kantian philosophy is admittedly somewhat misleading when applied to philosophies like those of the Madhyamaka and the Advaitavedānta, it has been used here because despite its shortcomings it has gained relative popularity among contemporary scholars.
4. *Op. cit.* p. 62.
5. The Madhyamaka sets froth the distinction between the two realities i.e. phenomenal (saṁvṛti) and ultimate (paramārtha). In the Advaitaveldānta a similar conception is expressed through the formulation of three realities which are successively transcended, i.e., prātibhāsika, saṁvyavahāra and paramārtha. The Vijñānavāda makes use of a division into three realities i.e. parikalpita, paratantra and pariniṣpanna.
6. The term prapañca in Madhyamaka philosophy refers to the experientially objective correlatives of concepts. In other words, it is the objects fabricated by imagination.
7. *Pratītyasamutpādahṛdayakārikā*, 5 commentary.
8. *Śūnyatāsaptati* 60; *Mūlamadhyamakakārikā* XVIII. 5.
9. *Prasannapadā* commentary to *Mūlamadhyamakakārikā* XVIII. 5.

10. *Ibid.*
11. This example which is most commonly associated with Advaitavedānta is also employed by the Madhyamaka. Āryadeva indeed uses it in the *Hastavālaprakaraṇa*. Murti, T. R. V., *The Central Philosophy of Buddhism*, p. 94.
12. Footnote 1 to Stcherbatsky, Th., *The Conception of Buddhist Nirvāṇa* p. 165.
13. The same is obviously true of the unconditioned ultimate reality.
14. *Ratnāvali*, II.112-113.
15. *Bodhicaryāvatāra*, IX.143.
16. *Op. cit.* II. 119.
17. *Mūlamadhyamakakārikā*, XXIV. 11.
18. *Ibid.* XXIV. 8, 9.
19. *Mūlamadhyamakakārikā*, maṅgalācaraṇam XXIV. 18; *Vigrahavyāvartanī* 70; *Śūnyatāsaptati*, Stanza 14 commentary.
20. *Vigrahavyāvartanī*, commentary to stanza I.
21. *Śūnyatāsaptati*, Stanza 3 and commentary.
22. This will be discussed in detail in chapter IX.
23. *Vigrahavyāvartanī*, Stanza 27 and commentary.
24. *Prasannapadā* commentary to *Mūlamadhyamakakārikā* XVIII. 8.
25. *Ibid.* XVIII., 9.
26. Stcherbatsky, Th., *The Conception of Buddhist Nirvāṇa*, pp. 207-208.
27. *Ibid.* 208.
28. *Mūlamadhyamakakārikā*, XV. 1.
29. *Śūnyatāsaptati*, Stanza 15, 16 and commentary.
30. *Op. cit.* II. V.
31. *Op. cit.* 27 and commentary.
32. *Mūlamadhyamakakārikā*, XVII. 21-33; *Śūnyatāsaptati*, 34, 36, 37, 38 and commentary.
33. For a detailed exposition of Nāgārjuna and Candrakirti's critique of the concept of the self see our article entitled The treatment of the self in Madhyamaka Philosophy' published in the *Journal of the Department of Buddhist Studies*, University of Delhi, 1976.
34. *Vigrahavyāvartanī*, Stanza 70; *Mūlamadhyamakakārikā*, XXIV. 18.

Chapter IV

INDIAN LOGIC AND THE MADHYAMAKA SYSTEM

Indian logic developed out of the practice which had existed from ancient times in India of engaging in public discussions of philosophical issues. In such discussions it was the object of the participants to convince their opponents of the correctness of the philosophical opinions which they favoured. In order to accomplish this, the participants naturally resorted to facts which were commonly approved by all the parties to the discussion as well as the public at large.

Thus, there were two principal factors which conditioned the origins and development of Indian logic. Firstly, it originated out of the context of public discussions or debates. Secondly, it relied heavily upon the data of common experience. Gradually, over the course of centuries, public discussions of philosophical issues became more formalised. Some considered it desirable or even necessary to lay down precise rules for the conduct of such discussions and criteria for determining the legitimacy of the arguments employed by the parties involved. This tendency eventually led to the emergence of systems of formal logic like those of the Naiyāyikas and the Buddhists Diṅnāga and Dharmakīrti. It is important to remember however that Indian logic despite this formalising tendency exhibited over the course of its development, never became purely formal in the sense that some systems of Occidental logic are purely formal. Nor did Indian logic ever completely abandon its intimate concern with the data of common experience.

The Madhyamaka system was not altogether unaffected by the formalising tendency of Indian logic as we shall show later in this chapter. Indeed, the Svātantrikamadhyamaka school founded by Bhāvaviveka may be seen to a large extent as an attempt to reconcile the Madhyamaka philosophy with the tenets of formal logic which were gaining increasing currency from the third century onward. Although the Prāsaṅgikamadhyamaka school was also undoubtedly influenced by the growing formality of

Indian logic, it tended to resist this development as far as possible.

As has been indicated, logic in India developed out of the context of public discussions of philosophical issues. If the procedure of public debate is considered it will be possible to isolate the fundamental elements of Indian formal logic which emerged out of the former. In any discussion in which one party (let us call him the proponent) seeks to convince the other (who may be called the opponent) of the correctness of the opinion he favours, two fundamental elements are immediately evident. Firstly, there is the initial opinion the correctness of which the proponent is desirous of demonstrating to the opponent. This element is termed the position (pakṣa) or the proposition (pratijñā) of the proponent. In fact the proposition contains two distinct elements, i.e., a subject and a predicate, however, for the time being it suffices to say that it constitutes the subject matter which is to be proved.

In support of his proposition, the proponent must adduce a reason (hetu) which compels the acceptance of the former. The reason in order to accomplish its object must be much as indisputably proves the correctness of the proposition, in the judgement of either the opponent or the public at large. Thus there are two most fundamental and indispensable elements of a syllogism of Indian logic, i.e., proposition and reason. An argument consisting of these two members may be termed a proto-syllogism.

It may so happen, however, that the reason adduced fails to immediately compel the acceptance of the proposition. The proponent may then take the help of an example (dṛṣṭānta or udāharaṇa) in order to bring home the compelling character of the reason to the opponent. The example is an analogous case, i.e., a fact given in common experience in which the coincidence of the reason and the predicate of the proposition is evident. The example serves to illustrate the necessary and invariable relationship which obtains between the presence of the reason and the presence of the predicate of the proposition. The addition of an example to the two-membered proto-syllogism we discussed earlier is significant because it hints both at the notion of universals and the conception of invariable concomitance which were to play an increasingly important part in Indian formal logic.

Thus, there is the formulation of a three-membered syllogism consisting of a proposition, reason and example. This kind of three-membered syllogism occupies a central place in the development of Indian logic. It evidently enjoyed great popularity among both Buddhist and non-Buddhist philosophers from the second to the sixth centuries C.E.

Now consider for a moment the conception of invariable concomitance which has been just mentioned. As has been suggested this conception gained increasing importance as Indian logic became more formal. In simple terms invariable concomitance means that the presence or existence of the reason is necessarily bound up with the existence of the predicate of the proposition. In other words, it is inconceivable that the reason could exist without the predicate also being present. This is termed the relationship of invariable concomitance obtaining between the two. This conception is expressed in the major premise of Occidental logic.

The help of the following illustration may be taken. Proposition—sound is impermanent. Reason—because sound is a product. The fact that sound is a product compels the acceptance of the predicate, i.e., the quality of being impermanent because the fact of being a product is invariably bound up with the fact of being impermanent. It is evident that this conception of invariable concomitance involves the use of universals. The general property of being a product is invariably bound up with the general property of impermanence. This is also indicated by the citation of an example—a jar. A jar is like sound a product and like sound it is impermanent. Thus, the relationship of invariable concomitance obtaining between the fact of being a product and impermanence is suggested by means of the citation of another fact of common experience in which the general rule is illustrated. Thus, it may be said, sound is impermanent because it is a product. Whatsoever is a product has been found to be impermanent as for instance a jar.

Before proceeding any further, the well known five-membered syllogism of the Naiyāyika ought to be mentioned. It is essentially an elaboration of the three-membered syllogism we have already discussed and does not differ substantially from the latter. Two additional members are simply appended to the three-membered syllogism we have described. They are application (upanaya) and conclusion (nigamana). Of these, the conclusion is hardly significant. It consists merely of a restatement of the proposition at the end of the argument. Application is however somewhat more interesting because it too makes even more explicit the implied presence of a relationship of invariable concomitance obtaining between two universals or general properties. Application identifies the presence of the reason in the example with its presence in the subject of the proposition. The reason is thus a universal property which both the example and the subject share. Moreover, the reason is invariably concomitant with another general property as is evidenced by its known presence in the example. We may note however that invariable concomitance expressed in the form of the major premise of Occidental logic, is not included in either the three-or five-membered syllogisms we have discussed. Nonetheless, its presence is clearly implicit in both types of syllogism and some philosophers did take up the practice of citing the invariable concomitance along with their arguments. By contrast the last two members of the five-membered Naiyāyika syllogism were frequently left unstated.

In the early sixth century, another type of three-membered syllogism was formulated by Diṅnāga. This reformed syllogism of Diṅnāga is perhaps the most formal of the syllogisms we have undertaken to consider. In it the conception of invariable concomitance acquires greater importance than in any of the other types of syllogisms we have discussed.

The Buddhist formal logic of Diṅnāga and Dharmakīrti has received considerable attention from modern scholars. The great Russian Buddhologist Theodor Stcherbatsky pioneered in this field with his publication of the mammoth work, *Buddhist Logic.*[1] In recent years Professor M. Hattori,[2] Professor S. Mookerjee, H. Nagaṣaki[3] and many others have contributed valuable studies on the logic of Diṅnāga and Dharmakīrti. Thanks to the efforts of these eminent scholars, Buddhist formal logic is relatively well known to modern students.

The logic of Diṅnāga and Dharmakīrti evidences a marked concern for the maintenance of quite formal criteria of the validity of arguments. The two Buddhist masters undoubtedly saw themselves as reformers in the field of logic. They believed that the five-membered Naiyāyika syllogism was clumsy and defective.

Diṅnāga constructed a reformed three-membered syllogism which he evidently believed was free of the imperfections of the earlier syllogistic formulations. The first member of the three-membered syllogism advocated by Diṅnāga and Dharmakīrti is in fact a partial combination of two members of the three types of syllogism we have discussed so far. Diṅnāga extracted the subject from the proposition of the earlier syllogisms and combined it with the reason. This combined syllogistic member he termed the pakṣadharma. In this context the term pakṣa which would normally mean the position or proposition as a whole is restricted to the sense of the subject of the proposition alone. This is combined with the property (dharma) which is the reason to form the first member of Diṅnāga and Dharmakīrti's syllogism. It can be said to correspond to the minor premise of Occidental logic.

As we have suggested, the conception of invariable concomitance acquired great importance in the logic of Diṅnāga and Dharmakīrti. It is therefore not surprising that the second and third members of the syllogism they advocated should be concerned with this conception. They are positive concomitance (anvaya) and negative concomitance (vyatireka). As has been indicated, the conception of invariable concomitance involves the cognition that the presence of the reason is necessarily bound up with the existence of the predicate of the proposition. This is termed positive concomitance. Its negative correlative is simply the cognition that the absence of the predicate of the proposition necessarily means the absence of the reason, and it is termed negative concomitance. Diṅnāga evidently intended the inclusion of both positive and negative concomitance as indispensable members of a correct syllogism of formal logic to exclude the possibility of uncertain reasons.

It is clear that the three-membered reformed syllogism of Diṅnāga and Dharmakīrti owes much to the syllogistic formulations which preceded it. Although the importance of the conception of invariable concomitance was stressed in their system, it was also certainly implicit in the earlier types of syllogism. What is peculiar about the logic of Diṅnāga and Dharmakīrti is its insistence upon the necessity of negative concomitance as well.

Interestingly enough, the conception of negative concomitance is at the heart of one of the criticisms which have been advanced against the syllogisms employed by Bhāvaviveka. It has been sometimes argued that Bhāvaviveka's syllogisms are invalid because they lack any demonstrable negative concomitance Bhāvaviveka argued that earth and so on do not possess self-existence (svabhāva) because they are interdependently originated like cloth.[4] The positive concomitance implied in the above three-membered syllogism may be stated, whatsoever is interdependently originated does not possess self-existence. However, inasmuch as according to the Madhyamaka all phenomena are interdependently originated, the argument lacks a demonstrable negative concomitance.

This however does not constitute a conclusive criticism of the syllogisms advanced by Bhāvaviveka. In the first place we have indicated that the stress laid upon the necessary presence of negative concomitance is peculiar to the formal logic of Diṅnāga and Dharmakīrti. It is evident that philosophers and logicians of the period to which Nāgārjuna, Bhāvaviveka and even Candrakīrti belonged were not particularly concerned with the conception of negative concomitance. It seems therefore that this criticism of the syllogisms of Bhāvaviveka originates from a later period of Buddhist scholarship when scholars had become used to thinking of valid syllogisms especially in the context of Buddhist philosophy as necessarily consisting of the three members advocated by Diṅnāga and Dharmakīrti.

Moreover, the problem of being able to consistently produce a demonstrable negative concomitance was a difficult one even for Diṅnāga and Dharmakīrti. Dharmakīrti in fact argues that the conception of negative concomitance is an ideal construction which follows directly and immediately from the cognition of positive concomitance.[5] Whether this reply of Dharmakīrti's be convincing or not as a defence of the conception of the necessity of the presence of negative concomitance in all cases, it is obvious that a similar defence can be made of the argument advanced by Bhāvaviveka. The criticism of Bhāvaviveka's syllogisms for lacking a demonstrable negative concomitance is therefore without much substance. Indeed, to our knowledge, this objection against Bhāvaviveka's syllogisms was not raised by any of the exponents of the Prāsaṅgika school in India or in Tibet up to the fifteenth century. Nor again, to our knowledge, does any contemporary Tibetan scholar object to Bhāvaviveka's syllogisms on this ground.

The gradual formalisation of Indian logic had its effect on the logic employed by Madhyamaka scholars. Nāgārjuna was undoubtedly familiar with the three-membered syllogism consisting of a proposition, reason and example which was in common use during his time. In all likelihood he was also cognisant of the five-membered Naiyāyika syllogism. Nonetheless, despite Nāgārjuna's evident acquaintance with the pre-Diṅnāga form of three-membered syllogism, he singularly refrains from employing it in any of his major works. Not a single instance of a regular three membered syllogism is to be found in the *Mūlamadhyamakakārikā*, *Śūnyatāsaptati* or *Vigrahavyāvartanī*. There are however contained in these works a very large number of two-membered arguments consisting of a proposition and reason which we mentioned earlier in this chapter and which we have termed proto-syllogisms.

The majority of these two-membered arguments employed by Nāgārjuna contain a negative proposition and a reason which compels the acceptance of the negation. We may cite the following examples. Nāgārjuna argues that causes and conditions do not really belong to existence, because they would then be superfluous.[6] Again, he declares that the sense of vision does not really perceive external objects because it lacks the capacity of introspection.[7] Nirvāṇa, he argues, is not existence because it would then be characterised by decay and death.[8]

Nāgārjuna does occasionally employ a two-membered positive argument utilising the conceptions of emptiness and interdependent origination. He argues at several places that phenomena are empty because they are interdependently originated.[9]

The above arguments which we have extracted from the works of Nāgārjuna are all instances of two-membered proto-syllogisms. They are capable of expansion into three- or even five-membered syllogisms, however Nāgārjuna evidently did not consider it necessary or desirable to do so in any of the works which have come to our notice.

Buddhapālita who commented on the *Mūlamadhyamakakārikā* of Nāgārjuna undertook to explain the intention of the latter in greater detail. However, he too strictly refrained from formulating any formal syllogisms of either the three- or the five-membered type.

Buddhapālita argues that phenomena do not originate from

themselves because they exist and hence their origination would be superfluous.[10] This argument advanced by Buddhapālita corresponds to that found in the first illustration cited above from the works of Nāgārjuna. While the argument undoubtedly constitutes an elaboration of Nāgārjuna's argument, it is still not presented in the form of either a three- or a five-membered syllogism.

Bhāvaviveka for his part formulated this argument of the Madhyamaka against the origination of existing phenomena in conformity with the requirements of the pre-Diṅnāga three-membered syllogism: He declares that the subjective poles of consciousness do not originate from themselves because they exist like the conscious principle.[11] This argument advanced by Bhāvaviveka clearly contains the elements of the pre-Diṅnāga three-membered syllogism: proposition, reason and example. It is an obvious compromise on the part of a Madhyamaka scholar with the increasing formalisation of Indian logic.

As has been already suggested, the influence of the tendency exhibited by Indian logic to become increasingly formal upon the Madhyamaka system is most evident in the emergence of the Svātantrika school founded by Bhāvaviveka. Nonetheless, even Candrakīrti the foremost advocate of the Prāsaṅgika philosophy had in some degree to respond to the increasing pressure of formalisation in Indian logic. After the advent of Bhāvaviveka this pressure emanated not only from the traditional opponents of the Madhyamaka, but also from within the system itself.

Candrakīrti met this challenge mounted against the standpoint of the Prāsaṅgikas by means of an expedient and purely formal compromise with the tenets of formal logic. At the same time, he rigorously disassociated the Prāsaṅgika philosophy from the ontological presuppositions which the use of formal logic in India normally implied. Thus, Candrakīrti compromised formally with the demands of syllogistic logic without surrendering in the least bit the characteristic philosophical attitude of the Madhyamaka.

Indeed, the characteristic philosophical attitudes of formal logic in India and the Madhyamaka were virtually opposite. As has been already said, Indian logic was founded upon the data of common experience. It employed facts which were mutually approved by all parties and it normally took it for granted that these facts were real. The Madhyamaka however on the contrary, when the nature of the ultimate truth was the subject of a discussion, did not admit the reality of such facts. Nonetheless, the Madhyamaka could legitimately employ the conventions of formal logic, so long as he did not himself admit the reality of the elements they contained, when the nature of the ultimate was to be determined.

Keeping this very important distinction in mind, Candrakīrti displays remarkable familiarity with and facility in the use of the most popular conventions of formal logic, i.e., the three-membered and the five-membered syllogisms. Indeed, in the works of Candrakīrti, the influence of the formalising tendency of Indian logic upon even the Prāsaṅgika school is quite evident. In the *Prasannapadā* we find many instances of both three- and five-membered syllogisms as well as frequent statements of invariable concomitance. These are not only quoted very freely in the work, but are also employed liberally by the author himself in defence of the Prāsaṅgikamadhyamaka philosophy.

Candrakīrti reformulates arguments used by Nāgārjuna and Buddhapālita in accord with the conventions of the three- and the five-membered syllogisms without admitting the reality of the elements they contain. He declares that the sense of vision does not perceive external objects because it lacks the capacity of introspection, like a jar.[12] The elements of the three-membered syllogism: proposition, reason and example, are clearly present in this argument. Moreover although the additional two members of the five-membered syllogism and the invariable concomitance are in this case left unstated, they can be easily derived from the elements presented. He also adduces the following formal three-membered syllogism against the Realist's insistence upon the verity of perception. Proposition—direct perception is delusive, reason—because it is perception, example—like the perception of two moons by one afflicted by a fault of vision.[13] As in the case of the earlier argument the two additional members of the five-membered syllogism and the invariable concomitance although unstated may be easily derived from the elements presented. Again, Candrakīrti reformulates Buddhapālita's argument against the origination of phenomena from themselves so as to reveal in it all the five members of the Naiyāyika syllogism.[14]

Candrakīrti did not employ, nor does he seem to have been

particularly concerned with the three-membered syllogism advocated by Diṅnāga. He was, however, undoubtedly familiar with Diṅnāga's logic because he takes up the question of the value of the logical reformations advocated by the latter.[15] It is possible that Diṅnāga's logic had not yet acquired any widespread popularity during the life of Candrakīrti and therefore the latter did not feel it necessary to devote much attention to it. In any case Candrakīrti seems to have concluded that the reforms urged by Diṅnāga did not have much value.

Thus, it is evident that the Madhyamaka system was influenced by the tendency of Indian logic to become more formal over the course of time. The final stage of the influence exercised by Indian formal logic upon the Madhyamaka system can perhaps be seen in the orthodox philosophy of the Tibetan Buddhist scholastic tradition. Although the Tibetan scholastic tradition now almost exclusively upholds the philosophy of the Prāsaṅgikamadhyamaka school, Indian formal logic has retained an important place within it. Not however as it is represented by the pre-Diṅnāga three-membered syllogism or the five-membered Naiyāyika syllogism which have fallen into disuse. It is the Buddhist formal logic of Diṅnāga and Dharmakīrti which has gained widespread acceptance among the adherents of the Tibetan Prāsaṅgikamadhyamaka system. Indeed, at present when Tibetan scholars speak of a three-membered syllogism of formal logic, they almost invariably mean the syllogism advocated by Diṅnāga and Dharmakīrti. This does not indicate however that the Tibetan Prāsaṅgikamadhyamakas have abandoned the critical attitude of the Prāsaṅgika philosopher toward formal logic. The Tibetan Prāsaṅgikamadhyamakas neither admit the syllogisms of formal logic nor the reality of the elements they contain when the nature of the ultimate truth is to be determined. The utility of the Buddhist formal logic of Diṅnāga and Dharmkīrti is explicitly restricted by the Tibetan Prāsaṅgikamadhyamaka system to the limits of the phenomenal.

References

1. Stcherbatsky, Th., *Buddhist Logic*, Dover Publications, New York, 1962. First published by the Academy of Sciences of the U.S.S.R., Leningrad, 1930.

2. Hattori, M., *Dignaga On Perception*, Cambridge, Massachusetts, 1968.

3. Mookerjee, S., Nagasaki, H., *The Pramāṇavārttikam* of Dharmakirti. *Nava Nālandā Mahāvihāra Publication.* Nalanda, 1964.

4. Shotaro Iida. *The nature of Samvṛti and the relationship of Paramārtha to it in Svātantrika Mādhyamika,* pp. 64-67 in '*Two Truths in Buddhism and Vedānta.*' Edited by M. Sprung. Dordrecht, Holland, 1973.

5. *Op. cit.* pp. 71-72.

6. *Mūlamadhyamakakārikā,* I. 6.

7. *Ibid.* III. 2.

8. *Ibid.* XXV. 4.

9. *Ibid.* XXIV. 18; *Śūnyatāsaptati,* 14.

10. Stcherbatsky, Th., *Conception of Buddhist Nirvāṇa,* p. 138; *dBu-ma-spyi-ston,* p. 263.

11. Stcherbatsky, Th., *Conception of Buddhist Nirvāṇa,* pp. 141-142; *dBu-ma-spyi-ston,* p. 345.

12. Stcherbatsky, Th., *Conception of Buddhist Nirvāṇa,* p. 176.

13. *Ibid.* p. 210.

14. *Ibid.* pp. 146-149.

15. *Ibid.* pp. 211- 215.

Chapter V

THE ORIGIN OF THE DIVISION

If we are to understand the nature and the development of the division which occurred in the Madhyamaka philosophy, and resulted in the appearance of the Prāsaṅgika and svatantrika schools, its origin must first be sought. Specifically what this means is that we must look to the works of Nāgārjuna who both Buddhapālita and Bhāvaviveka acknowledged to be their common master. Indeed, even Candrakīrti recognised that Bhāvaviveka was a follower of the Madhyamaka philosophy, though he relentlessly criticised his use of Independent syllogisms (svatantra-anumāna)[1], when the ultimate (paramārtha)[2] is examined.

It was with the explication of the intention of Nāgārjuna contained in the *Mūlamadhyamakakārikā* that Buddhapālita, Bhāvaviveka and Candrakīrti, all of whom wrote lengthy commentaries to Nāgārjuna's *Mūlamadhyamakakārikā*[3] were concerned. The *Vigrahavyāvartanī* also composed by Nāgārjuna is likewise vital to the issue which divided the two schools, though its significance is less obvious.

The original foundation upon which the dispute between the Prāsaṅgika and Svātantrika schools first took hold and grew was the first stanza of the first chapter of the *Mūlamadhyamakakārikā* of the Master Nāgārjuna. It was in the explication of these few lines that Buddhapālita and Bhāvaviveka differed characteristically.

It is this difference, which is equally present on the occasion of the explanation of the whole of the original text, i.e., the *Mūlamadhyamakakārikā* which constitutes the primary distinction between the two schools. The Prāsaṅgika and Svātantrika schools also differ with regard to their acceptance of the conventionally real (vyavahāra).[4] However, it is contended that the difference which arose with regard to the explanation of the intention of Nāgārjuna contained in the stanzas represents the most important division between the two schools, and that the disagreement with regard to the conventionally real is secondary. Moreover, the characteristic interpretations of the respective schools of the Madhyamaka philosophy as a whole may be extrapolated from an examination of the ways in which Buddhapālita, Bhāvaviveka and Candrakīrti interpreted the first stanza of the *Mūlamadhyamakakārikā*. The *Vigrahavyāvartanī* is significant with reference to the discussion of the validity and or orthodoxy of the explications of the intention of Nāgārjuna adopted by the two schools.

In the first stanza of the *Mūlamadhyamakakārikā*, which is the central treatise of the Madhyamaka school, the master Nāgārjuna declares that all entities are not originated from any of the four alternatives (catuṣkoṭi),[5] that is self, other, both or without cause. The refutation of origination reflects the characteristic view of the Madhyamaka and may be equated with the demonstration of emptiness (śūnyatā)[6] or the denial of own being (svabhāva).[7] On the occasion of investigating the ultimate truth (paramārthasatya)[8] by means of appropriate reasoning (yukti),[9] the Madhyamaka may declare that all entities are empty, or that they lack own being, or again that they are not originated. Formally these declarations may be termed the propositions (pratijñā)[10] of the Madhyamakas. That they may be distinguished from the propositions of other philosophers will become evident later.

In order to establish the proposition contained in the opening stanza of the *Mūlamadhyamakakārikā*, i.e., that all entities are not originated from themselves etc., the Prāsaṅgikas and Svātantrikas had recourse to distinct modes of argument. When the Madhyamaka philosopher is engaged in discussions with non-Madhyamakas, that is Realists (vastuvādins),[11] his acknowledged intention is to bring about an understanding of emptiness in the mind of the opponent, and to this end he has recourse to various arguments. The arguments advanced by Buddhapālita represent those of the Prāsaṅgika system. The Svātantrika system founded by Bhāvaviveka set forth an alternative mode of argument to that of Buddhapālita. The school developed in contradistinction to the Prāsaṅgika, and its characteristic mode of argument grew in part out of a criticism of the arguments advanced by Buddhapālita.

In order to explicate the statement made by the Master Nāgārjuna in the opening stanza of the *Mūlamadhyamakakārikā*, i.e., that entities are not originated from themselves, the Master Buddhapālita advanced the following arguments. Entities, he said, are not originated from themselves, since the origination of entities from themselves would serve no purpose and would lead to absurdity. Entities which exist in their own substantiality, (svātmatā)[12] are not in need of another origination, and if even though existent, they originate, their origination will go on *ad infinitum*.[13] The arguments given by Buddhapālita are characteristic of those employed by the Prāsaṅgika school of which he can be said to be the founder.

The Master Bhāvaviveka raised the following objections against the statement of Buddhapālita. He contended that the arguments advanced by Buddhapālita were deficient, since neither a reason (hetu)[14] nor an example (dṛṣṭānta)[15] had been stated. In addition, he maintained that the accusations of the opponent, the Sāṅkhya,[16] had not been answered by Buddhapālita. Finally, Bhāvaviveka believed that the arguments advanced by Buddhapālita implied the acceptance of the alternative proposition, i.e., that entities are originated from another.[17]

Bhāvaviveka undertook to establish the proposition expressed in the opening stanza of the *Mūlamadhyamakakārikā* by means of what may be termed independent syllogisms (svatantra-anumāna). He thought that in this way the opponent could be more effectively brought to accept the Madhyamaka view. His arguments take the form of regular syllogisms which are thought to be established by valid instruments of cognition (pramāṇa).[18] However, they are distinguished by a peculiar qualification which accompanies them. On the occasion of the refutation of origination from self, Bhāvaviveka advanced the following syllogism. Proposition (pratijñā)—ultimately (paramārthataḥ), the subjective poles of consciousness (ādhyātmikāyatana)[19] do not originate from themselves; reason (hetu)—because they exist (vidyamānatvāt)[20]; example (dṛṣṭānta)—like the conscious principle (caitanya).[21]

Thereafter the Master Candrakīrti defended the statements of Buddhapālita against the objections put forward by Bhāvaviveka and criticised the alternative mode of argument advocated by the latter. The comments of Candrakīrti came to be regarded as the primary and orthodox exposition of the Prāsaṅgika point of view. Candrakīrti argued that Buddhapālita was not at fault, though an independent reason and example had not been stated by him. He held that the opponent could be refuted by the arguments of the Prāsaṅgikas and hence the construction of independent syllogisms was unnecessary. He argued that if the application of the *reductio ad absurdum* (prasaṅga-vākya)[22] failed to convince an opponent, then the introduction of independent syllogisms would also be futile. Therefore, he concluded that the independent syllogism was powerless. Further Candrakīrti maintained that when Buddhapālita by means of the *reductio ad absurdum* refuted the proposition of the Sāṅkhyas, i.e., that entities originated from themselves, he had no proposition of his own to establish. Therefore, Candrakīrti held that the independent argument advocated by Bhāvaviveka was not only ineffective, but also incorrect.[23]

As has been seen the division between the Prāsaṅgika and Svātantrika schools first arose on the occasion of explicating the intention of the Master Nāgārjuna contained in the *Mūlamadhyamakakārikā*. It is maintained that this represents the fundamental difference between the two schools. In the opening stanza of that work Nāgārjuna declares, "Nowhere and at no time does any entity whatsoever originate from self, other, both or without cause."[24] In order to vindicate the four formal propositions of refutation contained in these lines, the Master Buddhapālita set forth the reasoning (yukti) of the Prāsaṅgika school. The Master Bhāvaviveka, having refuted Buddhapālita, constructed the Svātantrika system. The Master Candrakīrti defended the interpretation expressed by Buddhapālita and set forth his own explanation in agreement with that of the Prāsaṅgika school.[25] The characteristic argument employed by Buddhapālita and Candrakīrti was the *reductio ad absurdum* (prasaṅga-vākya), that of Bhāvaviveka was the independent syllogism (svatantra-anumāna). It is, thus, that the two schools derived their names, that is the Prāsaṅgika and the Svātantrika.

As the statement made by Nāgārjuna in the opening stanza of the *Mūlāmadhyamakakārikā* contains the initial proposition of the Madhyamaka, we may do well at this stage to examine it more closely. It constitutes one of the two elements, the other being the reason (hetu) with respect to which the interpretation adopted by the two schools differs.

The refutation of origination reflects the characteristic standpoint of the Madhyamaka. Soteriologically, it is intended to remove the naive belief in own being (svabhāva). The notion of own being represents the principal object of refutation of the Madhyamaka school in general. Indeed, it is for this reason that the school has sometimes received the name of Niḥsvabhāva-vāda.[26] The schools of Realists are convinced of the reality of own being and believe in the true existence of entities which are merely imputed (parikalpita).[27] The refutation of origination represents in substance the refutation of own being.

The four formal propositions of refutation contained in the opening stanza of the *Mūlamadhyamakakārikā* have been traditionally interpreted with reference to the doctrines of origination advocated by rival schools. Thus, it may be said that the Sāṅkhyas, Buddhist Realists,[28] Jainas[29] and Cārvākas[30] advocate the doctrines of origination from self, other, both and without cause which are the objects of refutation of the stanza.[31]

b Sod-nams Sen-ge supplies an additional explanation. He says, if entities originate, then their origination must be either with or without a cause. The latter view, i.e. that entities are originated without a cause, constitutes the fourth alternative of the tetralemma. The schools of materialists advocated the doctrine of origination without a cause. Again, if the former alternative is preferred and entities are originated with a cause, then in that case the cause ana effect must be either identical or different. The latter constitutes the second alternative of the tetralemma, advocated by the Buddhist Realists, while the former constitutes the first alternative of the tetralemma, the position held by the Sāṅkhyas. Finally, it might be maintained that cause and effect are both identical and different. This point of view constitutes the third alternative, and was advocated by the Jainas.[32]

The four alternatives of the tetralemma exhaust the possibility of origination. All theories of origination are extinguished by the refutation of the positions represented by the four alternatives. The refutation of origination is intended to remove attachment to the notion that entities exist in their own being.

The question of the nature of the four propositions of refutation expressed in the opening stanza of the *Mūlamadhyamakakārikā* played a significant role in the dispute between the Prāsaṅgika and Svātantrika schools. Formally, a proposition (pratijñā) consists of two elements—the minor term (dharmin)[33] and the property (dharma)[34] or more precisely the property to be established (sādhyadharma).[35] Though the minor term or substratum as such is not counted among the members of the five-membered inference[36] nor among those of either type of three-termed syllogism,[37] it represents the substratum (āśraya)[38] of inference. Literally, the term 'dharmin' may be translated as that object endowed with a property. It may be termed the ground of debate.[39]

As was stated above the minor term constitutes one of the two elements which make up a proposition. Similarly, its combination with the reason (hetu) and example (dṛṣṭānta) results in the first term of the Diṅnāga's three-termed syllogism, the so-called minor premise (pakṣadharma)[40] and in the fourth member of the five-membered inference, i.e., application (upanaya).[41] The minor term represents the subject of a proposition, while the property represents the predicate. For instance, in the proposition, "sound is impermanent", sound represents the substratum, while impermanence represents the property.

The propositions accepted by the Prāsaṅgikas and Svātantrikas differed both with respect to the substratum and with respect to the property. On the occasion of the refutation of origination from self, the Prāsaṅgikas accepted as the substratum any object whatsoever, which was believed to originate by the opponent without modifying the object of refutation, i.e., origination by the qualification ultimately (paramārthataḥ). On the other hand the Svātantrikas retained as the substratum the subjective poles of consciousness (ādhyātmikāyatana), and added the qualification ultimately to their propositions.[42]

However, there existed a still more fundamental problem. If the opening stanza of the *Mūlamadhyamakakārikā* contained four propositions of refutation, did it not contradict what the Master Nāgārjuna had declared in the *Vigrahavyāvartanī*, i.e., "If I had a proposition to establish, I could be at fault, but as I have none, I cannot be at fault. If I rejected or approved anything on the basis of perception and the like, I could be blamed, but as I apprehend none of these, I cannot be accused in such a way."[43] Indeed, this very question had been raised by the Master Candrakīrti who, it will be recalled had maintained that when the Master Buddhapālita refuted the proposition of the Sāṅkhyas, he had no proposition of his own.[44] In an attempt to resolve this apparent contradiction, some early Tibetan Prāsaṅgikamadhyamakas evidently maintained that the Madhyamakas accepted no propositions whatsoevei, notwithstanding the four formal poropositions contained in the opening stanza. The inconsistency was eventually to be removed by the precise definition of the nature of the propositions acceptable to the Madhyamakas in general and to the respective schools in particular. The solutions adopted by the Madhyamakas are not without relevance to the discussion of the nature of critical philosophy as a whole.

References

1. རང་རྒྱུད་ཀྱི་རྟགས།

2. དོན་དམ་པ།

3. Buddhapālita's commentary is entitled as *Madhyamakavṛtti*, Bhāvaviveka's the *Prajñāpradīpa* and Candrakirti's the *Prasannapadā*. See Chapter II.

4. ཐ་སྙད།

5. མཐའ་བཞི།

6. སྟོང་ཉིད།

7. རང་བཞིན།

8. དོན་དམ་བདེན་པ།

9. རིགས་པ།

10. དམ་བཅའ།

11. དངོས་པོར་སྨྲ་བ།

12. རང་གི་བདག་ཉིད།

13. dBu-ma-spyi-ston, p. 263.

14. རྒྱུ།

15. དཔེ།

16. གྲངས་ཅན་པ།

17. dBu-ma-spyi-ston, p. 263.

18. ཚད་མ།

19. ནང་གི་སྐྱེ་མཆེད།

20. འདོད་པའི་ཕྱིར།

21. ཤེས་རིག་གི་སྐྱེས་བུ།

22. Stcherbatsky, Th., *Conception of Buddhist Nirvāṇa*, p. 141.
23. *dBu-ma-spyi-ston*, p. 264.
24. *Mūlamadhyamakakārikā* I. 1.
25. *Op.cit.* pp. 253-264.

26. རང་བཞིན་མེད་པར་སྨྲ་བ།

27. ཀུན་བརྟགས།

dBu-ma-spyi-ston, p. 337.

28. དོན་སྨྲ་བ།

The term Buddhist Realist is applied by the Madhyamaka also to the Vijñānavāda since the latter advocates the real existence of consciousness, Vijñāna.

29. གཅེར་བུ་བ།

30. ཚུ་རོལ་མཛེས་པ་བ།

31. *dBu-ma-spyi-ston*, p. 338.
32. *Ibid.* p. 339.

33. ཆོས་ཅན།

34. ཆོས།

35. བསྒྲུབ་བྱའི་ཆོས།

36. ཡན་ལག་ལྔ་པའི་གཏན་ཚིགས།

37. ཚུལ་གསུམ་གྱི་རྟགས།

38. གཞི།

39. རྩོད་ཀྱི་ཆོས་ཅན།

40. ཕྱོགས་ཆོས།

41. ཉེ་བར་སྦྱོར་བ།

42. *dBu-ma-spyi-ston*, p. 339.
43. *Vigrahavyāvartanī*, 29, 30.
44. *Op.cit.* p. 264.

Chapter VI

THE DEVELOPMENT OF THE CONTROVERSY

The issues raised by the controversy between Buddhapālita and Bhāvaviveka were by no means finally set to rest by the interpretation offered by Candrakīrti. Though the adherents of the Prāsaṅgika school regarded Candrakīrti's comments as definitive and devoted themselves to the precise elaboration of them, the Svātantrika school continued to exercise a considerable influence which extended over several centuries upon Buddhist thought in India and Tibet. Indeed, the Svātantrika system manifestly preserved its popularity and philosophical respectability despite Candrakīrti's attack. In part this may have resulted from the increasing attention which had come to be paid to the formal logic of arguments. Logic and epistemology which had for many centuries been the subject of keen discussion in India, had witnessed rapid developments from the first century onward. Moreover, by the sixth century, Diṅnāga and Dharmakīrti had introduced a system of formal logic which they considered to be not incompatible with Buddhist thought. No doubt the works of Diṅnāga and Dharmakīrti have no direct bearing upon that which led to the division of the Madhyamaka system into the Prāsaṅgika and Svātantrika schools. Nonetheless, the emergence of a system of formal Buddhist logic is ample evidence of the growing concern with the formal logic of discourse.[1]

The Svātantrikas were eminently conscious of the community of human experience and affirmed the common character of cognitive processes. The Prāsaṅgikas on the contrary steadfastly refused to admit themselves the validity of the instruments of cognition (pramāṇa) or the objects cognised by them. They maintained that on the occasion of establishing emptiness the substratum (āśraya)[2] does not exist for the Madhyamaka, nor is there for him any reason established by valid instruments of cognition. Hence the arguments of the Prāsaṅgikas were constructed in agreement with the standpoint of the opponent and were valid for him alone. The Svātantrikas alleged that these conditions imposed by the Prāsaṅgikas vitiated the validity of their arguments. Moreover, they contended that a meaningful discussion between two parties presupposed the existence of a common point of reference. Thus, the existence or non-existence of a common substratum acceptable to both the Madhyamaka and the opponent upon the occasion of the examination of the nature of the ultimately real occupied a primary place among the issues about which the controversy developed.

The Svātantrikas maintained that an unqualified minor term (dharmin) should be acceptable to the Madhyamakas. They held that commonsense things, i.e., the objects of the six sense faculties like sound etc. were given commonly[3] in experience to both the proponent and the opponent. They believed that if disassociated from particular predicates, empirical facts such as these which were commonly available to all could be employed for the purposes of inference. Indeed, they argued that the rejection of such a commonly existing substratum by the Prāsaṅgikas was inadmissible, since in the absence of a common substratum the probative power of an argument could not be guaranteed. They, likewise, believed that the refusal to admit valid instruments of cognition was inconsistent because it denied the validity of those very processes of cognition by means of which the opponent was to be induced to accept emptiness.

The Prāsaṅgikas, for their part, refrained from according real validity to common processes of cognition which presupposed duality. They admitted the utility of arguments, but they did not believe them to possess consistency or reality of their own. Neither did they admit inference to lead to right knowledge in the ultimate sense. They maintained that arguments were efficacious through the power of illusion (māyā), however when examined critically they are found to be ultimately misleading. In accord with the critical reasoning which is competent to establish the ultimate truth the valid instruments of cognition along with their objects are not apprehended, for they do not in the ultimate sense exist.

The reasoning which is capable of establishing the nature of the ultimate truth may be termed analytic or critical. It consists of examining a given entity exhaustively from a variety of standpoints with the object of ascertaining whether or not it can be said to possess a nature or existence of its own. It is acknowledged that the arguments which are produced when the ultimate is in question merely afford an intellectual approximation of it. Through inference a mediate cognition of the ultimate is achieved.[4] Inasmuch as the knowledge obtained in this way is subject to duality, it does not really represent ultimate truth but is properly speaking said to belong to the conventional.

The Prāsaṅgikas did not affirm that their arguments possessed intrinsic validity, though no doubt they were calculated to produce with respect to a given opponent an understanding of the ultimate truth. The critical arguments of the Prāsaṅgikas are neither without object nor indiscriminate. They have a soteriological motivation. Nonetheless, they are philosophically consistent. They have as their paradigm the conduct of the Enlightened Ones who by means of appropriate arguments edify the ignorant.[5] In such a context, the validity of an argument is measured by its efficacy, not by its conformity to the principles of formal logic and epistemology. The Prāsaṅgikas alleged that the practice favoured by the Svātantrikas is either incompetable with the Madhyamaka philosophy, or logically inconsistent.

Jayānanda[6] who composed a commentary to Candrakīrti's autocommentary to the *Madhyamakāvatāra*[7] put the Prāsaṅgika position in the following way. "The particular purpose and character of the Prāsaṅgika argument is to admit provisionally the argument of the opponent, by means of which he establishes his proposition, and then to refute it. For instance, if the opponent maintains that entities originate from themselves, then sprouts and the like will be unoriginated.

Someone might ask, if it is accepted that the Prāsaṅgika argument is an argument which proceeds from valid instruments of cognition, or not? If the former, then it will be acceptable to both the opponent and the Madhyamaka. If the latter, then not even the opponent will accept it. It is replied, let us consider whether an argument which proceeds from valid instruments of cognition will be acceptable to both the proponent and the opponent. When the Madhyamaka expresses an argument, he will not apprehend whether the opponent accepts that argument as proceeding from valid instruments of cognition or not, for the very reason that the mind of the opponent is an object of neither of the valid instruments of cognition (perception and inference). Again he will not apprehend whether he himself accepts that argument as proceeding from valid instruments of cognition, since man has been in the grip of illusion since beginningless time and so there exists the possibility of error. Hence the Madhyamakas and their opponents accept objects themselves, accepting that they do so by means of valid instruments of cognition. It is not necessary that it be mutually agreed that it is so. It is sufficient if the opponent accepts the argument to proceed from valid instruments of cognition. Thus, by the strength of the opponent's acceptance, his argument can be refuted.

Moreover, if the reason (hetu) in an independent syllogism were established by valid instruments of cognition, the argument would be correct, however it is established by neither of the valid instruments of cognition, but exists merely through conventional acceptance. As this is so, why cannot the arguments of the Prāsaṅgikas refute those of the Sāṅkhyas and the like.[8]

Jayānanda begins by reviewing the character of the Prāsaṅgika argument which he says proceeds by admitting the standpoint of the opponent and then refuting it. That is to say, the Prāsaṅgika has no independent proposition of his own to establish. His argument is intended to induce the opponent to relinquish his position or theory. It is not considered necessary or expedient to establish a counterposition, as the ultimate truth for the Madhyamakas consists of the abandonment of all views.

However, a question may be raised. Is the argument of the Prāsaṅgikas established by valid instruments of cognition or not? This doubt had been expressed by logicians from the very beginning of the Madhyamaka philosophy, as is evident from the *Vigrahavyāvartanī*[9] and *Prasannapadā*.[10] The Prāsaṅgikas did not admit that their arguments proceeded from valid instruments of cognition for the very reason that they denied the ultimate existence of such cognitive faculties as well as the objects cognised by them. In this case, however, the question possesses an additional significance. The Prāsaṅgika maintained that his arguments were acceptable to the opponent alone, but it had become widely accepted that an argument could only be conclusive if it was accepted by both parties to a discussion. Diṅnāga had also endorsed this position.[11] Otherwise, it was maintained, the argument would remain uncertain.

Jayānanda's reply presupposes the criticism of valid instruments of cognition as it is found in the *Vigrahavyāvartanī*. The phenomenal is identified with the illusory, but this does not deprive it of efficacy. The same may be said of the instruments of cognition which derive their conventional efficiency from a prevalent illusion though they are ultimately unreal. Therefore, in the ultimate analysis the question of whether the Prāsaṅgika argument proceeds from valid instrument of cognition is irrelevant.

Finally, the argument against valid instruments of cognition in general may be applied to the independent syllogism itself, which claims to offer a proof of emptiness which is established by valid instruments of cognition. In the ultimate analysis, Jayānanda contends all such facts as may be produced as reasons, exist only in the sense that they are conventionally accepted, and so the Prāsaṅgika argument which produces an acceptance of the Madhyamaka standpoint on the part of the opponent is competent to establish the ultimate truth.

The Svātantrikas however firmly upheld the legitimacy of arguments which conformed to the requisites of formal logic. They believed that in this way the opponent could be effectively induced to accept the Madhyamaka philosophy. The Svātantrikas advocated the use of syllogisms whose members were admitted by them to be established by valid instruments of cognition,[12] though not truly established.[13] Generally, they employed a three-membered syllogism, the parts of which were essentially extracted from those of the five-membered inference. They rejected the refusal of the Prāsaṅgikas to accept a substratum. According to the Svātantrikas, the existence of a common substratum was indispensable if an argument were to result in a valid inference. In the absence of a common substratum, an argument would, they believed, remain inconclusive.

Thus Śrīgupta writes in the *Tattvāloka*, "That object which is endowed with the property that is to be established is always retained by the learned in logic as the substratum (āśraya). Hence a scholar must indicate his substratum. When the property that is to be established is emptiness, then at that time the object endowed with the property, emptiness is the substratum. Hence the objection of the Prāsaṅgikas is inadmissible."[14]

The point at issue is the following one. The Svātantrikas contended that for the purposes of inference the existence of a substratum must be acknowledged. Otherwise, in its absence, neither the reason of which it is the substratum nor the proposition of which it is the subject will be possible. This will become clearer if it is recalled that the substratum stands in a necessary relationship with two other essential members of an inference. That is to say, it is the locus of the property (dharma) which is the reason as-well as of the property which is to be established, i.e., the predicate of the proposition or probandum. The relation of invariable concomitance obtaining between these two properties which pertain to the logical subject is expressed in the major premise without which a valid argument is impossible. Thus, it can be easily seen that in the absence of an existent substratum, the whole process of inference topples.

It was, moreover, the consistent contention of the Svātantrikas that only the general nature of the terms employed in syllogisms should be taken into account. Otherwise, they argued, inference would become impossible, since no two schools were likely to agree about the metaphysical character of a fact given in experience. Jñānagarbha, who was a logician of no mean ability was also an adherent of the Svātantrika school. He composed a work on Madhyamaka philosophy entitled the *Madhyamakasatyadvaya* in which he states as follows, "Simply relying upon just those objects which appear to the minds of both debators (the proponent and the opponent) one can employ property (dharma) and subject (dharmin) etc. Then the argument will result in an inference. If the three, e.g., subject, property, etc.[15] are not present, the argument will fail to result in an inference. So who among the learned will dispute this?"[16]

Thus, it is evident that for the logician valid inference is founded upon facts given in experience. These objects of common sense appear commonly to all irrespective of the particular theories which may be entertained by different philosophers in regard to them. It is commonly known, the Svātantrikas argued, that the logical subject and reason of an inference must be facts available to all in experience. Only in that case can the argument be said to be conclusive.

Śāntarakṣita makes the position of the Svātantrikas clearer when he writes in the *Madhyamakālaṅkāra*, "Abandoning the particular logical subjects which originate from the texts (of various schools), entities well known to all from the learned to women and children may all be rightly employed as the actualit of the proposition and the reason. Otherwise, how is one to answer (when it is said) the substratum is not established etc."[17]

It is admitted the Svātantrikas urged that different schools advocate different theories about the ultimate nature of facts given in experience. However, the terms employed in inference should be disassociated from predicates which reflect a particular philosophical standpoint. The refusal of the Prāsaṅgikas to accept an unqualified subject and reason established by valid instruments of cognition on the occasion of establishing emptiness through inference, Svātantrikas contended, represents the introduction of a theoretical qualification. Such theoretical qualifications were out of place in a correct inference. Indeed, their introduction rendered valid inference impossible. The Svātantrikas were intent upon establishing emptiness by means of commonly accepted syllogisms for they believed that only in this way could the Madhyamaka philosophy be logically established.

Kamalaśīla sums up the position of the later Indian Svātantrikas when he writes in the *Madhyamakāloka*, "We do not demonstrate all elements to be emptiness only through Prāsaṅgika arguments, but rather by the strength of real logic. This also was only taught by the lord, so it is accepted. Thus, the Svātantrika system is established."[18]

The Indian Svātantrikas who followed Bhāvaviveka admittedly differed slightly with respect to what may be termed their ontological interpretations of Buddhist doctrine. Nevertheless, the mode of argument favoured by them was generally uniform. They believed that the principles of formal logic were not irrelevant to the demonstration of the Madhyamaka philosophy to an opponent. They employed syllogisms whose members were commonly admitted to be established by valid instruments of cognition. The Prāsaṅgikas rejected this practice because they maintained that on the occasion of ascertaining the nature of the ultimate truth, neither the subject of inference nor the reason exist for the Madhyamaka. Hence, they concluded it was inconsistent for the Madhyamaka philosophy to admit independent syllogisms, when the ultimate truth was investigated.

Ontologically the Indian Svātantrikas may be divided into those who generally accept the Sautrāntika conception of reality and those who favour the Yogācāra interpretation. A representative of the former is Bhāvaviveka. Representatives of the latter are Śāntarakṣita and Kamalaśīla. dKon-mchog-'Jigs-med-dbang-po writes in his exposition of philosophical system,[19] that, "The Yogācāramadhyamakasvātantrikas do not recognise external objects except as non-referential self-validating awareness. The Sautrāntikamadhyamakasvātantrikas do not recognise self-validating awareness and accept external objects."[20]

The Sautrāntikamadhyamakasvātantrikas represented by Bhāvaviveka followed the Sautrāntikas in that they accepted external objects to be built up of atoms.[21] They do not, according to dKon-mchog'-jigs-med-dbang-po, recognise the conceptualisation which believes in external objects as intellectual fog. The school also denied that Śrāvakas and Pratyekabuddhas had achieved realisation of the insubstantiality of elements (dharmanairātmya).[22]

Mi-pham in his summary of philosophical systems[23] divides the Svātantrikas into the so-called earlier Svātantrikas and the later. Among the former he includes Samudramegha and Śrīgupta. Samudramegha, he asserts, represents those early Svātantrikas who maintained that everything was an appearance, while Śrīgupta represents those who held that appearance and emptiness were different entities. Śrīgupta apparently held the view that the ultimate and the conventional, i.e., emptiness and appearance, do not coincide.[24]

The later Svātantrikas are represented according to Lama Mi-pham by Jñānagarbha, Śāntarakṣita and Kamalaśīla. They maintain that objects as they appear to commonsense are incontestable, though when examined critically they do not in the least exist. Accepting this proposition, they establish their own theory and refute others by means of syllogisms whose elements they consider to be constituted by themselves.[25]

The Svātantrikas generally accepted two valid instruments of cognition, i.e., perception and inference. They likewise divided the phenomenally real (saṁvṛtisatya) into the true phenomenal (tathyasaṁvṛti) and the false phenomenal (mithyāsaṁvṛti), inasmuch as the former was efficacious and the latter not so.

There does not seem to have existed any classification of the Prāsaṅgikas into different schools in India. The Prāsaṅgikas generally employ four instruments of cognition, e.g., perception, inference, testimony and comparison, which they admit to be conventionally accepted in the world. The Prāsaṅgikas do not themselves invest their arguments with real validity. They admit provisionally the standpoint of their opponent and then refute his contention by means of an argument whose elements are acceptable to the opponent alone. They believed this to be the only efficacious means of producing an understanding of the Madhyamaka philosophy in the mind of the opponent. The Prāsaṅgikas do not admit that inference can lead to right knowledge of the ultimate truth. Nevertheless, inference is applied on the occasion of demonstrating in a conventional way the nature of the ultimate.

It is evident from the development of the controversy between the Prāsaṅgika and Svātantrika schools in India, that the Svātantrikas occupied an important place in Buddhist thought in India. The Svātantrikas included many outstanding Buddhist philosophers who differed significantly in other respects, but who all felt the need to adopt the Svātantrika mode of argument on the occasion of establishing emptiness. Though the commingling of Sautrāntika, Yogācāra, Madhyamaka and Svātantrika philosophy which occurred in the two schools, i.e., Sautrāntikamadhyamakasvātantrika and Yogācāramadhyamakasvātantrika, may seem confusing, the position may be clarified if it is remembered that generally the schools can be said to be Madhyamakas in the sense that they accept the Madhyamaka view with respect to the ultimate, Yogācāra or Sautrāntika respectively inasmuch as they accept the Yogācāra or Sautrāntika ontology with respect to the phenomenally real and Svātantrika in that they employed the Svātantrika argument, on the occasion of establishing the ultimate truth. This last, i.e., the ultimate truth again points to their determination as Madhyamaka.

It is after all our fundamental contention that the essential difference between the Prāsaṅgika and Svātantrika schools lies in their acceptance or non-acceptance of the independent syllogism on the occasion of establishing the ultimate truth. It is, therefore, not our purpose to investigate in detail the ontological considerations which were entered into by Svātantrika philosophers inasmuch as they belonged to the Yogācāra or Sautrāntika schools. It is our aim in this study to concentrate upon the difference between the Prāsaṅgika and Svātantrika schools with respect to the mode of argument which they adopted in order to explicate the Madhyamaka philosophy. For this reason, the ontological distinctions which may be made with respect to the two schools are not to be explored at length, though they will be referred to again in greater detail later. We shall by and large confine ourselves to considering them as Madhyamakas and as Svātantrikas.

At any rate the situation may be summed up as follows. The Svātantrikas sought to establish a fact as the probandum certainly by means of an argument which was admitted to exist by virtue of valid instruments of cognition by both the Madhyamaka and the opponent. The Prāsaṅgikas, on the other hand, produced a consequence which was undesirable for the opponent by means of an argument whose three parts, e.g., subject, major premise and fallacious proposition, were acceptable to the opponent alone.[26]

References

1. See chapter IV.

2. Alternatively minor term or logical subject, dharmin. The two terms, i.e., dharmin (ཆོས་ཅན་) and āśraya (གཞི་) are functionally identical.

3. མཐུན་པར་སྣང་བ།

4. See chapter III.

5. *Ibid.*

6. Jayānanda was a scholar of Kashmir who lived in the twelfth century. He visited central Tibet where he acquired a large following. He is also said to have gone to China. He composed the *Tarkamudgara-kārikā.* Roerich, G. N., *The Blue Annals*, V. p. 272; XI. pp. 343-344.

7. *Madhyamakāvatāraṭīkā-nama.* Roerich, G. N., *The Blue Annals.* V. p. 334.

8. *dBu-ma-spyi-ston*, pp. 265-266.

9. See chapter IX.

10. Stcherbatsky, Th., *Conception of Buddhist Nirvāṇa*, pp. 208-211.

11. "Diṅnāga has also stated that the existence of the probans in the subject should be endorsed by both parties. This is meant to rebut those probanses which are endorsed only by one of the parties". Mookerjee, S., Nagasaki, H., *Translation of the Pramāṇavārttikam of Dharmakīrti*, p. 46.

12. ཚད་མ།

13. བདེན་པར་མ་གྲུབ་པ།

14. *dBu-ma-spyi-ston,* p. 267.

15. The third element referred to by Jñānagarbha may be either the probandum or the example. The term property (dharma) may also refer to the probandum however, here it almost certainly means the property which is the reason (hetu).

16. *Op. cit.* p. 267.

17. *Madhyamakālaṁkārakārikā,* Verses 76, 77 quoted in the *dBu-ma-spyi-Ston* pp. 267-268. A Translation of the *Madhyamakālaṅkārakārikā* and *Vṛtti* of Śāntarakṣita and *Pañjikā* of Kamalaśila has been made by the author under the auspices of the Institute for Advanced Studies of World Religions, U.S.A.

18. *Ibid.* p. 268.

19. Grub-pai mtha'i rnam-bzhag rin-po-che'i phreng-ba, *The Jewel Garland of the Dissertation on Philosophical Systems.* Guenther, H. V. (tr.), *Buddhist Philosophy in Theory and Practice.*

20. Guenther, H. V., *Buddhist Philosophy in Theory and Practice,* p. 131.

21. *Ibid.*

22. *Ibid.,* p. 136.

23. Yid bzhin-mdzod-kyi grub-mtha' bsdus pa, *The Summary of* Philosophical Systems. Guenther, H. V. (Tr.), *Buddhist Philosophy in Theory and Practice.*

24. Guenther, H. V., *Buddhist Philosophy in Theory and Practice,* p. 139.

25. *Ibid.* p. 139.

26. *dBu-ma-spyi-ston,* p. 268.

Chapter VII

THE DEVELOPMENT OE THE CONTROVERSY IN TIBET

At this point we propose to survey the interpretations of the ideas presented by the Indian Prāsaṅgikas and Svātantrikas which were offered by early Tibetan scholars. Through this we hope to accomplish two objectives. Firstly, it will enable us to explore more extensively the significance of the statements made by the Indian exponents of the schools on the basis of an authoritative analysis. The early Tibetan Madhyamakas were the immediate inheritors of the issues which had been raised in India. Notable exponents of both schools such as Śāntarakṣita, Kamalaśīla and Jayānanda had visited Tibet. The controversy between the Prāsaṅgikas and Svātantrikas received considerable attention in Tibet in the new Buddhist scholarly circles. Since the early Tibetan commentators were the most proximate, both historically and intellectually, to the philosophical dispute between the Prāsaṅgikas and the Svātantrikas, the opinions they expressed in any case deserve the consideration of a serious student of the problem.

Secondly, a survey of the interpretations offered by early Tibetan Madhyamaka scholars will enable us to bridge the chronological and intellectual distance which separates bSod-nams sen-ge from the historical nexus of the dispute in India. Thus, it serves to complete the picture of the development of the controversy throughout the centuries which preceded bSod-nams sen-ge. Though the latter devoted himself principally to the exposition of the original questions which had been raised by the interchange between the three Indian exponents of the schools, i.e., Buddhapālita, Bhāvaviveka and Candrakīrti, it will not be without profit to acquaint ourselves generally with the indigenous exegetical tradition which he inherited.

The introduction of Buddhist philosophy into Tibet from India may be divided into two more or less distinct periods. The former was roughly synchronous with the era of the three kings,

Sron-btsan sgam-po, Khri-sron Ide-btsan and Ral-pa-can[1] and may be termed the era of the old translations. Thereafter, during the reign of gLan Dar-ma (836-841 C.E.), Buddhism in Tibet suffered a serious persecution which temporarily crippled its growth in the new country. This intermediate period of decline was again superseded by a period of renewed religious and philosophical activity. The latter may be termed the era of the new translations.

The Svātantrika system which was introduced into Tibet along with systematic Buddhist philosophy by Śāntarakṣita and Kamalaśīla achieved an early and general acceptance there. The principal treatises of the school such as the *Prajñāpradipa* of Bhāvaviveka and others were rendered into Tibetan during the era of the old translations.

It was not until the era of the new translations that the Prāsaṅgika system was introduced into Tibet by sPa-tshab lo-tsāba,[2] who translated the texts of the Prāsaṅgikas and pondered upon their meaning. Then only were the outstanding treatises of the Prāsaṅgika school such as the *Prasannapadā* of Candrakīrti translated into Tibetan.

The length of time which in fact separated the two eras, that of the old and that of the new translations is a matter of doubt. Traditional Tibetan historians generally estimate it to have been as much as one hundred years. However, according to some modern opinions, it is not believed to have been more than fifty years.[3] Be that as it may, it remains certain that the Svātantrika system preceded the Prāsaṅgika system historically in Tibet. Although the Prāsaṅgika school eventually emerged victorious in Tibet in its contest with the Svātantrika system and came to be regarded there as the orthodox interpretation of the Madhyamaka philosophy as set forth by Nāgārjuna, it had to overcome the early advantage enjoyed by the Svātantrika school.

The early Tibetan Prāsaṅgikas assailed the Svātantrika doctrine with a vehemence which betrays their conviction that they were presenting a more accurate and more faithful interpretation of the Madhyamaka philosophy as set forth by the Master Nāgārjuna. Their attack was principally founded upon their understanding of the criticism of the Svātantrika system which had been advanced by Candrakīrti.

They declared that an independent argument which was constructed to fulfil one's own will and was accepted by one's self was inadmissible for the Madhyamakas. The early Tibetan Prāsaṅgikas pointed out again that the Prāsaṅgika argument, i.e., the argument *ad absurdum* proceeded by provisionally admitting the standpoint favoured by the opponent and then exposing its inconsistency. Therefore, they asserted an independent argument was unnecessary.

Again, they maintained that if the opponent refused to relinquish his proposition even when it had been shown to be contradictory, he could also not be persuaded to do so through the introduction of an independent argument. Therefore, they concluded an independent argument was powerless.

Finally, they contended that it was unreasonable for the Madhyamaka to employ an independent argument, since he neither accepted a proposition, nor valid instruments of cognition, nor yet again a substratum. The early Tibetan Prāsaṅgikas argued that on the occasion of the examination of the nature of the ultimate truth, an independent argument was unintelligible. They maintained that on that occasion, refutation by means of a *reductio ad absurdum* was the only reasonable method because the Madhyamaka did not accept a proposition of his own. They argued that the Madhyamaka did not accept a proposition because for one who was possessed of knowledge of the right vision,[4] or in conformity with the logic (yukti) which was competent to establish truly the nature of the ultimate, nothing from form to the omniscience of a Buddha, no entity or element can be said to exist, not to exist, both exist and not exist or neither exist nor not exist.[5]

Moreover, they affirmed the lord, the Buddha had declared in the holy discourses (Sūtra), that if one asserted the permanence or impermanence of form and the like, one relied upon instruments of cognition (pramāṇa) not upon emptiness (śūnyatā).[6]

The early Tibetan Prāsaṅgikas maintained that the phenomenal truth (saṁvṛti) did not conform to logic (yukti). The ultimate truth (paramārtha-satya) on the other hand transcended all thought and expression. Both truths they declared were empty of own being (svabhāva). Therefore the Master Nāgārjuna himself had said that one endowed with excellent qualities does not contend, such a one has no position (pakṣa) of his own.

When one has no position of one's own, how could one have another position.[7] He had likewise declared in the *Vigrahavyāvartanī*, "If I had a proposition of my own, I could be at fault, but as I have none, I cannot be at fault."[8] And again, "There exists for me no object to be negated, hence I do not undertake to negate anything. When I am accused of negating anything, I am falsely accused".[9]

Indeed, they continued, it may be thought by the opponent that when the Madhyamaka declares that all entities do not originate from themselves, he intends to affirm the positive counterpart of the refutation *ad absurdum*. However this consequence does not arise for the Madhyamaka because he has no position (pakṣa) of his own. It follows automatically that the Madhyamaka accepts no proposition (pratijñā) of his own. It is therefore incorrect, they contended, to vindicate a proposition by means of an independent syllogism. Thus it is evident, they concluded, that through arguments *ad absurdum* one can refute the proposition accepted by the opponent, without affirming any independent proposition of one's own. Indeed Candrakīrti had indicated in the *Prasannapadā* that an argument *ad absurdum* has for its effect only the refutation of the standpoint accepted by the opponent. Hence an alternative proposition in opposition to the one denied does not arise for the Madhyamaka.[10]

Thus, it is evident that the early Tibetan Prāsaṅgikas reaffirmed the inconceivable and inexpressible character of the ultimate truth which, as they indicated, transcends the four alternatives of existence, non-existence and the rest. Hence they maintained that the Madhyamaka does not himself accept any proposition refuting the existence of entities and so on. They similarly rejected the notion that the phenomenal truth possesses any logicality, or can be justified by reason (yukti). Hence they concluded that the Madhyamaka has no position or proposition of his own. Finally, Bhāvaviveka had maintained that an argument *ad absurdum* necessarily entails the emergence of a counter proposition. This contention of Bhāvaviveka's had already been rejected by Candrakīrti in the *Prasannapadā*. The early Tibetan Prāsaṅgikas reaffirmed the position which had been expressed by Candrakīrti and asserted that an argument *ad absurdum* results simply in the refutation of the position endorsed by the opponent. Therefore they declared, it does not in the least imply the Madhyamaka's acceptance of the alternative proposition.

Again the early Tibetan Prāsaṅgikas contended that an independent syllogism is inadmissible because the Madhyamaka does not accept the reality of valid instruments of cognition (pramāṇa). The status of the instruments of cognition will be discussed at length in a subsequent chapter. Hence at present it suffices to say that the ultimate validity of the instruments of cognition had been set aside by Nāgārjuna in the *Vigrahavyāvartanī*. In that work the Master had shown that as the instruments of cognition themselves stand in need of proof, they do not exist to establish anything.

Finally, the early Tibetan Prāsaṅgikas maintained that the Madhyamaka does not accept a substratum (dharmin). They declared that for the Madhyamaka ultimately nothing exists. Therefore, the subjective pole of eye consciousness (cakṣu-āyatana)[11] and the rest do not exist ultimately. The subjective pole of eye consciousness and the rest are also not established phenomenally because phenomena are only illusory.[12]

The Svātantrikas maintained that nonetheless simply the subjective pole of eye consciousness could be retained as the minor term for the purposes of argument. Indeed it will be recalled that the subjective poles of consciousness had been retained by Bhāvaviveka as the minor term in his syllogism refuting self-origination (sva-utpatti).[13]

The early Tibetan Prāsaṅgikas rejoined that it is inadmissible to accept even simply the subjective pole of eye consciousness as the minor term. They maintained that it is not inconsistent for the Realist who admits that entities exist to accept an unqualified sense faculty like the eye as the substratum of an inference. However, they pointed out, the case of the Madhyamaka is different for he does not accept the existence of entities. Therefore, it is inadmissible to accept as a substratum the subjective pole of eye consciousness and the rest which are not vindicated by either of the two truths. Moreover, they noted that the Master Bhāvaviveka had himself indicated in the *Prajñāpradipa* that when it is said that ultimately there is no origination, then at that time all the products of ignorance vanish. Hence, the early Tibetan Prāsaṅgikamadhyamakas concluded that there exists altogether no common substratum acceptable to both the Madhyamaka and the opponent.[14]

Thus, the early Tibetan Prāsaṅgikas maintained that an independent syllogism of three terms established by valid instruments of cognition, which seeks to establish certainly a fact as the probandum is unintelligible from the Madhyamaka standpoint. The proposition accepted by the opponent, they contended, is refuted through exposing its inherent inconsistency by means of an argument *ad absurdum*. Thus, the position advocated by the opponent is refuted indirectly. This, they affirmed, is the practice of the Prāsaṅgikas, and this alone is correct.[15]

Klu-mes,[16] an early Tibetan Svātantrika who achieved great renown just prior to the coming of Atīśa Dīpaṅkaraśrījñāna to Tibet, and others defended the Svātantrika system against the onslaught of the Prāsaṅgikas. They observed that though it might be the practice of the Prāsaṅgikas to accept neither a proposition nor a common substratum, it is incorrect not to do so.[17]

They asked, whether the non-existence of a jar in a place where no jar exists is accepted by the Prāsaṅgikas or not? If the non-existence of such a jar is not accepted, then there will be no refutation of the proposition advocated by the opponent. If on the other hand the non-existence of the jar is accepted, then why is not the proposition refuting the eternal self advocated by the opponent accepted. That is if the non-existence of an eternal self is admitted by the Madhyamaka then the formal proposition refuting it ought also to be accepted.[18]

In reply the Prāsaṅgika may insist that ultimately there exists no not-self (anātman) and the like to be established. Ultimately, he may say there is nothing to be refuted, hence there is no refutation.

Nonetheless, the Svātantrikas rejoined, the Master Nāgārjuna himself accepted the proposition of the negation of origination. He had declared, "The nature (svabhāva) of sugar is sweet, that of fire hot; similarly the nature of all elements (dharmas) is emptiness (śūnyatā). The twelve constituents of interdependent origination from ignorance through old age and death originate interdependently. I see them to be like dream and illusion."[19]

The Svātantrikas maintained that the proposition refuting own being ought to be accepted by the Madhyamaka. The proposition refuting own being, they said, possesses the three characteristics definitive of a proposition. A proposition, they declared, should first contain something of which the opponent is ignorant. Second, it should not be fallacious. Finally, he who advances a proposition should desire to prove it to the opponent. The proposition refuting own being, they contended, possesses these three characteristics. Hence it ought to be accepted by the Madhyamaka.[20]

The Svātantrikas argued that form and the like originate interdependently. Therefore, they may legitimately be employed as the logical subject (dharmin) of an argument. Similarly, they maintained that the fact of Interdependent Origination could function as the reason or middle term of an inference refuting own being. They constructed syllogisms like the following one. Proposition (pratijñā)—the minor term (dharmin), i.e., a jar is devoid of own being. Reason (hetu)—because it is interdependently originated. Example (dṛṣṭānta)—like form.

The Prāsaṅgikas replied that form and interdependent origination alike are apprehended only through intellectual delusion,[21] therefore, they are not admissible when the nature of the ultimate is investigated. To this the Svātantrikas replied, that in that case, the opponent who admits a contradictory position must also be apprehended only through intellectual delusion.[22]

Klu-mes also maintained that when the subject of debate[23] is something well known and commonly accepted, an independent syllogism ought to be employed. However, he said, when the subject of an argument is a non-entity (abhāva), like the eternal self or the primordial matter (pradhāna)[24] admitted by the Sāṅkhyas, an argument *ad absurdum* is applicable, since in that case it is impossible to have a commonly accepted subject of debate.[25]

The Prāsaṅgikas contended that no common substratum exists acceptable to both the Madhyamaka and the Realist. The Realist, they maintained, accepts that form and the like are established in their own being, while, for the Madhyamaka, they are illusory. Hence the two are altogether dissimilar and no common substratum is possible.

The Svātantrikas countered that they do not admit a substratum which is merely imputed, but rather one which is given in experience; form and the like, they argued, are not given as truly existent even to the Realist. His contention that they existed truly is simply a false ascription. For instance, they said, even though one might hold that the five aggregates (skandhas) are the self (ātman), that very self does not appear. Similarly, though non-Buddhists affirm the eternality of sound while it is denied by Buddhists, sound alone is given commonly to both. Again though non-Buddhists held that sound is a property of space, while for Buddhists it is generated from the four great elements (mahābhūtāni), still sound itself is experienced commonly by Buddhists and non-Buddhists alike.

The Prāsaṅgikas responded characteristically to this line of argument advanced by the Svātantrikas. To two persons, both afflicted by double vision, they said, two moons will appear commonly. The case is exactly parallel. Hence it is inadmissible to accept a common substratum when the nature of the ultimate truth is examined.

The Svātantrikas rejoined that even if it were so and the entity which is the substratum does not exist, it might still be legitimately imputed for the purposes of assertion and refutation.[26]

The Master Phyā-pa[27] was without doubt one of the most acute philosophers among the Tibetan Svātantrikas. Though the intricacy and subtlety of his arguments may sometimes baffle his readers, it must nonetheless be admitted that he offers an eminently convincing defence of the Svātantrika doctrine. In addition he raises some very significant questions regarding the method of argument favoured by the Prāsaṅgikas.

It is especially interesting to note that the Master Phyā-pa was a contemporary of Jayānanda, the Indian Prāsaṅgika whose ideas were presented in the foregoing chapter. Indeed Phyā-pa is said to have met Jayānanda in a philosophical debate and defeated him, when the latter was in Tibet.[28] This encounter provides added evidence of the intimate acquaintance which the early Tibetan Madhyamakas had with the controversy between the Prāsaṅgika and the Svātantrika schools.

Phyā-pa maintained that entities are not to be accepted as truly existent or otherwise, without recourse to examination. If a conclusion is accepted following upon a thorough examination, then it can be said to be truly proved. Examination, he said, is the method by means of which the opponent is induced to accept emptiness. When the method is initiated, he contended, it is inadmissible to accept its result.[29]

Thus while the subject is in the process of being examined or analysed, it should not be accepted by the Madhyamaka to be empty (śūnya). The emptiness of the logical subject or substratum should be accepted only after its examination has been completed.

Similarly, a substratum which is believed to be illusory is likewise unacceptable. The theories entertained by the Realist regarding the ultimate nature of the substratum are also inadmissible at the time of analysis, since it is through the process of examination that the reality or unreality of the substratum is to be determined.

Thus, form and the like qualified as truly existent or illusory alike are unacceptable as subjects of valid arguments. Disassociated from the predicates of permanence and impermanence, objects which are equally well known to the learned and to cowherds alike are acceptable as the subjects of debate.

If it is not so, he argued, then the substratum of all that one may wish to establish will not exist, because a substratum qualified by predicates like permanence and the like is essentially unproven. In that case it would be impossible even to establish the existence of fire from that of smoke, and the impermanence of sound from the fact that it is a product.[30]

Again Phyā-pa questioned the contention of the Prāsaṅgikas, that their arguments derived their legitimacy from the acceptance of the opponent. He asked, is the object to be refuted[31] rendered altogether non-existent simply through the power of the opponent's acceptance of a concept which contradicts the object's existence ? Is it for instance the mere acceptance of the non-existence of fire which negates the existence of smoke ? If the logical consequence of absolute negation can be secured simply through the acceptance of a concept which contradicts the existence of the object to be refuted, then the acceptance of the permanence of entities by non-Buddhists can negate their phenomenal efficacy, since permanence and efficacy are believed to be mutually contradictory. However, this is unacceptable.[32]

Alternatively, if the acceptance of a contradictory concept merely hinders the acceptance of the object of refutation, then the possibility of its existence cannot be altogether disposed of. Thus, though one may accept that one's own mother is a barren woman, her motherhood which is a fact well known to all cannot be negated.[33]

Thus, in either case the conclusion is inescapable, that mere acceptance cannot constitute an adequate criterion for determining the validity of an argument. Otherwise any argument, however absurd, can be vindicated on the ground that it is accepted by someone. However, it is universally admitted that a valid argument must in some sense correspond to real or objective facts.

In defence of the standpoint of the Prāsaṅgika, it can only be said that it is not after all his intention to negate the apparent reality of individual facts of experience as such. The object of the arguments of the Prāsaṅgikas is to induce an opponent to relinquish the dogmatic interpretation which he has superimposed upon the simple data of common experience and which he invests with ultimate reality.

Thus for instance, the doctrine advocated by the Sāṅkhyas of an ultimate identity between cause and effect, is only a theoretical construction which is not in the least vindicated by an appeal to observable phenomena. When the Sāṅkhya is induced to abandon his theory of a substantial identity between cause and effect, as a result of his acceptance of an argument which contradicts it, it does not affect the status of empirical causality as it is approved by commonsense. Finally, it is not the case that the argument of the Madhyamaka, or even its acceptance by the opponent renders an object non-existent. The argument serves merely to communicate the factual absence of the object to the opponent.

The Tibetan Svatantrikas like their Indian counterparts stressed the community of human experience and the similarity of human volitional activity. They held that if the objects of the six sense faculties do not exist commonly, the inconsistency entailed by the doctrine advocated by the opponent would not be apparent to both the Madhyamaka and the opponent.[34]

They asserted that both the Madhyamaka and the opponent to whom objects were presented in experience, approached or withdrew from them alike. If there were altogether nothing commonly given, they contended, it would be futile for one person to address himself to another. In that case the intention of the former could not be apprehended by the latter. Hence communication between individuals would become impossible.[35]

Moreover, the Svâtantrikas contended that if the substratum and reason does not exist for the Madhyamaka the argument will be incapable of achieving its object. That is to say that an argument which does not exist will be without the causal efficiency required to bring about an understanding of emptiness in the mind of the opponent.[36]

Therefore, they maintained in order to convince an opponent of the truth of emptiness, it is reasonable to rely upon an independent syllogism containing a minor term and a major premise commonly established by valid instruments of cognition.[37] The great early Tibetan Prâsangika Khu-mdo-sde-bar,[38] also maintained that the Madhyamaka accepts no proposition of his own. Then the ultimate truth, the negation of origination and emptiness, are the subjects of discussion, he held the Madhyamaka does not accept any proposition whatsoever. However he does admit that generally, i.e., when the nature of the ultimate truth is not in question, the Madhyamaka has a proposition which he himself favours.

When the correct conventional truth is to be determined, he affirmed, the Madhyamaka accepts a proposition. Though the Madhyamaka does not accept an independent syllogism when the nature of the ultimate truth is to be determined, an independent ogism is acceptable within the limits of phenomenal reality.[39]

The ultimate truth, he maintained, transcends the four alternatives of existence, non-existence and the rest. In the absence of determinations like existent and non-existent, the object determined also does not exist.[40]

Moreover the objects cognised through perception and inference do not exist ultimately. Therefore, perception and inference are also not established.[41]

Therefore, since the ultimate truth transcends the four alternatives, and does not admit of any proposition, an independent syllogism is not competent to establish its nature. The objects which are grasped by the mind, he held, are only phenomenal. Hence an independent syllogism is only acceptable with reference to the phenomenally real.[42]

Ultimately, nothing at all is to be admitted. As for the theories admitted by the Realists, they can be refuted by means of an argument *ad absurdum*, which exposes their inherent inconsistency.[43]

For instance, one school of the Yogâcâra[44] advocates the theory that the objects of the six senses do not exist. They however affirm the sole existence of consciousness.[45] It is pointed out that if the objects of the six senses do not exist altogether, they cannot be related to consciousness which does exist. In that case they will not even be apprehended by consciousness. However, if the objects of the six sense faculties are related to consciousness and are apprehended by it, they cannot be altogether non-existent. Thus the sole reality of consciousness advocated by the school is refuted by means of an argument *ad absurdum.*[46]

Again, the Ābhidharmikas advocate the doctrine that atoms are not composite, i.e., that they are unitary and indivisible entities. However, they also maintained that through conjunction with other atoms they become perceivable. It is observed that if atoms are indeed non-composite, i.e., do not possess parts, their conjunction with other atoms is unintelligible. Again, if they become perceivable through conjunction with other atoms, they cannot be devoid of parts or indivisible as the opponent asserts. Thus, the indivisibility of atoms advocated by the Buddhist Realists is set aside.[47]

In this way the doctrine accepted by the opponent is refuted through exposing its inherent inconsistency. In other words the contradiction involved in the simultaneous acceptance of the initial proposition, the minor premise, i.e., the combination of the minor term with the reason or probans[48] and the major premise, i.e., invariable concomitance is revealed by means of an argument *ad absurdum.*[49]

This may be clarified through reference to one of the illustrations cited above. The Ābhidharmikas accept the proposition that atoms are indivisible, i.e., that they do not possess parts. They likewise accept that atoms became perceivable through conjunction with other atoms. This constitutes the minor premise, i.e., the minor term (atoms) become visible through conjunction with other atoms, which is the probans, i.e., their conjunction with other atoms. The minor premise is accepted by the Ābhidharmikas who, as has been seen, admit that atoms become visible through conjunction with other atoms. The major premise or invariable concomitance may be stated as follows—whatsoever is capable of conjunction with others, is possessed of parts, i.e., is not indivisible, or conversely, whatsoever is not possessed of parts, i.e., is indivisible is not capable of conjunction with others. The major premise is conventionally established by valid instruments of cognition and is accepted as such by the opponent.

Thus it has been shown that the early Tibetan Prāsaṅgikas like their Indian counterparts consistently rejected the applicability of the valid instruments of cognition at least when the nature of the ultimate truth is to be determined. The great rMa-ḅya[50], a Tibetan Prāsaṅgika, however, believed that there were valid instruments of cognition acceptable to the Madhyamaka.

He maintained that the characteristic standpoint of the Madhyamaka is not achieved without recourse to valid instruments of cognition. He asserted that the three parts of an argument *ad absurdum*, i.e., proposition, minor premise and major premise are established by the four conventionally accepted valid instruments of cognition (lokaprasiddhi-pramāṇa),[51] i.e., perception, inference, testimony and comparison. He apparently thought that the acceptability of the conventionally accepted valid instruments of cognition for the Madhyamaka had been taught by Candrakīrti in the *Prasannapadā*.

He was aware of the fact that his acceptance of valid instruments of cognition left him open to the charge that his doctrine amounted to an admission of the position advocated by the Svātantrikas. However, he sharply distinguished the valid instruments of cognition which he admitted. It was his contention that while the conventionally accepted valid instruments of cognition are acceptable to the Madhyamaka, the objective valid instruments of cognition,[52] i.e., perception and inference inasmuch as they are conceived to correspond to real objects (vastu) are altogether rejected by the Madhyamaka.

He believed that the defining property of an independent syllogism and the Svātantrika doctrine is the acceptance of the objective valid instruments of cognition and that the three terms of an independent syllogism, i.e., proposition, reason and example, or alternatively minor premise, positive concomitance and negative concomitance, are established by the objective valid instruments of cognition. rMa-bya held that it is because it is constituted by the objective valid instruments of cognition that an independent syllogism is unacceptable to the Madhyamaka. He even denied the acceptability of an independent syllogism established by the objective valid instruments of cognition within the limits of the phenomenally real.[53]

References

1. Sroṅ-btsan sgam-po—569/629-650 C. E.
Khri-ston-lde-btsan—755-780 C. E.
Ral-pa-Can 814-836 C.E. Roerich G. N., *The Blue Annal*, Introduction, xix.

2. sPa-tshab lo-tsā-ba Ñi-ma-grags who lived in twelfth century is credited with playing the most important role in the introduction of the Prāsaṅgika system into Tibet. sPa-tshab, a native of 'Phan-yul went to Kashmir as a youth. The date of his departure for India is given as 1137 C. E. In Kashmir sPa-tshab studied under many scholars including the two sons of Sañjana. He remained in India for twenty three years. According to Śākya mChog-lDan, he also studied under Hasumati and Kanakavarman. He represented the exegetical tradition of Hasumati, Parūhita, Ratnavajra, Devacandra, Mañjukīrti, Candrakīrti, Nāgārjuna, Rāhulabhadra and Munīndra. In Tibet sPa-tshab taught the six treatises of Nāgārjuna. Eventually he gathered many disciples. He translated the *Prasannapadā*, *Madhyamakāvatāra* and its auto-commentary as well as Candrakīrti's commentary to the *Yuktiṣaṣṭikā* with the help of Kanakavarman. He is also credited with the revision of the translation of Candrakīrti's commentary to the *Śūnyatāsaptati*. He translated with the Kashmirian Jayānanda and Khu-mdo-sde-'bar the *Sūtrasamuccaya*. He also translated the *Uttaratantra* and its commentary. Roerich, G. N., *The Blue Annals*, pp. 230, 236, 272, 341-342, 344, 350; *The complete works of Śākya mChog-lDan*, Vol. XIV, p. 518.

3. The controversy revolves around the question of the date of the persecution of the doctrine under gLan dar-ma. Gos-lo-tsā ba gives the date of the persecution as 841 C. E., while other sources mention 901 C. E. The latter date in fact seems more probable.

4. གཟིགས་པ་དག་པའི་ལོ་ཆེས།

5. *dBu-ma-spyi-ston*, pp. 269-271.
6. *Ibid.* p. 272.
7. Quoted in the *dBu-ma-spyi-ston*, p. 272 from *Yuktiṣaṣṭikā*.
8. Quoted in the *dBu-ma-spyi-ston*, p. 272. *Vigrahavyāvartanī*, Stanza 29.
9. *Vigrahavyāvartanī*, Stanza 63.
10. *Op. cit.* p. 273.

11. མིག་གི་སྐྱེ་མཆེད།

12. *dBu-ma-spyi-ston*, p. 271.

13. བདག་སྐྱེས།

14. *Op.cit.* pp. 270-271.
15. *dBu-ma-spyi-ston*, p. 274.

16. Klu-mes belonged to the tradition of Nāgārjuna, Bhāvaviveka, Śrīgupta, Jñānagarbha, Śāntarakṣita, sBa, Ratna and Dgons-pa rab-gsal. He lived in the later part of tenth century and the first part of the eleventh century C. E. Klu-mes is one of the six or ten men from dBu gTsan who are credited with the reintroduction of the monastic tradition into central Tibet from

Khams after the persecution of the doctrine instigated by gLan-dar-ma. Klu-mes took over many monasteries and constructed many temples in Central Tibet. Klu-mes is primarily known for his preaching of the Vinaya: He taught the *Vinaya Sūtra-ṭikā*, the *Pratimokṣasūtraṭikāvinayasamuccaya*. He resided at the se-ra cave of Tshe-spon. He died on his way to Than and his remains are enshrined in the Stupa of 'Od-can. Roerich., G. N., *The Blue Annals*, pp. 34, 75, 77.

17. *Op. cit.* p. 275.
18. *dBu-ma-spyi-ston*, p. 275.
19. *Ibid.*
20. *Ibid.* p. 276.
21. སྣོ་འཁྲུལ་བ།
22. *dBu-ma-spyi-ston*, pp. 276-277.
23. རྟོད་ཀྱི་ཚོས་ཅན།
24. གཙོ་བོ།
25. *dBu-ma-spyi-ston*, p. 278.
26. *Ibid.* pp. 278-279.
27. The Master Phyā-pa lived in the twelfth century. Most of the great scholars of his period were at one time or other his disciples. He composed commentaries, on the 'Five Treatises' of Maitreya, the *Pramāṇaviniścaya*, the *Madhyamakadvayasatya*, the *Madhyamakālaṅkāra* and the *Madhyamakāloka*. He wrote a work on logic in verse and its autocommentary. He also wrote large and short abridged expositions of the Madhyamaka system. He also wrote many works refuting the interpretation of the Madhyamaka philosophy given by Candrakīrti. He died in 1169 C. E. Roerich, G. N., *The Blue Annals*, pp. 332-334.
28. According to Śakya mChog-lDan, Phyā-pa met Jayānanda in a debate in which Khu-mdo-sde-'bar acted as interpretor. *The complete works of Śākya mChog-lDan*, Vol. XIV, p. 518.
29. *dBu-ma-spyi-ston*, pp. 279-280.
30. *Ibid.* pp. 280-281.
31. དགག་བྱ།
32. *dBu-ma-spyi-ston*, p. 287.
33. *Ibid.* p. 288.
34. *Ibid.* p. 281.
35. *Ibid.*
36. *Ibid.* p. 282.
37. *Ibid.* p. 289.
38. Khu-mdo-sde'bar was a contemporary of sPa-tshab lo-tsā-ba, the Kashmirian Jayānanda and the Master Phyā-pa. He taught the Madhyamaka system. Roerich, G. N., *The Blue Annals*, p. 94.
39. *dBu-ma-spyi-ston*, p. 283.
40. *Ibid.*

41. *Ibid.*
42. *Ibid.* pp. 283-284.
43. *Ibid.* p. 284.

44. སེམས་ཙམ་པ།

45. The Yogācāra is divided into two schools. One denies the reality of the objects of the six sense faculties. Representatives of this school are Diṅnāga and Dharmakīrti. The other maintains the reality of the objects of the six senses. A representative of the latter is Śāntarakṣita.

46. *dBu-ma-spyi-ston,* p. 284.

47. The concept of conjunction entails compositeness because if it is held that a number of atoms conjoined to form a perceivable mass, then it must be admitted that each atom has at least six distinguishable parts, i.e., front, sides, back, top and bottom which come into contact with other atoms which similarly possess parts. *dBu-ma-spyi-ston,* pp. 284-285.

48. ཁྱབ་བྱ།

49. *Op.cit.* p. 285.

50. The great rMa-bya-Byan-brtson lived in the twelfth century. He studied under the Master Phyā-pa, but then later became a disciple of sPa-tshab, Khu-mdo-sde-'bar and Jayānanda. He resided at Yar-Kluns. He wrote a commentary on the *Tarkamudgara-kārikā* of Jayānanda. He also wrote works on the *Prasannapadā,* the *Madhyamakāvatāra* and an abridged exposition of the Madhyamaka system. Roerich, G. N., *The Blue Annals,* p. 343.

51. འཇིག་རྟེན་ལ་གྲགས་པའི་ཚད་མ།

52. དངོས་པོ་སྟོབས་ཞུགས་ཀྱི་ཚད་མ།

53. *dBu-ma-spyi-ston,* pp. 293-295.

Chapter VIII

THE SIGNIFICANCE OF THESE INTERPRETATIONS ASSESSED

It is evident from our survey of the interpretations offered by the early Tibetan Madhyamaka scholars that in Tibet, as in India, the controversy between the Prāsaṅgika and Svātantrika schools centred around three principal issues. They were, firstly the character of the proposition as a whole, secondly, the character of the subject which it contains and lastly, the nature of the logical ground or reason by means of which the proposition is sought to be established. Moreover, the problem of the relevance and nature of the valid instruments of cognition had again to be faced in the attempt to determine the nature of the subject and reason.

It is clear that the early Tibetan Prāsaṅgikas uniformly maintained that the Madhyamaka had no proposition of his own. Their interpretation was founded upon the evidence of those stanzas composed by the Master Nāgārjuna, in which he disavows the acceptance of a position (pakṣa) or proposition (pratijñā). They also had before them the statements of Candrakīrti who likewise had rejected the notion that the Madhyamaka accepted any proposition of his own.

The early Tibetan Prāsaṅgikas uncritically accepted these utterances of Nāgārjuna and Candrakīrti, and as a result they were led to deny altogether that the Madhyamaka accepted any proposition. They seem to have ignored the problem presented by the existence of numerous formal propositions in the works of the master Nāgārjuna. This was a fact which Svātantrikas like Klu-mes were quick to point out.

Though the early Tibetan Prāsaṅgikas maintained that the Madhyamaka had no preferred proposition of his own, this interpretation is untenable according to bSod-nams Seṅ-ge. He asks if it is that the proposition refuting origination from the four alternatives which is advanced in the opening stanza of the *Mūlamadhyamakakārikā* is produced by the Madhyamaka, though it is not preferred by him. If so, then the proposition affirming origination from the four alternatives will be equally acceptable. In that case both propositions would be on an equal footing, since neither of them would be preferable to the Madhyamaka. However this is inadmissible.[1]

Moreover it is not the case that what is preferable[2] is necessarily accepted to be truly existent.[3] A preferable proposition may be truly existent or not.

Again, it is unreasonable to hold that stanzas like the following—"One endowed with excellent qualities does not contend, such a one has no position of his own. When one has no position of one's own, how could one have another's position"—are evidence of the fact that there is altogether no proposition acceptable to the Madhyamaka. That stanza and others like it only indicate that on the occasion of determining the nature of the ultimate truth, an independent proposition is unacceptable.[4]

The acceptance of a preferred proposition does not entail the acceptance of an independent proposition, because there is no relation of invariable concomitance obtaining between the two.[5]

Moreover, it is not through the mere rejection of a proposition as such that the erroneous doctrines of the Realists are refuted. Khu-mdo-sde-'bar advocated the theory that ultimately the Madhyamaka accepted no proposition of the negation of origination or the negation of self-existence (svabhāva). However, he admitted that when the reality of the phenomenal truth is to be determined, a preferred proposition existed for the Madhyamaka. bSod-nams Señ-ge believes this distinction to be irrelevant. He maintains that if it is held that ultimately no proposition as such exists, then in that case, it will not exist phenomenally either.

Again if it is meant that when the negation of the origination of an entity like a sprout is to be established, the Madhyamaka accepts no preferred proposition of his own, then the proposition refuting origination from the four alternatives set forth by Nāgārjuna will be contradicted.[6]

In short it must be admitted that the Madhyamaka accepts a preferable proposition of his own even when the nature of the ultimate is in question. The acceptance of a preferred proposition of this kind, however, does not involve the Madhyamaka in any inconsistency because it is not believed by him to possess independent reality.

Then it may be asked, how are the preferred propositions of the Madhyamaka arrived at ? Firstly it must be recalled that it is the Realist who affirms the real origination or existence of entities. It is with reference to this assertion of the Realist that the Madhyamaka expresses his proposition of refutation. The refutation of the notion of the real existence of entities is soteriologically necessary because it is attachment to this notion which is the primary cause of ignorance, bondage and suffering.

The Svātantrikas justified their acceptance of an independent proposition, i.e., a proposition the subject of which is established commonly by valid instruments of cognition, because such a proposition does not seek to affirm a truly established fact (dharma). The Prāsaṅgikas who were also obliged to accept the existence of preferred proposition avoided the apparent inconsistency which existed between the admission of such a preferred proposition, and the statements of Nāgārjuna, because they did not accept an independent proposition as defined above. It need hardly be said that the Prāsaṅgikas also rejected a proposition of a truly existent fact, for it was a proposition of a truly established fact which it is the intention of the Madhyamaka to refute.[7]

While Klu-mes's criticism of the categorical rejection of any proposition whatsoever by the early Tibetan Prāsaṅgikas was without doubt well founded, the theory which he propounded regarding the respective applicability ofthe independent syllogism and the argument *ad absurdum*, seems to be untenable. It will be recalled that Klu-mes had advocated the view that when the subject of debate existed as something commonly known, an independent syllogism ought to be employed. However, when the subject of debate is a non-entity not found in experience, like the primordial matter of the Sāṅkhyas or the changeless self of the Brāhmaṇical schools, an argument *ad absurdum* is needed.

bSod-nams Sen-ge assails this contention of Klu-mes's. He points out that the Master Nāgārjuna declared in the *Mūlamadhyamakakārikā*, "If form exists disassociated from the cause of form, then that form will be without a cause. However, there is no object found anywhere disassociated from a cause."[8] Hence it is evident, bSod-nams Sen-ge concludes that, for the most part, a generally accepted subject was employed by the Master in arguments *ad absurdum*. It follows that the theory advanced by Klu-mes, is an instance of ill considered speech.[9]

The early Tibetan Prāsaṅgikas generally refused to admit the existence of a common subject (dharmin) or substratum (āśraya) of discussion. They contended that, as the refutation of origination necessarily entails the rejection of an existent substratum, an independent syllogism is incorrect. The existence of a fact which could serve as the common substratum of an inference, they maintained, is not sanctioned by either of the two truths. Since the Madhyamaka maintains that the objects of common sense possess only an illusory nature, while the Realist accepts them as truly real, they could not be considered commonly established subjects of valid independent syllogisms. Therefore, they concluded that there is altogether no common substratum acceptable to both the Madhyamaka and the opponent.

The Svātantrikas countered that objects as they presented themselves in experience ought to be commonly acceptable to both the Madhyamaka and the Realist. They believed that the similarity of human experience and volitional behaviour is sufficient evidence of the necessary existence of commonly accepted objects. Without such commonly existing facts, they contended, communication between individuals would be impossible. Moreover in such a situation, the inconsistency admitted by the opponent would not be apparent to both parties to a discussion. Therefore they argued that the position of the Prāsaṅgikas renders meaningful discourse impossible.

This attack of the Svātantrikas however is ill founded, because the community of human experience does not for the Prāsaṅgika imply its logical validity or acceptability. An illusion may also be commonly experienced. The efficacy of dialogue may be secured simply through the power of common illusion. Hence the Prāsaṅgika's ability to communicate effectively is not in the least impaired by his rejection of the logical reality of the unqualified data of experience.

Again, the Master Phyā-pa asserted that if a substratum does not exist commonly, the reliability of even ordinary syllogism such as that through which the existence of fire is established from the existence of smoke would be impaired. This argument however does not affect the position of the Prāsaṅgikas. When the correct conventional truth is to be determined, the Prāsaṅgikas also accept an unqualified independent substratum. The Prāsaṅgika, however, does not accept the existence of an independent substratum, when the nature of the ultimate truth is under consideration.[10]

While the master Phyā-pa maintained that an unqualified substratum exists commonly for both the Madhyamaka and the opponent during the critical examination of a given entity, bSod-nams Sen-ge holds that such a substratum exists for the Madhyamaka only before the critical examination is begun.[11] This interpretation of the conventional acceptability of an independent substratum offered by bSod-nams Sen-ge will be expanded upon later in the text.[12]

The question of the reason or argument to be employed by the Madhyamaka was also raised in Tibet. The Svātantrikas contended that if the reason like the subject does not exist for the Madhyamaka the refutation of opposing views would not occur. The objection of the Svātantrikas, however, can be met in large part by applying the considerations which were urged in connection with the dispute about the existence of the logical subject.

bSod-nams Sen-ge's explication of this point brings into clear relief the soteriological character of the arguments employed by the Madhyamakas. He says that when the Madhyamaka having comprehended the nature of the substratum, produces an argument, the reason as well as the substratum do not then exist for the Madhyamaka. The arguments however are not constructed for the benefit of the Madhyamaka himself. The arguments are meant to be efficient for the opponent, for whom the reason adduced by the Madhyamaka does indeed exist. Once the argument has exercised its efficiency with regard to the opponent and he has comprehended the nature of emptiness, the argument will cease to exist for the opponent as well.[13]

Once again, it is interesting to note that the question of the efficacy of the Madhyamaka's arguments, if they are considered unreal or not existent (asat), was also raised by Nāgārjuna's Realist opponent in the *Vigrahavyāvartanī*. Nāgārjuna replies that efficiency is indeed only a property of conditioned phenomena, which are in their own being empty. Hence though the arguments employed by the Madhyamakas are empty or ultimately not existent, they are nonetheless capable of exercising their causal efficiency and achieving their intended objective.

The Master Phyā-pa asked what is it that imparts probative power to an argument? He questioned the contention of the

Prāsaṅgikas that the opponent's acceptance of a logical ground accomplished the refutation of its contradictory correlative. His question probes at the heart of the problem of logic in general. It seeks to avoid a wholly subjective interpretation of the dynamics of argument. Characteristically Phyā-pa's criticism is substantiated through an appeal to common experience.

The objections raised by the Master Phyā-pa however seem to be in large part a result of a misunderstanding of the level on which the Prāsaṅgika dialectic operates. Indeed Phyā-pa apparently thought that the Prāsaṅgika's rejection of the elements of formal logic pervaded the conventional sphere as well. He believed that the standpoint of the Prāsaṅgika's destroyed the credibility and efficacy of empirical logic. However, this is not the case.

The arguments produced by the Prāsaṅgika when his intention is to demonstrate to an opponent the nature of the ultimate truth do not strike at the conventional efficiency and legitimacy of logical relationships, corresponding in some sense to objects presented in experience. The Madhyamaka's contention is not with the pragmatic interpretation of phenomena commonly accepted in the world. His arguments assail dogmatic or theoretical interpretations which are credited by their proponents with ultimate reality. Interpretations of this kind are not only superfluous for the requirements of practical utility, but in fact render phenomenal efficiency unintelligible.

The specific illustrations of the functioning of the argument *ad absurdum* given by Khu-mdo-sde-'bar are interesting in that they indicate clearly the character of the arguments employed by the Prāsaṅgikas. It is immediately apparent that the objects of refutation of both the representative arguments cited by Khu-mdo-sde-'bar are examples of theoretical postulates which have no reference to the world of commonsense. In the first case it is the sole and ultimate existence of consciousness affirmed by one school of the Vijñānavāda which it is the intention of the Prāsaṅgika to refute. In the second case it is the notion of the indivisibility of atoms advocated by the Buddhist Realists. These propositions endorsed by the opponent are opposed by the Prāsaṅgika through drawing the opponent's attention to other conditions or grounds which he is inclined or constrained to accept. All three terms, i.e., fallacious proposition, minor premise and major premise of an argument *ad absurdum* are acceptable to the opponent alone, not to the Madhyamaka. The proposition and reason are endorsed by the opponent while the positive concomitance of the major premise is conventionally established by valid instruments of cognition. It is not incumbent upon the Madhyamaka himself, the Prāsaṅgikas maintain, to endorse any of the parts of the argument. The intention of the Madhyamaka is simply to reject the theoretical interpretations advanced by dogmatic philosophers.

It was seen that the great rMa-bya departed from the interpretation favoured by the majority of Tibetan Prāsaṅgikas according to which there were no valid instruments of cognition acceptable to the Madhyamaka when the nature of the ultimate was to be determined. rMa-bya, it will be recalled, held that the four conventionally accepted valid instruments of cognition, viz., perception, inference, testimony and comparison, were acceptable when the nature of ultimate reality was under consideration. He seems to have even gone so far as to admit the existence of a substratum established by these valid instruments of cognition when the ultimate was examined.[14]

bSod-nams Sen-ge rejects this theory advocated by rMa-bya. He observes that Candrakīrti, far from approving the validity of the conventionally accepted instruments of cognition, offers the significant thirtieth stanza of the *Vigrahavyāvartanī* as evidence that on the occasion of the investigation of the ultimately real a substratum established by the conventionally accepted valid instruments of cognition does not exist for the Madhyamaka. If rMa-bya intended to affirm that the three parts of an argument *ad absurdum* were established by the conventionally accepted valid instruments of cognition for the Madhyamaka, his interpretation is clearly at variance with that offered by Candrakīrti.[15]

Again, bSod-nams Sen-ge adds, if rMa-bya intended to affirm that the three parts of an argument *ad absurdum* are established by the conventionally accepted valid instruments of cognition for the opponent, then even in that case his explanation is in error. Indeed, it is an inconsistency or contradiction not vindicated by the conventionally accepted valid instruments of cognition which is advocated by the opponent, and is revealed by an argument *ad absurdum*.[16]

rMa-bya sought to justify his approval of the conventionally accepted valid instruments of cognition by distinguishing them from what are termed the objective valid instruments of cognition.[17] rMa-bya maintained that it was because it was constituted by the objective valid instruments of cognition that the independent syllogism was objectionable. rMa-bya refused to admit independent syllogism even within the limits of phenomenal reality.

bSod-nams Sen-ge however affirms that independent syllogisms as well as what are termed the objective valid instruments of cognition are conventionally acceptable for the Madhyamaka. When for instance, a Madhyamaka proponent wishes to establish, for the benefit of a Madhyamaka opponent, the existence of fire on a hill and produces the reason—because there is smoke—the elements of the syllogism including the substratum necessarily exist commonly. Hence it is not other than a case of the employment of an independent syllogism, and moreover one which may be considered to be established by the objective valid instruments of cognition.[18]

The objective valid instruments of cognition are so called be cause they are said to correspond to objects (vastu). The schools of Realists for whom objects exist ultimately, similarly admit the ultimate existence of the instruments of cognition corresponding to them. rMa-bya believed this to be the unalterable definition of the objective valid instruments of cognition, and this led him to reject them categorically.

However, while the Realist admits the ultimate reality of the objective valid instruments of cognition, the Madhyamaka may admit only their conventional reality. For the Madhyamaka the object to which the instruments of cognition correspond is itself illusory. Nonetheless the objective valid instruments of cognition are accepted conventionally by the Madhyamaka. This interpretation, endorsed by bSod-nams Sen-ge, was also given by the great Śākya Paṇḍita before him.[19]

A syllogism constituted by the objective valid instruments of cognition may be defined as one in which the probans derives its probative force either from a relationship of identity (svabhāva) or causality (kārya) with the probandum. When the logical relationship in question is of causality, the probans is produced from the probandum, i.e., the probans is the effect of the probandum, e.g., smoke of fire. When the logical relationship is one of identity, the probans and the probandum are essentially identical, their discrimination as two distinct terms of a syllogism being only a consequence of linguistic expression. Such is the case with the concepts of being a product and being impermanent.[20]

References

1. *dBu-ma-spyi-ston*, p. 295.
2. ཞེ་འདོད་
3. བདེན་པར་གྲུབ་པ།
4. *dBu-ma-spyi-ston*, p. 296.
5. *Ibid.*
6. *Ibid.* p. 299.
7. *Ibid.* p. 339.
8. *Mūlamadhyamakakārikā*, IV. 2.
9. *dBu-ma-spyi-ston*, p. 297.
10. *Ibid.*
11. *Ibid.*
12. See chapter XV.
13. *dBu-ma-spyi-ston*, p. 298.
14. *Ibid.* p. 300.
15. *Ibid.* p. 301.
16. *Ibid.*
17. དངོས་པོ་སྟོབས་ཞུགས་ཀྱི་ཚད་མ།
18. *dBu-ma-spyi-ston*, pp. 302-303.
19. *Ibid.* p. 304.
20. *Ibid.* pp. 303-304.

Chapter IX

THE VIGRAHAVYĀVARTANĪ AND THE EXPOSITION OF THE STATUS OF THE VALID INSTRUMENTS OF COGNITION (PRAMĀṆA)

As we have already noted in a preceding chapter, the *Vigrahavyāvartanī*, composed by the Master Nāgārjuna is particularly relevant to a study of the division between the Prāsaṅgika and the Svātantrika schools. The *Vigrahavyāvartanī* represents the fundamental treatise on logic and epistemology of the Madhyamaka system. Inasmuch as it was composed by Nāgārjuna himself, the historical founder of the school, its orthodoxy is unassailable. Though short, comprising only seventy-one stanzas and their autocommentary, the work is regarded even today as of primary importance within the Buddhist scholastic tradition and so clearly deserves careful attention.

The *Vigrahavyāvartanī* tested the orthodoxy of the Svātantrika doctrine on the crucial questions of the acceptability of a proposition and of a substratum of inference. The interpretation of the *Vigrahavyāvartanī* presented difficulties not only to Svātantrika expositors, but to Prāsaṅgika scholars also. Of special importance is the detailed exposition which the work contains of the standpoint of the Madhyamaka with respect to the valid instruments of cognition.

The *Vigrahavyāvartanī* provides an extraordinarily comprehensive picture of a classical encounter between the Realist philosopher who advocates the doctrine of self-existence (svabhāva), and the critical philosopher, i.e., the Madhyamaka who rejects the notion of self-existence. Nāgārjuna devotes the first twenty stanzas of his work together with their prose commentary to an exposition of the objections raised by the Realist against the doctrine of emptiness (śūnyavāda). He presents the reply of the Madhyamaka in the subsequent stanzas and prose commentary. In this, Nāgārjuna has followed the accepted practice of dividing the subject matter of philosophical discussion into pūrvapakṣa and uttarapakṣa.

It is usually believed that the opponent whose objections are presented by Nāgārjuna in the first twenty stanzas of his work, must have been a Naiyāyika. Certainly the opponent does indeed advocate the acceptability of four valid instruments of cognition—perception, inference, testimony and comparison. In addition the doctrine that an object of negation, i.e., negatum must have a real existence is characteristic of the Naiyāyika school. Thus, it may be held that the opponent belonged to the Naiyāvika school, a conclusion which is rendered even more plausible when it is considered that the school is perhaps the foremost example of classical Indian realism.

Notwithstanding the evidence of Naiyāyika tenets in the objections put forward by the opponent. it may be that the views presented represent those of a relatively heterogeneous realism which included Buddhist as well as non-Buddhist elements. Evidence for this may be supplied by the seventh and eighth stanzas and their commentary, in which the opponent objects that the doctrine of emptiness will prejudice the designation of one hundred and nineteen ethically wholesome factors (kuśala-dharma) which are prescribed in Buddhist scriptures such as the *Abhidharmakośa*, and which were traditionally taught by spiritual masters conversant with Buddhist doctrine. One fails to see why this objection could not have come from the Buddhist Realists themselves. Indeed it is evident from reference to other works of Nāgārjuna like the *Mūlamadhyamakakārikā* and *Śūnyatāsaptati*, that the views which Nāgārjuna refutes are more often than not those of the Ābhidharmika. It may be suggested in fact that the *Vigrahavyāvartani* presents a compendium of the current objections which were advanced by naive realism in general against the standpoint of the Madhyamaka.

The natural affinity which exists between the standpoint of the classical logician and that of the Realist inasmuch as they are both pre-eminently concerned with the world of experience may account for the similarity which is felt between at least some of the questions raised by the opponent in the *Vigrahavyāvartani* and those presented by Svātantrika logicians. It seems inevitable that a recourse to the canons of formal logic which derive their efficiency from a conventionally accepted empirical pattern tends to lead to a certain commitment to the logical reality of objects (vastu). In this connection it may be recalled that even the formal Buddhist logic of Diṅnāga and Dharmakīrti is constructed upon a realistic ontology, i.e., that of the Sautrāntrika.

The Svātantrika logicians stressed the importance of the world of common experience. Much of their criticism of the Prāsaṅgikas seems to have been prompted by their concern with the regularity and community of experience which they accused the Prāsaṅgikas of arbitrarily disparaging. The fundamental questions regarding the nature and admissibility of a proposition (pratijñā), for the Madhyamaka and of the subject (dharmin) it contains are met with in the *Vigrahavyāvartanī*, as is also the problem of the valid instruments of cognition. It is evident from the fact that they occur in other texts as well, such as in the *Prasannapadā* of Candrakīrti that these were important questions which were persistently asked by opponents of the Madhyamakas.[1]

More than simply providing an exposition of the Madhyamaka standpoint in the area of epistemology and logic, the *Vigrahavyāvartanī* also offers a defence of the Madhyamaka philosophy. The Madhyamaka maintains that inasmuch as all entities are devoid of self-existence (svabhāva), they are empty (śūnya). It is moreover affirmed that the law of interdependent origination (pratītyasamutpāda), the doctrine of emptiness (śūnyatā) and the middle path (madhyamapratipada) are of one import.

The standpoint of the Madhyamaka is expressed in the prose commentary to the first stanza of the work. "It may be maintained that the self-existence of all entities (bhāvāḥ), is not to be found among their corresponding causes and conditions (hetupratyaya), either collectively or individually. Since in all of these the self-existence of entities is not found, they are empty (śūnya).

"Further, it might be said that in a seed, which is a cause, a sprout does not exist. Nor is the sprout found in the earth, water, fire, air, etc. which are termed conditions. Nor again is it to be found in all the conditions either taken together or separately. The sprout neither exists in the causes and conditions, nor does it exist apart from the causes and conditions. Since at all of these places self-existence is not to be found, the sprout which originates is devoid of self-existence. As the sprout is devoid of self-existence, it is empty (śūnya). Just as the sprout is empty inasmuch as it is devoid of self-existence, so also all entities which are similarly devoid of self-existence are empty."

This exposition of the fundamental standpoint of the Madhyamaka may be compared with that given by Nāgārjuna in the

Śūnyatāsaptati. "Since the own-being of all entities is not in (the individual) causes and conditions, nor in the aggregation of causes and conditions, nor in any entity whatsoever, i.e., not in all (of these), therefore, all entities are empty in their own-being".[2]

These passages express the initial proposition (pratijñā) of the Madhyamaka. It is this very standpoint which is likewise expressed by the proposition contained in the opening stanza of the *Mūlamadhyamakakārikā* which was discussed in Chapter V. Inasmuch as the self-existence of the sprout is not to be found, the sprout is properly speaking unoriginated.

The inseparable relationship which binds the demonstration of non-origination to that of emptiness is again suggested by the succeeding stanza of the *Śūnyatāsaptati* which states, "The existent does not-originate since it is existent; the non-existent does not originate since it is non-existent; the (both) existent and non-existent also does not (originate) since these properties are dissimilar. Since there is no origination, there is no duration and no destruction."[3]

One may compare Nāgārjuna's argument, i.e., the existent does not originate because it is already existent, with that given by Buddhapālita, against the doctrine of a pre-existent effect, (satkāryavāda), i.e., entities which exist in their own substantiality (svātmatā) do not require origination. The argument is an example of an argument *ad absurdum* (prasaṅgavākya) which elicits an undesirable consequence for the opponent upon the basis of his own premises.

The Realist opponent whose objections are presented by Nāgārjuna in the *Vigrahavyāvartanī* first assails the reality of the statement or proposition of the Madhyamaka. The opponent believes he has detected an inherent fallacy in the standpoint expressed by the Madhyamaka. He contends, the Madhyamaka holds that all entities are empty because their self-existence is not found among all the causes and conditions. In that case, he proceeds, your statement also which is included within the class of all entities, is equally vacuous. How then, the opponent asks, can the Madhyamaka hope to achieve anything by means of what is itself unreal and vacuous. Indeed, an unreal fire does not burn, nor does an unreal weapon cut.

Alternatively, if the Madhyamaka should wish to distinguish his statement in some way from the general class of all entities, he is in that case obligated to state the ground of distinction (viśiṣṭa-hetu), which he has not done.

Indeed, the attack made by the Realist is conditioned by an initial misunderstanding which leads him to identify efficiency with ultimate reality. On the contrary, the Madhyamaka holds that efficiency is a property of conditioned phenomena only but inasmuch as conditioned phenomena are devoid of self-existence, they are ultimately unreal. Their causal efficiency is indeed compatible with their emptiness, but not with their supposed ultimate reality.

As for the consequential assertion that a ground of distinction ought to have been stated, it does not arise. Certainly the Madhyamaka does not in any way distinguish his statement from the class of all entities. He admits that his statement which exists dependent upon a combination of corresponding causes and conditions is empty just as are all entities.

The Realist opponent puts forward a supposed analogy which he thinks illustrates the position of the Madhyamaka. He suggests, it might so happen that to prevent the production of a sound in the future, one pronounces the words, "don't make sound." In that case oneself makes a sound, the object of which is to prevent the emergence of sound in the future. However, even in this case, the opponent concludes, the emergence of a real sound in the future is prevented by another real sound. The contention of the Madhyamaka, i.e., that through an unreal statement the intended object is achieved, is unjustified.

This analogy put forward by the opponent also betrays the same fundamental confusion of the concepts of reality with efficiency. When the Madhyamaka makes the statement that all entities are empty, it is to demonstrate that the self-existence of all entities is not among the corresponding causes and conditions upon which they are relationally dependent. The statement of the Madhyamaka is in this respect not in any way different from other entities. Nevertheless, just as in the world objects like a chariot, cloth and the like perform their respective functions though they are empty so also through the statement of the Madhyamaka which is equally empty the refutation of the reality of all entities is justified.

In the twenty-third stanza of the *Vigrahavyāvartanī* Nāgārjuna presents an illustration of his own. It might so happen that a man created by the art of a sorcerer or the like deters another illusory man similarly created by magical art from pursuing a certain course of conduct. Though in such a case, the agent of the prevention and the object of it are equally unreal, the prevention is nonetheless successful. This the Madhyamaka holds to be an accurate illustration of the operation of his statement. Since in this way the Madhyamaka does not in the least distinguish his statement from other entities, he is not obligated to state any ground of distinction.

The analogy proposed by the opponent, i.e. with the statement, "don't make sound", is not at all admitted by the Madhyamaka. In the example advanced by the opponent, the emergence of a real sound in the future is prevented by another real sound. If the Madhyamaka through his unreal statement intended to controvert, i.e., negate the unreality of all entities, the example would be relevant; however, the unreal argument of the Madhyamaka affirms the unreality of all entities, and hence no inconsistency is entailed.

In the twenty-seventh stanza and its prose commentary Nāgārjuna sets forth another illustration of the way in which the arguments of the Madhyamaka function. It might so happen that an artificial man (nirmita puruṣa) becomes subject to the affliction of lust with respect to an equally artificial woman. In order to free him from the bonds of his affliction, a man artificially created by the Tathāgata or a Śrāvaka might instruct him in the artificiality and unreality of his attachment. In this analogy the artificially created woman represents all entities, the artificial man who becomes subject to lust with respect to her, living beings subject to ignorance or delusion. The discourse delivered by the artificial man created by the Buddha or one of his disciples represents the argument employed by the Madhyamaka to controvert the belief in the real existence of entities.

The methodology of the Madhyamaka argument is further illustrated by Nāgārjuna. "It is not as though the Madhyamaka makes any statement like that rejecting the reality of all entities, without having taken note of conventional reality (saṁvyavahāra). Without having apprehended conventionality the instruction of living beings with respect to the religious truth (dharma) would be impossible."[4] At this point Nāgārjuna interjects the tenth stanza taken from the Chapter XXIV of the

Mūlamadhyamakakārikā, "Without recourse to the conventionally real, ultimate truth is not taught. Without obtaining the ultimate truth, Nirvāṇa is not attained." The successful interpretation of this stanza supplies the key to an understanding of the initial acceptance by the Madhyamaka of a conventionally existent substratum, as will be seen later.[5]

The twenty-ninth stanza of the *Vigrahavyāvartanī* has already been referred to several times in foregoing chapters. It is in this stanza and its prose commentary that Nāgārjuna expresses the Madhyamaka's refusal to accept a proposition (pratijñā).

The prose commentary to the twenty-ninth stanza reads as follows, "Inasmuch as all entities are empty, totally quiescent and devoid of any nature of their own, how indeed could there be any proposition."

Since for the Madhyamaka no real proposition exists, he is not guilty of any inconsistency. He makes the statement, all entities, being devoid of self-existence are empty, having had recourse to conventional usage, for the purpose of emancipating unenlightened living beings subject to deeds (karma) and afflictions (kleśa).

In the fifth and sixth stanzas of the *Vigrahavyāvartanī* the Realist opponent presents the objection which leads to the discussion of the status of the valid instruments of cognition. The opponent contends that the Madhyamaka cannot have recourse to any of the valid instruments of cognition (pramāṇa) to support his initial rejection of the reality of entities. Since the four valid instruments of cognition—perception, inference, testimony and comparison—are included within the class of all entities, they cannot serve to establish the proposition advanced by the Madhyamaka. Moreover, the percipient, i.e., the subject of perception also will be unreal so there will be no one who perceives objects. Hence there will not be any proposition at all regarding them. The same will be true in the case of inference and the other valid instruments of cognition. Again as there is no subject who perceives and the like there will be no cognition whatsoever. Therefore, reality or unreality cannot be asserted of objects which are not cognised. So the initial proposition is impossible. This, the opponent contends, is a case of blatant self-contradiction on the part of the Madhyamaka, because it places him in the position of refuting the reality of entities which he does not at all cognise.

In the thirtieth stanza of the *Vigrahavyāvartanī* the discussion of the status of the valid instruments of cognition is initiated by Nāgārjuna. Again there has already been occasion to refer to the thirtieth stanza. The stanza was also cited by Candrakīrti in the *Prasannapadā* in support of his contention that an unqualified substratum like the subjective poles of consciousness is inadmissible when the ultimate truth is to be determined.

Nāgārjuna states, "If I apprehended anything through perception and the like, and were to approve it or reject it then only could an inconsistency arise with respect to my standpoint. However, as I apprehend none of these I cannot be assailed on such a basis."[6] If the Madhyamaka were to apprehend any object through the four valid instruments of cognition—perception, inference, testimony and comparison or through any one of them and were on that ground to affirm or reject it, the attack of the opponent would be justified. However, the Madhyamaka neither apprehends any object through the valid instruments of cognition, nor does he affirm or reject it. Hence the objection raised by the realist, i.e., that having cognised entities through the valid instruments of cognition the Madhyamaka rejects entities, is without foundation. For the Madhyamaka neither the valid instruments of cognition, nor their respective objects exist in truth.

Nāgārjuna proceeds to pose a counter-question to the opponent. He asks, "If it is held that all entities must necessarily be established through the valid instruments of cognition, then it may be inquired from whence the valid instruments of cognition themselves are established or proved. It is the position of the Realist that the existence of objects is established through the valid instruments of cognition, but how are the valid instruments of cognition themselves to be established? If the valid instruments of cognition are thought to be established without recourse to any proof, then the initial standpoint expressed by the opponent, i.e., that all entities are established to exist through the valid instruments of cognition is contradicted."[7]

Nāgārjuna develops his criticism of the valid instruments of cognition further. "It might be held that the valid instruments of cognition are established through other valid instruments of cognition. However, this will result in an infinite regress (anavasthā), i.e., an infinite series of relationally dependent members none of which is established. If the opponent contends that through the valid instruments of cognition objects are established and that through other valid instruments of cognition altogether, those very valid instruments of cognition are justified, an infinite regress will result. It may be asked, what fault is entailed by an infinite regress ? It is replied, a fault occurs because in that case there is proof neither of the first member of the series, nor of the intermediate, nor of the last. Of the first member of the series, there is no proof, because those very valid instruments of cognition are supposed to be proved through other valid instruments of cognition. Again it is claimed that there is proof of those other valid instruments of cognition through some other valid instruments of cognition altogether. Since the first of this series is not in the least admitted, how can the notion of an intermediate or a last be entertained. It follows that the position expressed, i.e., that the valid instruments of cognition are established through other valid instruments of cognition, is not justified."[8]

Alternatively, it might be held that the valid instruments of cognition are established without resort to any proof. In that case the Realist's own standpoint which he expressed earlier, i.e., that objects are established through the valid instruments of cognition, is negated. In other words, a discrepancy occurs in the position expressed by the opponent, inasmuch as some objects are established through the valid instruments of cognition, while some others are not so established, i.e., require no proof. A ground of distinction ought to have been stated by the opponent, which might justify why special treatment should be accorded to the valid instruments of cognition. However, no such ground of distinction has been indicated by the opponent. How is it then that with regard to some entities there is proof through a reason, while other entities are established without recourse to a reason ?[9]

The foregoing paragraphs contain classic examples of the application of arguments *ad absurdum* to the position advocated by the Realist, by Nāgārjuna. Arguments resembling these were employed by Prāsaṅgika scholars like Buddhapālita and Candrakīrti. Such arguments became accepted components of the Madhyamaka canon of argumentation and will be discussed formally and in greater detail later.[10]

The Realist might attempt the following vindication of his

position. He might maintain that it is the valid instruments of cognition themselves which establish, i.e., prove themselves and also establish the existence of other entities. He puts forward the following supposed analogy. Just as fire illuminates itself as well as other objects, so also the valid instruments of cognition prove themselves as well as other entities. This analogical defence offered by the Realist, however, is altogether ineffective.

Nāgārjuna states, "It is not the case that fire illumines itself. Hence, the analogy is altogether irrelevant. It cannot be maintained that fire is illumined by fire, in a manner comparable to that in which a jar which exists uncognised in darkness, is illumined by fire and is then cognised. If fire could be said to pre-exist unillumined in darkness, then only could it be said that fire illumines itself. However, this is not acceptable."[11]

Nāgārjuna presents two analogies, comparable to that advanced by the opponent, neither of which is admissible. His arguments are designed to elicit the unacceptability of the analogy presented by the Realist. "If it were the case that fire illumines itself as well as other objects, then fire ought also to consume itself as well as fuel. Again darkness ought to obscure itself as well as other objects. However, nothing of the kind is seen."[12]

Nāgārjuna's criticism of the theory of self-validating valid instruments of cognition as defended by the spurious analogy of fire, i.e., the supposed self-illumination of fire, supply the pattern for the arguments employed by later Prāsaṅgika scholars like Śāntideva. The latter criticised the theory of the self-awareness of consciousness, advocated by the Vijñānavāda through similar arguments.[13]

Nāgārjuna presses his argument further. "It is not the case that in the being or locus of fire, darkness can be said to exist, since as it is well known, light is the very opposite of darkness. Since in this way in fire darkness does not exist, nor does darkness exist wherever fire is present, how can it be maintained that fire destroys darkness."[14]

At this point the Realist may attempt the following defence. He may fall in with the contention of the Madhyamaka that in fire or in the locus of fire darkness does not exist. However, he may hold that at the moment when fire is kindled, fire illumines itself as well as other objects.

Nāgārjuna argues that this view expressed by the Realist is

unacceptable. "It is not the case that at the moment when fire is kindled, fire obtains to, i.e., reaches darkness. Since fire does not obtain darkness how can it destroy it. In such a situation darkness would persist undestroyed and so light could not exist."[15]

Moreover, Nāgārjuna urgues, "If it were the case that fire destroys darkness without obtaining it, then a fire existing at one place in the world, could destroy the darkness in the whole world; however nothing of the kind is seen. Hence the notion that fire destroys darkness without obtaining it is unjustified."[16]

Nāgārjuna concludes his attack on the notion that the valid instruments of cognition could be proved by themselves. "If, indeed, it were true that the valid instruments of cognition are proved by themselves, then in that case they would have no necessary reference to the objects of cognition (prameya). It is not as though something which is established by itself requires anything else to support it. If, indeed, a support is necessary, then the valid instruments of cognition cannot be said to be proved by themselves.

"If the valid instruments of cognition were established without reference to their respective objects of cognition, they could not then be said to correspond necessarily to any object. In that case the very definition of cognition would be contradicted. Moreover, such a theory would entail the absurdity that cognitions, *qua* pramāṇas exist antecedent to the objects of cognition. If it is held that cognitions do indeed exist antecedent to the objects of cognitions, it cannot then also be held that cognitions occur with reference to and dependent upon corresponding objects, because what exists independently cannot be said to require any other entity for its existence."[17]

Nāgārjuna criticises the alternative position, i.e., that the valid instruments of cognition are proved by the objects of cognition. "It is not the case that dependent upon the objects of cognition the valid instruments of cognition are established, because in that case the object which is to be established, i.e., the object of cognition (prameya), would have to be supposed to prove the instrument of cognition, through which the object itself was initially supposed to be proved. If the objects of cognition could be supposed to exist independent of the valid instruments of cognition so that they might be able to furnish proof of the latter, ther of what use are the valid instruments of cognition themselves? If the objects of cognition were already known without recourse to the services of the instruments of cognition, then the instruments of cognition would be altogether unnecessary.

"Moreover, if it should be maintained that the objects of cognition furnish proof of the instruments of cognition, then in that case, the respective functions of the two, object and instrument, will be reversed. In such a situation the objects of cognition would function as instruments of cognition inasmuch as through them the instruments of cognition are established. Again, the instruments of cognition would assume the character of objects of cognition inasmuch as they are proved through recourse to the objects of cognition.

"If the objects of cognition are supposed to be proved through the instruments of cognition and in turn the objects of cognition are supposed to furnish proof of the existence of the instruments of cognition, then in that case the objects of cognition would be required to prove the existence of the instruments of cognition. However, inasmuch as the existence of the objects of cognition is said to be established through the instruments of cognition, the latter, i.e., the objects of cognition will not be capable of establishing the existence of the instruments of cognition since the objects themselves in that case remain unproved."[18]

Nāgārjuna sums up his criticism of the valid instruments of cognition as follows "If through the objects of cognition, the instruments of cognition are proved, while in their turn the instruments of cognition are supposed to furnish proof of the existence of the objects of cognition, then inasmuch as the instruments of cognition are unproved, the objects of cognition remain unproved. Therefore, the objects of cognition themselves unproved, cannot be thought to establish the existence of the instruments of cognition. If the instruments of cognition and the objects of cognition are mutually dependent upon each other, then neither of them can be said to exist independently, i.e., to have a real or ultimate existence.

"Thus it might be said that by the father the son is produced, and again that by that very son the father is produced. In such a situation let it be said who is the father and who the son. Similarly, the Realist holds that the objects of cognition exist through the instruments of cognition. Again, he holds that the existence of the instruments of cognition is established through their objects. In such a case it may be asked, which is to be proved by which?

"In the analogy cited above, who is the father and who the son. Inasmuch as each is endowed with the characteristic mark of producing the other, they both share the characteristic of fatherhood. However, inasmuch as each is produced by the other, they both partake of the nature of being the son.

"Similarly, among the entities which the realist accepts as objects and instruments of cognition, which are the objects and which the instruments?"

Both sets of entities possess the character of instruments of cognition inasmuch as they are supposed to establish the other. Again both are objects inasmuch as they are supposed to be proved by the other. Thus it may be asked, which are the instruments and which the objects of cognition?

"It is not the case that of a given perception proof is possible through that very perception. Nor again is proof possible of a given inference, testimony or comparison through those very instruments of cognition respectively. Again, it is not possible to establish the existence of the four valid instruments of cognition taken collectively. It is not possible to establish inference through perception, testimony or comparison. Nor again is it possible to establish comparison through an appeal to perception, inference or testimony etc. Nor can it be supposed that the valid instruments of cognition are established through other valid instruments of cognition altogether. Hence, the instruments of cognition are unestablished."[19]

Again, it was demonstrated by Nāgārjuna, that there can be no proof of the instruments of cognition through recourse to the objects of cognition. Hence the position advocated by the Realist, according to which the existence of entities which are objects of cognition is established through valid instruments of cognition which are also real is unacceptable.

Thus Nāgārjuna concludes his sustained criticism of the notion of the ultimate reality of the valid instruments of cognition. According to the Madhyamaka neither the instruments of cognition nor their objects are real. Thus the Madhyamaka assails the idea that the existence of entities is established through valid instruments of cognition. For him the instruments and objects of cognition inasmuch as they are relative and mutually dependent upon each other are empty.

In the fifty-second and succeeding stanzas and commentary, Nāgārjuna devotes himself to the refutation of the objection raised by the Realist in the seventh and eighth stanzas, i.e., that the doctrine of śūnyatā will undermine the foundations of spiritual discipline. The refutation of this objection, already alluded to, although not without philosophical interest, lies outside the limits of the study, and so will not be dealt with. The same may be said of the objection based upon the assumption of the reality of nomenclature presented by the opponent in the ninth stanza and that presented in the tenth stanza. Nāgārjuna rejects these objections in the succeeding stanzas and commentary concluding with the sixtieth stanza.

The objection raised by the Realist in the eleventh and twelfth stanzas however is to a certain degree relevant to this study. Nāgārjuna replies to the objection as follows. The opponent had objected that a meaningful negation must necessarily have reference to a real object of negation, i.e., negatum. Nāgārjuna replies that the contention of the opponent betrays an inconsistency, because given the opponent's acceptance of the theory that negation is only possible with reference to a real negatum, his negation of emptiness (śūnyatā) really implies his acceptance of its reality.

Certainly, the Madhyamaka does not admit the reality of objects of negation. Nāgārjuna expresses the standpoint of the Madhyamaka in regard to the negatum. He states, "There exists for me no object to be negated (pratiṣedhya), hence, I do not undertake to negate anything. When I am accused of nagating anything, I am falsely accused."[20] Since for the Madhyamaka all entities, inasmuch as they are devoid of self-existence are empty, there can be no occasion for the notion of a real negatum to arise. In the absence of any negatum, it follows, there can be no negation. The sixty-third stanza just cited stands in a somewhat complementary relationship with the twenty-ninth stanza in which Nāgārjuna rejects the existence of a proposition. The assertion of the emptiness of all entities and the negation or refutation of the self-existence of all entities are in substance identical. The difference is only one of verbal formulation.

Again, Nāgārjuna clarifies the *modus operandi* of the Madhyamaka's statements. "It is not the case that the negation of the real existence of all entities functions as the causal condition of their unreality. All entities are empty inasmuch as self-existence is not to be found in any of them. The statements of the Madhyamaka simply serve to communicate the actual absence of reality in all entities."

Nāgārjuna clarifies the Madhyamaka's position by presenting an illustration. "It might so happen that when somebody, e.g., Devadatta, is in fact not at home, somebody asserts, Devadatta is at home. A knowledgeable person might correct him by the statement, no, he is not at home. The statement is not the causal condition of Devadatta's absence from home. It merely serves to communicate his actual absence." The same may be said of the statements of the Madhyamaka which simply communicate the absence of reality in entities.[21]

Again in the seventeenth and eighteenth stanzas, the Realist presents the objection that inasmuch as the logical ground (hetu) presented by the Madhyamaka is unreal, his statement amounts to an unproved assertion. In addition, the opponent contends in the twentieth stanza that negation, considered as the causal condition of the non-existence of the object negated, is impossible whether it be antecedent, synchronous or subsequent to the negatum.

The objection raised by the opponent in nineteenth stanza, about the unreality of the logical ground does not affect the position of the Madhyamaka because it is already admitted by him.

The objection that negation, taken as a causal condition, is impossible is inconsequential. It is clear from the evidence of the sixty-third and sixty-fourth stanzas and their commentary that negation, interpreted as a causal condition, is admitted to be impossible, by the Madhyamaka. Indeed, Nāgārjuna employs substantially the same criticism of the causal relation in general.[22]

In the penultimate and final stanzas of the *Vigrahavyāvartanī* and their commentary, Nāgārjuna expresses the central idea of the Madhyamaka doctrine. The fundamental principle of Buddhist religion and philosophy is the law of interdependent origination or causation (pratītyasamutpāda). According to this law, entities originate dependent upon a corresponding combination of causes and conditions. The doctrine of inter-dependent origination is the fundamental principle of all relative existence. Moreover, the doctrine vindicates the law of ethical responsibility, i.e., the regular succession of actions and their effects.

Again, the relative existence of all entities which originate dependent upon corresponding causes and conditions is identical with śūnyatā, inasmuch as all entities are devoid of self-existence. Thus the doctrine of śūnyatā expresses the ultimate unreality of all relatively existing conditioned entities.

The middle path (madhyamapratipada) taught by the Buddha, the Madhyamaka maintains, means the avoidance of the two alternatives of eternalism (śāśvatavāda) and nihilism (ucchedavāda). The doctrine which avoids the alternatives is believed by Nāgārjuna to be the quintessence of the teaching of the Buddha. Understanding the relative existence of all entities which originate dependently, the Madhyamaka successfully avoids the alternative of non-existence or nihilism. Again, understanding that all conditioned entities, though they appear in common experience, are empty inasmuch as self-existence is not to be found in them, he successfully avoids the alternative of existence or eternalism.

Nāgārjuna reaffirms the identity of these three principal tenets of Buddhist philosophy in the final stanza of the *Vigrahavyāvartanī*. He states, "I offer my obeisance to the Enlightened One who is without an equal, who has declared that interdependent origination, emptiness and the middle path are identical in import."[23]

References

1. Stcherbatsky, Th., *Conception of Buddhist Nirvāṇa*, pp. 203-211.
2. *Śūnyatāsaptati*, Stanza 3.
3. *Ibid.* Stanza 4.
4. *Vigrahavyāvartanī*, Stanza 28 and commentary.
5. See Chapter XV.
6. *Vigrahavyāvartanī*, Stanza 30.
7. *Ibid.* Stanza 31 and commentary.
8. *Ibid.* Stanza 32 and commentary.
9. *Ibid.* Stanza 33 and commentary.
10. See Chapter XVI.
11. *Vigrahavyāvartanī*, Stanza 34 and commentary.
12. *Ibid.* Stanzas 35, 36 and commentary.

13. *Bodhicaryāvatāra*, Chapter IX. Verses 17 and 18.
14. *Vigrahavyāvartanī*, Stanza 37 and commentary.
15. *Ibid.* Stanzas 37, 38 and commentary.
16. *Ibid.* Stanza 39 and commentary.
17. *Ibid.* Stanzas 40-42 and commentary.
18. *Ibid.* Stanzas 43-47 and commentary.
19. *Ibid.* Stanzas 48-51 and commentary.
20. *Ibid.* Stanza 63.
21. *Ibid.* Stanzas 61-64 and commentary.
22. *Śūnyatāsaptati*, Stanza 6 and commentary.
23. *Vigrahavyāvartanī*, Stanza 71.

Chapter X

THE REFUTATION OF ORIGINATION

It may be said that the definitive characteristic of the Madhyamaka philosophy is its rejection of the ultimate existence of all elements (dharmas). As has been indicated, the standpoint of the Madhyamaka is arrived at through a sustained and systematic examination of the existential status of all elements. By means of a dialectic analysis of the notions of self-existence (svabhāva) and origination (utpatti), the Madhyamaka seeks to establish the ultimate emptiness of all entities.

While the refutation of origination and the refutation of self-existence are of co-equal status, i.e., are identical in import, it is a matter of documented fact that the Madhyamaka often chose to stress the refutation of origination. The central position which the refutation of this notion occupies in the Madhyamaka philosophy is evident from the fact that Nāgārjuna takes up the question in the first of the twentyseven chapters, which constitute the *Mūlamadhyamakakārikā*, entitled the examination of conditions (pratyaya-parīkṣā). He reserves the critique of the notion of self-existence for the fifteenth chapter, entitled the examination of self-existence (svabhāva-parīkṣā). It must be said that the importance of the first chapter of the *Mūlamadhyamakakārikā* has also not escaped the notice of respected scholars like Theodor Stcherbatsky.

As it was indicated in a previous chapter, the opening stanza of the *Mūlamadhyamakakārikā* expresses the fundamental contention of the Madhyamaka. According to it, the origination of all entities is ultimately not possible, either by themselves, from others, by themselves and from others or without causes. It was pointed out that this stanza presents the initial proposition, which the Madhyamaka intends to support through arguments.

In addition, it was also suggested that a correct appraisal of the nature of the division between the Prāsaṅgika and Svātantrika schools could be achieved through a consideration of the arguments advanced by Madhyamaka scholars against the notion of origination. Thus, it is proposed to consider the arguments against the notion of origination presented by Nāgārjuna, Buddhapālita, Bhāvaviveka and Candrakīrti as well as the internal polemics which were employed against each other by the exponents of the respective schools.

It is important to remember that the alternatives, isolated by the structure of the dialectic analysis, are not solely determined by the context of doctrinal disputation. While they are no doubt capable of being co-related with historical schools they may also be derived analytically, as was shown in Chapter V. This is because the alternatives represent categories of thought, which are *a priori* and reflect the structure of the faculty of reason.

Nāgārjuna undertakes to analyse the notion of origination in works like the *Mūlamadhyamakakārikā*, the *Śūnyatāsaptati*, the *Yuktiṣaṣṭikā* and others. These stanzas constitute the scriptural foundation upon which the exegetical works of subsequent Madhyamaka scholars were constructed. They likewise indicate the structure of the analysis to be applied and the character of the arguments to be employed in the refutation of the alternatives isolated. Hence, it is at this point necessary to consider Nāgārjuna's criticism of the notion of origination as it is found in the *Mūlamadhyamakakārikā* and the *Śūnyatāsaptati*.

It will be found that Nāgārjuna undertakes to refute the notion of origination through an examination of the idea of causality, i.e., the relation between cause and effect. The arguments are intended to elicit the ultimate unintelligibility of cause and effect, considered either as co-present or disassociated. Cause and effect are analysed through the categories of existence and non-existence, conjunction and disjunction, as well as through the temporal categories of antecedence, subsequence and simultaneity.

The importance of the first stanza of the chapter on conditions, inasmuch as it expresses the standpoint of the Madhyamaka, has already been noted in several places. The stanza, however, is a simple statement of the proposition advanced by the Madhyamaka and as such it contains no argument or reason (hetu). In other stanzas Nāgārjuna suggests a variety of arguments in support of his initial position.

Thus he writes, "Conditions (pratyaya) do not in fact pertain to either existence or non-existence. If to existence what purpose do they serve, if to non-existence, whose purpose do they serve."[1] The arguments suggested in the stanza may be elucidated as follows. Conditions cannot truly be said to pertain to an existent effect, since in that case, inasmuch as the effect already exists, the conditions are superfluous. On the other hand in the absence of an effect conditions are not obtained.

The application of the principle of dialectic analysis in terms of hypothetical co-presence and disassociation is evident. Thus, if conditions pertain to an existent effect, the cause and effect will be co-present. However, this entails the mutual dissolution of the conceptual integrity of the related elements, i.e., cause and effect. Alternatively, if conditions pertain to a non-existent effect, then in that case, the cause will be altogether disassociated from the effect. This situation is no more satisfactory than the former, since apart from an effect, conditions are unintelligible and vacuous.

Again, Nāgārjuna indicates in the subsequent stanza that, inasmuch as an effect does not originate from existence, non-existence or both existence and non-existence, the notion of an efficient cause must be discarded.[2] The following clarification of the stanza may be supplied. The effect does not originate from a condition of existence, since in that case its origination would be unnecessary. Similarly, it cannot be maintained that an effect originates from a condition of non-existence, since then a single entity would have to be supposed to be non-existent at one time and existent at another; a fact, which entails the distraction of the notion of an integrated entity.

The argument pre-supposes an acceptance of the logical law, according to which contradictory predicates cannot be asserted of a single entity.[3] The third alternative mentioned in the stanza is untenable as a consequence of the same law.[4]

The tenth stanza of the chapter clearly indicates the close interconnection which exists between the notions of origination and self-existence. It also expresses the Madhyamaka standpoint, which proposes the ultimate rejection of the conventional causal formula. Nāgārjuna writes, "As entities without self-existence (svabhāva) do not exist in truth, it is not justified (upapadyate) that from the existence of that, this comes about."[5] This stanza leaves no room for doubt that, for the Madhyamaka, the absence of self-existence in entities, amounts to the negation of their origination.

The subsequent stanzas again contain instances of the analysis of cause and effect in terms of hypothetical co-presence and dis-association. While the notion of an effect is obtained in relation to that of a cause, the former is unintelligible, either co-present with the cause or disassociated from it. Hence, it does not exist ultimately. The same may be said of the cause which only exists relative to the effect. Thus, the vacuity of entities, which exist relative to each other, is revealed through the foregoing analysis.

Nāgārjuna also undertakes to criticise the notion of origination in the seventh chapter entitled, the examination of the conditioned (Saṁskṛta-parīkṣā). Nāgārjuna explains that the notion of origination is not justified whether it be relative to existence or to non-existence. Again, origination cannot be relative to both existence and non-existence, for as was shown above two mutually contradictory predicates cannot be asserted of an identical entity.[6]

The twentieth chapter of the *Mūlamadhyamakakārikā*, entitled the examination of assembly (samagra-parīkṣā) contains a number of stanzas which analyse the cause and effect, by means of the categories of conjunction and disjunction. The fact that both the Tibetan and Chinese translations render the title of the chapter as the examination of cause and effect is an indication that the chapter is concerned with the analysis of the causal relationship.

In the fifteenth stanza of the chapter Nāgārjuna writes, "Without existing in conjunction with the cause, how does the effect arise? Existing in conjunction with the cause, how does the effect arise?"[7] The arguments suggested in the stanza may be interpreted as follows. The conjunction of a cause with an effect entails the co-presence of the cause and the effect, while their disjunction equals their total disassociation. Thus, if the effect does not exist in conjunction with the cause, its origination from the latter is inconceivable, since it is altogether disassociated from it. Alternatively, if the effect exists in conjunction with the cause, it follows that the cause and the effect are co-present. In that case, the origination of the effect is likewise impossible for a variety of reasons. Here too, the analysis of two interdependently related entities through the dialectical principle of co-presence and disassociation is exhibited.

Nāgārjuna presents essentially the same analysis, substituting the categories of empty (śūnya) and non-empty (aśūnya), for those of conjunction and disjunction in the subsequent stanza. He states, "If the cause is empty of the effect, how does the effect arise ? If the cause is not empty of the effect, how does the effect arise ?"[8] Here also, if the cause is empty of the effect, it follows that the cause and the effect are totally disassociated. In that case, the origination of the effect from the cause is impossible. Alternatively, if the cause is not empty of the effect, i.e., the effect exists in some way in the cause, then the cause and effect will be co-present. This again precludes the origination of the effect because of the consequences which have been suggested.

In the nineteenth stanza of the chapter, Nāgārjuna analyses the notions of cause and effect through the categories of identity and difference. Like the categories of existence and non-existence, the categories of identity and difference presuppose the analytical principle of co-presence and disassociation. Thus, according to Nāgārjuna, the cause and effect cannot be thought to be either identical or different. He develops his criticism in the twentieth stanza. "If the cause and effect are identical, then the producer and the produced will also be identical. However, if the cause and effect are different, then the cause will be equal to a non-cause." The stanza presents two arguments *ad absurdum*, which elicit undesirable logical consequences. On the first alternative, if the cause and effect are indeed identical, such a notion entails the identity of other similarly related entities, like the producer and the produced. However, this will result in the dissolution of the conceptual integrity of the entities involved. On the second alternative, if the cause and effect are believed to be altogether different, i.e., disassociated, this also leads to undesirable consequences. In that case, the supposed cause would be as good as a non-cause, since it would be unrelated to the effect.

Nāgārjuna reiterates the position of the Madhyamaka in a stanza which is reminiscent of the opening stanza of the *Mūlamadhyamakakārikā*. He writes, "Existence arises neither from itself nor from another; it does not arise from both; how then does it arise ?"[9] The stanza summarises the conclusion obtained through the dialectical analysis of the notion of origination. Inasmuch as origination, in any of the ways suggested, is impossible when analysed, the ultimate origination of entities is refuted. Hence, the phenomenal appearance of origination is not at all vindicated when subjected to rigorous critical examination.

Nāgārjuna also rejects the notion of origination in the *Mūlamadhyamakakārikā* by means of similes. Thus, he describes the notion of origination and the consequential notions of duration and destruction in the following way. "Like illusion, a dream and a fairy city, thus origination, duration, and destruction have been described."[10] This stanza exhibits an analogical argument, employed by Nāgārjuna in consonance with the fourth conventionally accepted valid instrument of cognition, i.e., that of comparison (upamāna).

The analysis of the notion of origination found in the *Śūnyatāsaptati* of Nāgārjuna is in many ways similar to that presented in the *Mūlamadhyamakakārikā*. For instance, in the fourth stanza of the work Nāgārjuna states, "Existent does not originate since it is existent. Non-existent does not originate since it is non-existent. The (both) existent and non-existent also does not (originate) since these properties are dissimilar."[11] Here also, as in the *Mūlamadhyamakakārikā*, the notion of origination is examined through the dialectic categories of existence and non-existence. Origination cannot be believed to be either of the existent or of the non-existent. The former alternative entails the futility of origination, while as a consequence of the latter origination is altogether unintelligible. Again, the third alternative in which the two preceding alternatives are conjunctively affirmed is explicitly denied for the reason stated above.

In the subsequent stanza, Nāgārjuna substitutes the categories of origination and non-origination for those of existence and non-existence. The structure of the analysis contained in the stanza is identical with that found in the preceding one. It differs from the former, however, in that like the opening stanza in the *Mūlamadhyamakakārikā* it contains no arguments in support of the position it affirms. Nonetheless, the stanza indicates the structure of the dialectic analysis to be adopted and also states the proposition of the Madhyamaka.

Nāgārjuna writes, "The originated is not the (entity) which is to be originated; the not-originated is also not the (entity) which is to be originated; the (entity) which is in the process of origination is also not the (entity) which is to be originated, since it would (then) be originated and not originated."[12] In this stanza the alternatives presented constitute a variation within the same analytical pattern, which obtained in the case of the categories of existence and non-existence. The fourth alternative advanced in the stanza is adoptable to the arguments employed on the occasion of the refutation of the third alternative, inasmuch as the so-called process of origination may be reduced to the simultaneously originated and unoriginated.

Nāgārjuna also analyses the existential status of a cause in the *Śūnyatāsaptati* and rejects the notion of origination inasmuch as a cause is not admitted. The sixth stanza of the work contains the following statement. "If the effect is existent, the cause which possesses the effect is not a cause; if non-existent, the cause will be equal to a non-cause; if neither existent nor non-existent, it is contradictory; nor again is a cause justified in the three times."[13] Here again, the analysis follows the familiar practice of examining mutually related entities, through the dialectic principle of co-presence and disassociation. As is evident, the stanza very closely resembles some of those met within the *Mūlamadhyamaka-kārikā.*

Nāgārjuna then proceeds to analyse the notion of a cause in terms of the three temporal relations of antecedence, subsequence and simultaneity as follows. "First, if it is supposed that the cause is prior (to the effect) of what is it the cause? Yet, if it is supposed that (the cause is) subsequent (to the effect) then what need is there for a cause as the effect is already complete? Yet (again) if it is supposed that the cause and effect are simultaneous, then among the cause and effect which originate simultaneously, which is the cause of which ? Which is the effect of which ? Thus in all three times, a cause is not justified."[14] The notion of a cause which is subsequent in time to an effect, must be interpreted, as having reference to the fact that the conceptual judgement, which determines an entity as a cause, occurs only after the perception of the effect. Thus, the judgement which determines the seed to be the cause of the sprout, is possible only subsequent to the perception of the effect, i.e., the sprout. Again, though the analysis functions through the three temporal categories, it nonetheless depends upon the dialectic principle of co-presence and disassociation. The first alternative presented represents a variety of disassociation, since if the cause is antecedent in time to the effect, it follows that the effect does not exist co-present with the cause. The second and third alternatives, on the other hand, present a hypothetical situation in which cause and effect exist together. Such a state of affairs is, however, inadmissible, since in that case, origination would be superfluous or it would be impossible to discriminate which of two entities is the cause and which the effect. In other words, in the latter case the integrity of the relative notions of cause and effect would be destroyed.

The dialectic principle of analysis in terms of co-presence and disassociation, which is applicable to all related phenomena, is clearly revealed in the tenth stanza of the eighteenth chapter of the *Mūlamadhyamakakārikā*. Nāgārjuna writes, "Whatever is dependent, i.e., relative is neither identical with nor different from, the related object. Hence, it is neither eternal nor annihilated." The stanza indicates the inexpressible nature of all relative entities, which are not intelligible either in terms of co-presence or disassociation. Indeed, as Nāgārjuna writes in the *Śūnyatāsaptati*, "Neither that which originates dependently nor that upon which it depends are existent."[15] The inexpressibility and ultimate non-existence of all phenomena results in the negation of the two alternatives of eternity (śāśvata) and annihilation (uccheda), which is in fact the middle way (madhyamapratipada) advocated by the Madhyamaka.

The cause and effect are entities, which exist dependent upon and relative to each other. Hence, they are unintelligible either in terms of co-presence or disassociation. Thus, if it is examined ultimately the causal relationship cannot be expressed through the categories of thought, nor is it justified. Nonetheless, the conventional reality of causal origination, which springs from habitual imputation conditioned by ignorance, remains unaffected. All attempts, however, to describe it in terms of ultimate categories are futile.

This is clearly indicated by the following statement of Nāgārjuna contained in the *Pratityasamutpādahṛdayakārikā*. "The instructions, given by the Master, are the cause of the instructions possessed by the disciple. However, whether those of the disciple are identical with or different from those of the Master, is inexpressible."[16] The same may also be said of the causal relation between a seed and a sprout. Thus, the phenomenal appearance of origination from causes is not subject to assertions imposed by the categories of thought. Again, when phenomenal origination is analysed dialectically, it is found to be ultimately impossible.

As is evident from the passages, which have been considered, the structural components of the dialectic analysis are principally three in number. They are affirmation, negation and the conjunctive affirmation of the two preceding alternatives. The first alternative entails co-presence while the second entails disassociation. The third alternative entails the assertion of contradictory predicates of a single subject; thus destroying the notion of an integrated entity altogether. The fourth alternative, particularly in the case of the analysis of origination or causality, stands in a somewhat different position from that of the three other alternatives. The refutation of origination without causes is thus undertaken from the phenomenal, rather than from the ultimate standpoint, so as to vindicate the regularity of phenomenal appearance relative to causes. Thus, the pragmatic certainty of the causal relationship is secured, as well as its eithical infallibility.

The stanzas, which have been adduced contain the essence of Nāgārjuna's criticism of the notion of origination. The formal structure of the dialectic analysis, employed by the Madhyamaka, emerges from a consideration of the stanzas. In them, the proposition favoured by the Madhyamaka is enunciated and the categorical alternatives isolated. It must be admitted, however, that for the most part the arguments contained in the stanzas are suggestive or germinal in character. If they are to be explicated Nāgārjuna's autocommentary to the *Śūnyatāsaptati*, as well as the exegetical works of commentators like Buddhapālita and Candrakīrti must be investigated. Only then will the full implications of the arguments appropriate to the alternatives isolated in the stanzas become apparent.

In conclusion, it may be noted that the dialectic principle of analysing related entities in terms of co-presence and disassociation is also applicable to categories like existence and non-existence. The *Śūnyatāsaptati* indicates that existence and non-existence cannot exist together (i.e., cannot be co-present). Alternatively, disassociated from non-existence, existence is not obtained. Similarly existence always suggests non-existence and vice versa. Thus, disassociated from existence there is no non-existence. Again, existence and non-existence cannot exist together, since existence and non-existence at one time and in one object are impossible.[17]

While the notions of existence and non-existence are obtained relative to each other, they are unintelligible, if examined dialectically in terms of co-presence and disassociation. If existence and non-existence are disassociated from each other, the notions become vacuous. On the other hand, the supposition of their co-presence involves contradiction. Indeed, analysis in terms of co-presence and disassociation is applicable to all relative phenomena, including the notions of origination and destruction, permanence and impermanence, unity and multiplicity and the like.

References

1. *Mūlamadhyamakakārikā*, I.6.
2. *Ibid.* I.7.
3. This principle is central to many of the Madhyamaka arguments.
4. That is an entity cannot originate from both existence and non-existence because this entails contradiction. Also see chapter XV.
5. *Mūlamadhyamakakārikā*, I.10.
6. *Ibid.* VII.20.
7. *Ibid.* XX.15.
8. *Ibid.* XX.16.
9. *Ibid.* XXI.13.
10. *Ibid.* VII.34.
11. *Śūnyatāsaptati*, Stanza 4. Many of the stanzas contained in the seventh chapter of the *Mūlamadhyamakakārikā* cover the same ground as this citation adduced from *Śūnyatāsaptati*. The latter has been chosen because the exposition in the *Śūnyatāsaptati* seems to be more easily intelligible than that found in the other work.
12. *Śūnyatāsaptati*, Stanza 5 and commentary
13. *Ibid.* Stanza 6.
14. Ibid. Stanza 6 and commentary.
15. *Ibid.* Stanza 14.
16. *Pratītyasamutpādahṛdayakārikā*, Stanza 5 and commentary.
17. *Śūnyatāsaptati*, Stanza 19 and commentary.

Chapter XI

THE REFUTATION OF THE FIRST ALTERNATIVE

It has been shown that the dialectical structure of the Madhyamaka analysis results in the isolation of three or four alternatives. While the alternatives may be co-related with the doctrines advocated by rival schools, they are not solely determined by them. The fact that the alternatives may also be derived analytically indicates that they reflect the dialectical nature of the faculty of reason.

The dichotomising activity of the faculty of reason results in the emergence of mutually opposed conclusions to philosophical problems. Thus, it is not surprising that the dialectical alternatives isolated by the Madhyamaka analysis should have been concretely expressed in the contemporary philosophical systems of the day. Indeed, Professor T. R. V. Murti rightly remarks that the four sets of views represented by the four alternatives serve as schema for the classification of all philosophical systems.[1]

Thus, it may be said that the four alternatives express fundamental philosophical attitudes which have appeared and reappeared in widely differing traditions throughout the history of philosophical thought. The philosophical attitudes represented by the four alternatives may be designated as—the affirmative, the negative, the synthetic and the agnostic or sceptic respectively. The fundamental conceptual attitudes, expressed by the four alternatives, in turn determine the nature of the systems of speculative philosophy associated with them.

The first alternative represents the philosophical attitude which affirms existence, permanence, identity, substantiality and the like. The position expressed by the first alternative was most commonly termed the doctrine of eternalism (Śāśvatavāda) by the Buddhists. In Indian philosophy, this fundamental conceptual attitude was developed in the doctrines of the Sāṅkhya and the Vedānta.

In regard to the problem of causality, the acceptance of the first alternative implies the affirmation of the identity of cause and effect, i.e., the doctrine of Satkāryavāda. According to the doctrine, the effect pre-exists in its material cause. It was the Sāṅkhya school that advocated the doctrine of Satkāryavāda, with which it was particularly associated.

Thus for the Madhyamaka, the school most clearly exemplified the acceptance of the first alternative in the area of the interpretation of causality. The Madhyamaka masters, from Buddhapālita onward, invariably referred to the Sāṅkhya doctrine when they refuted the notion of the identity of cause and effect. Indeed, it is evident that the theory advocated by the Sāṅkhya corresponds exactly with the first alternative cited in the opening stanza of the *Mūlamadhyamakakārikā*. Hence a brief recapitulation of the origins and doctrine of the Sāṅkhya system and particularly of its theory of the pre-existence of the effect in the cause will not be out of place before proceeding with the exposition of its refutation.

The Sāṅkhya whose beginnings are clearly pre-Buddhist, was probably the earliest systematic philosophy formulated in India. The characteristic approach of the Sāṅkhya was rational and independent. It rejected the authority of the Vedas and attempted to explain certain apparent inconsistencies in the nature of reality through its bifurcation into spirit (puruṣa) and matter (prakṛti). The Sāṅkhya recognised two kinds of existence, the unchanging existence of the subject (Kūṭastha-nitya) and the changing existence of the object (pariṇāmi-nitya).[2] The Sāṅkhya constitutes the philosophical matrix, out of which both the Nyāya-Vaiśeṣika and the Vedānta grew and developed. It is evident that the Sāṅkhya system exercised considerable influence in contemporary philosophical circles, if only from the persistence with which its opponents who included both Buddhists as well as Vedāntins like Śaṅkara undertook to refute ts doctrine.

bSod-nams Seṅ-ge gives the following summary of the position advocated by the Sāṅkhya in regard to the problem of causality. The Sāṅkhya system maintains that it is irrational to believe that entities do not originate from themselves. Surely, the Sāṅkhyas argue, entities do not originate without cause nor do they originate from causes which are other to them. Therefore, entities originate from themselves, i.e., from their own substance or essence.[3] Again they contend, the origination of entities from themselves will not be without purpose, because that which existed in an unmanifest form becomes manifest. Nor again does an infinite series of originations occur, since once an entity has become manifest, it does not require a second manifestation.[4]

Professor Murti gives a similar interpretation of the doctrine advocated by the Sāṅkhya. He writes that, for the Sāṅkhyas, change is self-manifestation. The same thing is the stuff which changes and the efficient cause of its change. That which changes and that into which it changes are identical. The difference is of two states of one thing. The effect is the actualised state of the potential cause.[5]

Nāgārjuna refers not infrequently to the notion of the pre-existence of the effect co-incident with the cause. The first alternative presented in the opening stanza of the *Mūlamadhyamakakārikā* was also invariably interpreted, by Madhyamaka commentators, as having reference to the Sāṅkhya doctrine. However, inasmuch as Nāgārjuna was principally occupied with the refutation of the doctrines of the Ābhidharmika schools, there is little or no explicit criticism of the Sāṅkhya to be found in his works. Nonetheless, it is clear that many passages contain refutations of the notion of a pre-existent effect.

The criticism applicable to the doctrine advocated by the Sāṅkhya may be legitimately extrapolated, even from arguments which appear to be generally directed against the Ābhidharmika philosophy, for as it has been urged, the alternatives represent fundamental attitudes of thought and not merely the particular doctrine advocated by a given school. This approach was, indeed, adopted by the subsequent exponents of the Madhyamaka system, who constructed their arguments against the Sāṅkhya theory of causality, in consonance with the criticism of the notion of a pre-existent effect, as outlined by Nāgārjuna in a variety of passages.

A number of citations from the works of Nāgārjuna, suggesting arguments against the notion of a pre-existent effect, have already been presented in the foregoing chapter. Reference may here, again, be made to the following passages. Nāgārjuna has said in the *Mūlamadhyamakakārikā*, "How could an origination which is unoriginated arise by itself? On the other hand, if the originated arises, how is it that it arises again?"[6] He has also said in the *Śūnyatāsaptati* that an existent entity does not originate because it already exists, and that the originated, i.e., an originated entity does not originate because its origination is already complete.[7] Again, the Master has said, "If the cause and effect are identical, then the producer and the produced will also be identical."[8] He has also said, "If the effect exists in the assembly of cause and conditions, it should be apprehended, i.e., grasped within the assembly. However, in fact it is not apprehended."[9]

In addition, it may be mentioned that the origination of an entity which already exists or is originated, alluded to in the arguments cited from the *Śūnyatāsaptati*, implies an infinite regress. This consequence, as it will be seen, was explicitly mentioned by subsequent commentators like Buddhapālita and Candrakīrti. The latter also elaborated, at length, the other arguments suggested by Nāgārjuna.

At this point, it will be appropriate to review the arguments advanced by Buddhapālita against the notion of self-origination. Buddhapālita was the first commentator to attempt the explication of the Madhyamaka refutation of the theory of the preexistent effect as set forth by Nāgārjuna. Hence his comments function as the point of departure for the subsequent interpretations offered by Madhyamaka scholars. It may also be recalled that it was against the opinion of Buddhapālita that Bhāvaviveka directed his criticism and that it was likewise in defence of Buddhapālita that Candrakīrti undertook to refute the allegations of Bhāvaviveka.

Buddhapālita proposes to vindicate the favoured proposition of the Madhyamaka through the following arguments. He says that entities do not originate from themselves, i.e., from their own substantiality, since the origination of such entities will be without purpose and will result in absurdity, inasmuch as an infinite regress will occur. Entities which exist by themselves, i.e., in their own substantiality, he argues, do not require another origination and if even though they exist, they nonetheless originate, then in that case, never so long as they exist, will they fail to originate.[10]

While it may be said that the comments of Buddhapālita contain nothing which was not implicit in the statements of Nāgārjuna, they nonetheless serve to clarify the criticism of the notion of self-origination suggested by the latter. The infinite regress implied by the proposition of self-origination, which does not seem to have been explicitly mentioned by Nāgārjuna,[11] emerges as an important element of the refutation of self-origination in the interpretation offered by Buddhapālita.

The arguments of Buddhapālita are constructed upon the premises supplied by the doctrine of his opponent, the Sāṅkhya, against whom they are directed. Thus, his interpretation may be regarded as the commencement of the Prāsaṅgika tradition of textual exegesis.

The Madhyamaka arguments against self-origination suggested by Nāgārjuna and Buddhapālita were extensively elaborated by Candrakīrti in the *Prasannapadā* and the *Madhyamakāvatāra.* Candrakīrti follows the practice, established by Buddhapālita, of refuting the doctrine favoured by the opponent through arguments *ad absurdum* which elicit the undesirable consequences entailed by his position. Indeed, it may be said with justification that the refutation of opposing views through the *reductio ad absurdum* is brought to its greatest perfection in the works of Candrakīrti.

Like Buddhapālita Candrakīrti argues that it will be without purpose if entities which exist by themselves, i.e., exist substantially originate, since if entities do indeed exist, their repeated origination is non-sensical. If the entity which is the cause already exists substantially, it does not require another origination as the effect, as in the case of a manifest jar.

Moreover, Candrakīrti contends that the contradictory character of the position advocated by the opponent involves the admission of consequences which are not commonly accepted. Again, propositions generally approved by commonsense will be unacceptable for the same reason. Again, he argues, if the cause and effect are identical, the integrity of the entities concerned will be lost. Finally, if in fact the effect does exist in the cause, then it ought to be apprehended when the cause is apprehended. However, this is not the case.

Candrakīrti argues that if indeed entities originate from themselves, then the sprout which is green in colour ought to originate from itself, while its cause, the white seed, ought also to originate from itself alone. If so, then at all times the seed ought to originate only from the seed; however, this involves the acceptance of a state of affairs which is not commonly admitted.

Moreover, if the seed originates from the seed itself, then its extinction is inconceivable. In that case, the sprout will not originate since the extinction of the cause must necessarily precede the emergence of the effect. Again, if the non-extinction of the seed is admitted, it will then be eternal. However, the doctrine of eternalism is seen through the *reductio ad absurdum* to entail a variety of faults.

The Sāṅkhya mayattempt to improve his position in the following way. He may hold that conditions such as earth, water and the like assist the seed in the production of the sprout. Thus when the effect, i.e., the sprout, emerges, its cause, i.e., the seed, is extinguished.

This defence, however, is of no avail, since for the Sāṅkhya himself not only the cause and effect, i.e., the seed and sprout, but the conditions, i.e., earth, water etc., as well, are essentially identical. Hence, it cannot be maintained that the conditions assist the primary cause in the production of the effect, since inasmuch as the cause and the conditions are thought to be identical, the latter cannot be supposed to assist the former. Indeed, just as fire does not consume itself, nor does the blade of a sword cut itself, so also no entity can be supposed to exercise its causal efficiency upon its very self.

Again, Candrakīrti writes that though dependent upon a seed, earth and other conditions the sprout originates, it cannot be maintained that the seed and the sprout are identical. The seed and the sprout are not identical, since in that case through the *reductio ad absurdum*, it will follow that the producer and the produced are likewise identical. Similarly, the father and the son will also be one. The resemblance of this argument advanced by Candrakīrti to that employed by Nāgārjuna in the *Mūlamadhyamakakārikā* is immediately apparent.[12]

Candrakīrti also argues that if the seed and the sprout are, in fact, identical, then the attributes of the seed ought to be apprehended in the sprout and alternatively those of the sprout ought to be apprehended in the seed. However, this is not the case. The five attributes of the seed are not found in the sprout, nor are those of the sprout found in the seed. The shape of the seed is semicircular like a half moon; its colour is white; its taste is sweet; its latent potentiality is to produce the sprout, and when it is matured its taste becomes bitter. These are the five attributes which are apprehended in the seed. On the contrary, the shape of the sprout is long and thin; its colour is green; its taste is bitter; its latent potentiality is to produce shade and when it is matured, its taste becomes sweet. These are the five attributes of the sprout.

Finally, Candrakīrti observes that inasmuch as the seed and the sprout are thought to be identical, whenever the sprout is apprehended, the seed ought also to be apprehended. Similarly, when the seed is not apprehended, so also the sprout ought not to be apprehended.[13] Once more this argument somewhat resembles that given in the *Mūlamadhyamakakārikā*[14] which was cited earlier in this chapter.

The arguments advanced by Candrakīrti against the notion of a pre-existent effect rely exclusively upon the *reductio ad absurdum* through which the undesirable consequences of the position endorsed by the opponent are exposed. While Candrakīrti's arguments reveal a manifest affinity with those suggested by Nāgārjuna, it must be admitted that they constitute a substantial elaboration of the latter. It was indeed Candrakīrti's genius as a critical philosopher which earned him his place as the preeminent exponent of the Prāsaṅgika school. The *reductio ad absurdum* which was used so effectively by Candrakīrti continued to be employed by the Prāsaṅgika scholars like Śāntideva who followed him.

The following stanza contained in the ninth chapter of the *Bodhicaryāvatāra* presents two arguments *ad absurdum* against the notion of a pre-existent effect exhibiting the ruthless sarcasm which the *reductio ad absurdum* can achieve in the hands of a master debator. Śāntideva writes, "If the effect exists in the cause, to eat food will be to eat excrement. Again, having bought cotton seed with the price of cloth you ought to clothe yourself with it instead."[15]

The arguments advanced by Buddhapālita, Candrakīrti and Śāntideva which have been considered represent those of the Prāsaṅgika school of which they are the foremost exponents. They undertook to refute the notion of self-origination advocated by the Sāṅkhya system through exposing the undesirable consequences which the doctrine entailed, thus revealing the inherent inconsistency of the Sāṅkhya theory. All their arguments without exception represent varieties of the *reductio ad absurdum*. They advanced no independent syllogisms whatsoever.

The primary argument *ad absurdum* advanced by Buddhapālita and Candrakīrti against the doctrine of self-origination advocated by the Sāṅkhya system may be summarised as follows. Entities do not originate from themselves. This statement constitutes the proposition of refutation advanced by the Madhyamaka. If it is otherwise, the origination advocated by the Sāṅkhya will be futile and will go on *ad infinitum*, since even though entities exist, they nonetheless originate. The major premise suggested by the words, even though entities exist, may be stated in the following way—whatsoever exists is not in need of origination.

It has been said that the Prāsaṅgika commentators, from Buddhapālita through Śāntideva, altogether avoided independent syllogisms and refuted the doctrine of their opponents solely through arguments *ad absurdum*. The argument *ad absurdum*, however, does admit of an alternative formulation, consistent with the practice of the Prāsaṅgikas.

The argument *ad absurdum* may also be stated in the form of an inference familiar to the opponent (paraprasiddhānumāna). Formally, the inference familiar to the opponent corresponds exactly to the five-membered inference of the Naiyāyika. The five-membered Naiyāyika inference constitutes an independent syllogism, as does the three-membered inference advocated by Diṅnāga and Dharmakīrti. Thus the inference familiar to the opponent, the five-membered Naiyāyika inference and the so called independent syllogism are formally identical.

The inference familiar to the opponent, however, differs from the latter two in one crucial respect. The canons of formal logic unanimously insist that the elements of an independent syllogism, be it of five members or of three, be commonly admitted by both parties to a debate. This is emphatically not true in the case of the inference familiar to the opponent.

The terms of the inference familiar to the opponent, as is suggested by its very appellation, are acceptable to the opponent alone. Hence, the inference familiar to the opponent does not constitute an independent syllogism. However, it is for this very reason that the inference familiar to the opponent may be consistently admitted even by the Prāsaṅgika school. Since the Prāsaṅgika himself need not accept the terms of the inference, he may legitimately employ it to refute the doctrine advocated by his opponent.

Indeed, the arguments of Buddhapālita may also be expressed in the form of an inference familiar to the opponent. Thus it may be said that entities such as jars and the like, effects which exist in the substance of the cause, constitute the subject of the proposition (sādhya-dharmin). It is argued that entities do not originate from themselves because they exist in their own substantiality, just as a jar. The reason (hetu) may be stated as—because they exist in their own substantiality. Through the words, "Entities which exist in their own substantiality do not require origination, and if even though they exist, they nonetheless originate, their origination will go on *ad infinitum*", the example (dṛṣṭānta) is indicated, i.e., a jar which exists in its own substantiality. The reason is understood indirectly, when it is shown that it pervades the example. The reason is then applied to the logical subject in the minor premise, i.e., entities exist in their own substantiality. Thus it is said, "The origination of entities which exist in their own substantiality will be futile and if even though they exist, they nonetheless originate, their origination will go on *ad infinitum*", just as in the case of the origination of a manifest jar. The words, "Entities which exist in their own substantiality do not require origination", indicate the major premise, i.e., whatsoever exists in its own substantiality does not require origination.[16]

It may seem paradoxical that the Prāsaṅgika school, which relentlessly criticised the independent syllogisms, advocated by the exponents of the Svātantrika system, should itself have employed inferential arguments of the kind just outlined. It must be stressed, however, that the inference familiar to the opponent resembles the independent syllogism only formally. As it has been already said, the terms of the inference familiar to the opponent are not admitted by the Prāsaṅgika himself. The inference is constructed in accord with the conventions accepted by the opponent, utilising terms admitted by him alone. Thus, the inference familiar to the opponent represents a logical extension of the traditional method of argument; employed by the Prāsṅagika school, according to which the proposition advocated by the opponent is refuted on grounds acceptable to the opponent alone.

References

1. Murti, T. R. V., *The Central Philosophy of Buddhism*, p. 130.
2. *Ibid.* pp. 55-56.
3. The Sāṅkhyas established the theory of Satkāryavāda through the refutation of Asatkāryavāda.
4. *dBu-ma-spyi-ston,* pp. 339-340.
5. Murti, T.R.V., *The Central Philosophy of Buddhism*, p. 61.
6. *Mūlamadhyamakakārikā,* VII.13.
7. *Śūnyatāsaptati,* Stanzas 4, 5 and commentary.
8. *Op. cit.* XX.20.
9. *Mūlamadhyamakakārikā,* XX. 3.
10. *dBu-ma-spyi-ston,* pp. 342-343.
11. The infinite regress was, however, frequently used by Nāgārjuna as an argument on other occasions. See chapter IX.
12. *Mūlamadhyamakakārikā,* XX.20.
13. Quoted in the *dBu-ma-spyi-ston,* pp. 340-342 from the *Madhyamakāvatāra*; *Prasannapadā* commentary to *Mūlamadhyamakakārikā,* XVIII. 10.
14. *Op.cit.* XX.3.
15. *Bodhicaryāvatāra,* IX. 135 and 136.
16. *dBu-ma-spyi-ston,* pp. 342-343.

Chapter XII

THE CONTROVERSY BETWEEN BHĀVAVIVEKA AND CANDRAKĪRTI

As it was indicated in a previous chapter, Bhāvaviveka criticised the arguments advanced by Buddhapālita against self-origination on a number of grounds. He alleged that Buddhapālita had failed to state a reason and example. Again, he maintained that Buddhapālita had not answered the objections raised by the Sāṅkhyas. Finally, Bhāvaviveka contended that if the argument adduced by Buddhapālita had been a simple *reductio ad absurdum*, a positive counter-proposition would emerge by implication. Thus, it would follow that entities originate from entities which are other to them which would contradict the doctrine of the Madhyamaka system.[1]

Bhāvaviveka advocated an alternative method of argument to that employed by Buddhapālita. He constructed independent syllogisms composed of three members and modified by a special qualification. In this way, he hoped to avoid the errors which he believed he had detected in the arguments advanced by Buddhapālita. The independent syllogism proposed by Bhāvaviveka established the pattern of the arguments employed by the adherents of the Svātantrika system of which he was the founder.

Candrakīrti, in defence of the interpretation offered by Buddhapālita, undertook to refute the objections which had been raised by Bhāvaviveka against the opinion of the latter. In his turn, he criticised the alternative method of argument proposed by Bhāvaviveka and raised a number of objections against the independent syllogism advocated by the latter. His observations represent the definitive reply of the Prāsaṅgika school to the challenge posed by the Svātantrika system.

Candrakīrti's principal polemic against Bhāvaviveka and the independent syllogism proposed by him is contained in the opening portions of his commentary to the *Mūlamadhyamakakārikā* the *Prasannapadā*.[2] bSod-nams-Sen-ge's interpretation of the controversy between Bhāvaviveka and the Prāsaṅgikas is in large part founded upon the treatment accorded to the problem by Candrakīrti in the *Prasannapadā*. His comments contained in the *dBu-ma-spyi-ston* constitute an explanation of the interpretation expressed by Candrakīrti in the *Prasannapadā*. Thus, the exposition of the controversy with Bhāvaviveka presented in this and in the subsequent chapter generally follows the pattern encountered in the *Prasannapadā*. Nonetheless, the order of the presentation of the topics has been to some extent altered and interpolations, supported by textual evidence, have been resorted to in the hope that in this way the significance of the controversy will emerge more clearly.

The objections raised by Bhāvaviveka must be seen in the following context. When Buddhapālita refuted the notion of self-origination advocated by the Sāṅkhya, was the argument which he advanced intended to be an independent syllogism or an argument *ad absurdum* ? If it was intended to be an independent syllogism, then Buddhapālita's argument ought to have been stated in the following way. "Ultimately the subjective poles of consciousness do not originate from themselves because they exist, as for example, the conscious principle (caitanya)." The introduction of the special qualification "ultimately" in the independent syllogism given above may be noted. In that case, however, Buddhapālita failed to produce the reason "because they exist" and the example "like the conscious principle." Therefore, his argument was incorrect.[3]

Again, if the argument advanced by Buddhapālita was intended to be an independent syllogism, then he failed to reply to the objections raised by the Sāṅkhya. The Sāṅkhya indeed objected that the reason adduced, "because they exist", either proved the opposite of what was intended, or proved what was already established. These objections raised by the Sāṅkhya, Bhāvaviveka contended, were not answered by Buddhapālita. Hence, his argument was deficient.[4]

The Sāṅkhya assailed the Madhyamaka argument against self-origination in the following way. They asked, when it is said that entities do not originate from themselves because they exist, what is intended ? Is it meant that manifest effects which pre-existed in the substance of their causes do not originate from themselves because they exist or is it meant that unmanifested effects which exist in the substance of the cause do not originate from themselves because they exist? If the former is intended, then the argument amounts to a case of proving what is already established (siddha-sādhana), since the Sāṅkhya also admits that manifest effects do not originate again. If the latter is meant, then it is a case of proving the opposite of what is intended, since in that case all entities which originate exist precisely in the substance of their causes. If entities are acknowledged to exist in the substance of their causes, then it must consequently be admitted that they surely originate from themselves.[5]

Alternatively, if the argument advanced by Buddhapālita was not intended to be an independent syllogism, but was merely a *reductio ad absurdum*, then in that case, Bhāvaviveka contended, it was associated with its positive counterpart. It was said, "Entities do not originate from themselves, since their origination will then be futile and will go on *ad infinitum*." The implied positive counter-proposition will then affirm that entities originate from entities which are other to them. Similarly, the positive counterpart of the reason presented in the above argument, "since their origination will then be futile and will go on *ad infinitum*" will be stated as follows, "since their origination will then not be futile and will not go on *ad infinitum*." Thus the positive counterpart of the argument *ad absurdum* attributed to Buddhapālita will run "Entities originate from entities which are other to them, since their origination will then not be futile and will not go on *ad infinitum*." This argument, however, contradicts the Madhyamaka doctrine, according to which the ultimate origination of entities from entities which are other to them is also not admitted.[6]

The Prāsaṅgikas responded to the first objection raised by Bhāvaviveka as follows. They contended that if Bhāvaviveka had assailed Buddhapālita for failing to present a reason and example compatible with the requisites of an independent syllogism, his attack was irrelevant. The Sāṅkhya system, the Prāsaṅgikas repeated, advocates the doctrine that entities originate from themselves. They maintain that the effect pre-exists in its material cause. According to the Sāṅkhya, entities such as a jar and the like exist in an unmanifested condition in the substance of their causes. Thus, they hold that the effect which pre-exists in the substance of the cause itself originates. This constitutes the doctrine of self-origination advocated by the Sāṅkhya.[7]

It is replied that the origination of entities will then be futile and will go on *ad infinitum*, since they sxist in their own substantiality. The repeated origination of entities which already exist in their own substantiality is therefore absurd. The inconsistency of the position accepted by the Sāṅkhya is exposed through an argument *ad absurdum*. Thus, the erroneous doctrine of self-origination is refuted.[8]

The Prāsaṅgikas held that in itself this constitutes a sufficient refutation of the Sāṅkhya doctrine of self-origination, inasmuch as the Sāṅkhya also does not desire the reproduction of entities which already exist, nor does he admit an infinite series of originations. Hence, it follows that the doctrine advocated by the Sāṅkhya of the pre-existence of the effect in the cause is untenable. The Prāsaṅgikas argued that if the Sāṅkhya refused to abandon his doctrine even after it had been shown to be inconsistent it was of no use to pursue the discussion with him. In such a situation, they contended, the introduction of further arguments and examples would also not avail, since the opponent's obstinacy arose from his impudence.[9]

Moreover, the Sāṅkhya cannot hope to avoid the refutation of the doctrine of self-origination advanced by the Madhyamaka on the ground that he, the Sāṅkhya, advocates the view that causality consists of the manifestation of entities which pre-existed in an unmanifest condition. The term origination applies equally to the notion of manifestation, since both share the common characteristic of denoting the apprehension of an entity which was previously not apprehended.

The Sāṅkhya, indeed, affirms the existence of the effect though not apprehended, in the cause. Thus, he maintains that the sprout exists in the seed though it is not apprehended in the latter. He undertakes to vindicate his assertion through the argument, existence alone originates because non-existence does not originate. The inference is an example of an apologetic proof by means of which the position favoured by the proponent is sought to be established through the negation of the position opposed to it. In fact, it is well-known that the Sāṅkhya established its doctrine of Satkāryavāda through a refutation of the doctrine of Asatkāryavāda.[10]

The argument advanced by the Sāṅkhya in support of the doctrine of the pre-existence of the effect in the cause is, however, inadmissible, since the reason adduced in it is as unproven as the proposition. The assertion that entities originate from themselves is moreover not supported by any example or precedent met with in common experience. Thus, the Sāṅkhya is himself incapable of logically vindicating his theory of the pre-existence of the effect in the cause, though unperceived, which is shown to be merely a dogmatic assertion.[11]

Again, the Prāsaṅgikas held that Buddhapālita had indeed indicated a reason and example, though he had not produced an independent syllogism. Buddhapālita's argument, the Prāsaṅgikas contended, could also be expressed in the form of an inference familiar to the opponent. Thus, it may be said that entities such as a jar and the like which pre-exist in an unmanifested condition in the substance of their causes do not originate from themselves because they exist in their own substantiality. Whatsoever exists in its own substantiality does not require origination or originate from itself as in the case of a manifest jar. According to the Sāṅkhya, a jar which exists in an unmanifest condition in the substance of the cause also exists in its own substantiality. Therefore, such a jar also does not require origination or originate from itself. Thus, the Prāsaṅgikas argued, the five-membered inference familiar to the opponent is suggested in the statements of Buddhapālita. Hence Bhāvaviveka's assertion that he failed to indicate a reason and example is without justification.[12]

Explicitly, the five-membered inference may be extrapolated as follows from the arguments presented by Buddhapālita. It has been said, "Entities such as a jar and the like which exist in an unmanifest condition in the substance of their causes do not originate from themselves, since their origination will then be futile and will go on *ad infinitum*." In this statement the proposition is indicated. Entities, such as a jar and the like constitute the subject of proposition (sādhya-dharmin). "They do not originate from themselves, since their origination will then be futile and will go on *ad infinitum*." These words indicate the predicates, i.e., the properties (dharma) of the major term (sādhya) or proposition (pratijñā). Thus, if entities which exist in their own substantiality do indeed originate, then their origination will be futile and will go on *ad infinitum*. The major premise or invariable concomitance (vyāpti) may be expressed through the words, "whatsoever exists in its own substantiality does not require origination or originate from itself." Thus, entities which exist in their own substantiality, such as a manifest jar, do not require another origination, and if even though they exist they nonetheless originate, their origination will go on *ad infinitum.* The major premise, "whatsoever exists in its own substantiality does not require origination or originate from itself", is applied to the example (dṛṣṭānta), i.e., a manifest jar. It may likewise be understood that entities, such as a jar and the like which exist in an unmanifested condition in the substance of their causes, also exist in their own substantiality. Thus, the reason (hetu), "because they exist in their own substantiality", which applies equally to manifest and unmanifest entities is indicated. The reason is thus applied to the subject in the minor premise (pakṣadharma), "entities such as a jar and the like which exist in an unmanifested condition in the substance of their causes, exist in their own substantiality." The major premise, "Whatsoever exists in its own substantiality does not require origination or originate from itself" is applied to the example of a manifest jar which indicates the application (upanaya) of the reason or probans (vyāpya) to the subject of the example (dṛṣṭāntadharmin) and to the subject of proposition. Finally, the conclusion may be stated, "entities do not originate from themselves," which is indicated by the proposition. Therefore, the five members of an inference familiar to the opponent—proposition, reason, example, application and conclusion—are implicitly present in the statements of Buddhapālita.[13]

The analysis just presented may become more easily comprehensible if applied to a simpler argument. Thus, a parallel case, that of the familiar argument establishing the impermanence of sound, may be used to clarify the procedure which is to be adopted. In this instance also it may be said, "Sound is impermanent because it is the product of an effort. Whatsoever is the product of an effort is known to be impermanent, as for example a jar." In this argument, the five-membered inference is not immediately evident. Indeed, an argument may be stated briefly, as in this case, or in detail.

Here also, the proposition is indicated through the words, "Sound is impermanent." Sound is the subject, while "impermanence" is the predicate. The major premise may be stated, "Whatsoever is the product of an effort is known to be impermanent." The reason,—"because it is the product of an effort", is applied to the example,—"a jar" and to the subject, "sound." Thus the reason, "because it is a product of an effort," is revealed in the application (upanaya) of the reason to the subject of the example and to the subject. Again, the conclusion, "therefore sound is impermanent," is indicated by the proposition.[14]

So also in the former case it was said, "entities which exist in their own substantiality do not originate from themselves, since their origination will then be futile and will go on *ad infinitum*." Again, it is known that entities, such as a jar and the like, which exist in their own substantiality do not require another origination. Moreover, inasmuch as, for the Sāṅkhya, entities such as a jar and the like exist in their own substantiality even in an unmanifest condition, their origination is similarly refuted, because they exist in their own substantiality.

The two arguments just discussed, that refuting the doctrine of self-origination and that establishing the impermanence of sound, are in fact exactly parallel. The complexity of Buddhapālita's argument results from the fact that it contains multiple predicates, rather than a single predicate. Thus, the proposition in Buddhapālita's argument against self-origination includes three distinct predicates or properties. The primary predicate or consequence, which the Madhyamaka intends through his argument to induce the opponent to accept, is non-origination from self. The opponent is constrained to admit this consequence on pain of two other undesirable consequences, i.e., purposeless origination and origination *ad infinitum*, which constitute the secondary predicates or properties of the major term. In other words, the non-acceptance of the primary predicate, i.e., non-origination from self, entails the acceptance of the secondary predicates, i.e., purposeless origination and origination *ad infinitum*. The reason adduced, "because they exist in their own substantiality, " functions as the probans of all the three predicates which constitute the properties of the major term. The opponent is thus compelled to admit the conclusion that entities do not originate from themselves, since his refusal to do so will involve him in absurdity. This analysis reveals again the *modus operandi* of the argument *ad absurdum*.

Again, it may be objected that the reason adduced in the inference familiar to the opponent, "because they exist in their own substantiality," is uncertain, inasmuch as when the positive concomitance (anvaya) was indicated, the jar alone was stated as an example. Thus, the origination of cloth and the like which also exist in their own substantiality is not necessarily refuted since the reason adduced applies equally to dissimilar objects.

This objection, however, is without foundation because when the example was presented, it was said, "a jar and the like." The phrase, "and the like", indicates the inclusion of all entities without exception which may be thought to originate.[15]

In addition, an alternative argument against the doctrine of self-origination advocated by the Sāṅkhya is suggested by Candrakīrti. The argument is similar to that adduced by Buddhapālita. The Sāṅkhya system advocates the theory that all objects of cognition may be included in the conscious and the material. They hold that all material objects exist in the nature of primordial matter, i.e., in the nature of the Pradhāna. It is said, "material objects do not originate from themselves, because they exist in their own substantiality, as for example, the eternal spirit (puruṣa)." In this argument, the existence of material objects in their own substantiality is exemplified by the existence of the eternal spirit of the opponent. Thus, the refutation of the Sāṅkhya doctrine of self-origination advanced by the Madhyamaka is altogether conclusive.[16]

Again, Bhāvaviveka alleged that Buddhapālita had failed to refute the objections raised by the Sāṅkhya. It will be recalled that the Sāṅkhya had contended that the reason adduced by the Madhyamaka either proved what was already established or proved the opposite of what was intended. Bhāvaviveka held that these objections ought to have been answered by Buddhapālita but were not and hence his argument was deficient.

The Prāsaṅgikas replied that the errors alleged by the Sāṅkhya applied only to those who produced an independent syllogism like the following one. "The subjective poles of consciousness, do not originate from themselves because they exist." The Prāsaṅgikas maintained that in their case the foundation of the errors alleged by the Sāṅkhya was not admitted. Hence, the Sāṅkhya's objections did not affect the arguments produced by the Prāsaṅgikas.

The Svātantrikas advanced the argument, "Entities do not originate from themselves because they exist." The reason adduced is, "because they exist." Is it then meant that entities exist in an unmanifest condition in the substance of their cause, or is it meant that they exist in a manifest condition in the substance of effects ?

If it is held that entities exist in an unmanifest condition in the substance of their causes and that they do not originate from themselves because they exist, then in that case, the reason adduced is contradictory. That is to say, the reason adduced contradicts the predicate, i.e., the negation of self-origination, contained in the proposition, "entities do not originate from themselves," since if entities exist in an unmanifest condition in the substance of their causes, it is proved that they originate from themselves. Therefore, the reason adduced in fact proves the opposite of what is intended.

Alternatively, if it is held that entities which exist in a manifest condition in the substance of effects do not originate from themselves because they exist, then in that case, the proposition is already admitted by the Sāṅkhya. The Sāṅkhya, indeed, agrees that entities which exist in a manifest condition as effects do not themselves originate again. Therefore, the argument is pointless, since it seeks to prove something which, for the opponent, is already established independent of the argument.

Bhāvaviveka, indeed, responded to the objections raised by the Sāṅkhya in the following way. The terms employed in syllogisms, he maintained, ought to be disassociated from specific predicates imposed by the interpretations favoured by different schools. Thus, the term existence ought not to be qualified as existence in an unmanifest condition in the substance of the cause, or existence in a manifest condition in the substance of the effect, but ought to be understood in its generalised signification only. He also availed himself of the argument that existence in an unmanifest condition and existence in a manifest condition are essentially identical, since for the Sāṅkhya both in any case exist in their own substantiality.[17]

The Prāsaṅgikas contended that when self-origination was to be refuted neither a proposition, reason, nor example existed for the Madhyamaka. They held that the doctrine of self-origination advocated by the Sāṅkhya was not refuted by the Madhyamaka through an independent syllogism whose terms existed commonly for both the proponent and the opponent by virtue of valid instruments of cognition.[18]

Nonetheless, it might be objected that even in the case of an inference familiar to the opponent, the proposition, minor premise and major premise ought to be accepted by the opponent. Thus, the argument through which the doctrine advocated by the Sāṅkhya is refuted ought to be free from the logical errors of a proposition which affirms what is already established, a contradictory reason and an example in which the property of the proposition is not found. Even in the case of an inference familiar to the opponent, the argument ought to be stated in conformity with the established criteria of a correct argument. However, a reason and example were not cited and the errors alleged by the Sāṅkhya were not refuted, hence the argument *ad absurdum* produced by Buddhapālita was faulty.

It has already been shown that the Prāsaṅgikas argued that an inference familiar to the opponent including a reason and example had in fact been indicated by Buddhapālita. Moreover, they contended, the errors alleged by the Sāṅkhya did not arise in the case of the inference familiar to the opponent produced by the Prāsaṅgikas. When it is demonstrated, they said, that a jar and the like which exist in an unmanifest condition in the substance of their causes do not originate from themselves the error of proving what is already established does not occur. Again, the positive concomitance was applied to the example of a jar and the like which exist in a manifest condition. Hence, the logical error of a contradictory reason also does not occur. Thus, the errors alleged by the Sāṅkhya do not exist in the case of the inference familiar to the opponent produced by the Prāsaṅgikas. Therefore, Bhāvaviveka's accusation that Buddhapālita failed to answer the objections raised by the Sāṅkhya is out of place.[19]

Finally, Bhāvaviveka had asserted that if the argument advanced by Buddhapālita had been a simple *reductio ad absurdum*, a counter-proposition would be implicitly affirmed. Thus, the argument that entities do not originate from themselves, since their origination will then be futile and will go on *ad infinitum* really implied the affirmation of the proposition that entities originate from entities which are other to them. This consequence is however unacceptable, since it contradicts the Madhyamaka doctrine.[20]

The Prāsaṅgikas countered that though the argument advanced by Buddhapālita had been a *reductio ad absurdum* the acceptance of a counter-proposition was not in the least implied. The Madhyamaka argument indeed expresses an absolute negation (prasajya-pratiṣedha), not a relative negation (paryudāsa-pratiṣedha). Therefore, the refutation of the position advocated by the opponent, through an argument *ad absurdum* does not imply the affirmation of the alternative position.[21]

When the doctrine of self-origination advocated by the Sāṅkhya is refuted through an argument *ad absurdum*, the fallacious proposition and major premise are established conventionally by valid instruments of cognition, while the minor premise is established by the acceptance of the opponent. Thus, when it is said that entities which exist in their own substantiality do not originate from themselves, since their origination will then be futile and will go on *ad infinitum*, the major premise, "Whatsoever exists in its own substantiality does not require origination or originate from itself", and the fallacious proposition, "Entities which exist in their own substantiality originate from themselves", are established conventionally by valid instruments of cognition. The minor premise, "Entities exist in their own substantiality" is established by the acceptance of the opponent.[22]

The argument does not imply any affirmation to the contrary on the part of the Madhyamaka. An argument *ad absurdum* consisting of the three members just indicated, i.e., fallacious proposition, major premise and minor premise directly negates the position advocated by the opponent. Such an argument may also in certain cases indirectly affirm an independent position. However, when the doctrine of self-origination advocated by the Sāṅkhya is refuted by the Madhyamaka through an argument *ad absurdum*, an independent proposition is not accepted by the latter.

Nonetheless, when it is said that entities do not originate from themselves, the opponent may conclude that the origination of entities from entities which are other to them is implicitly affirmed. While this is no doubt possible, it does not affect the position of the Madhyamaka who advocates the doctrine of emptiness since, for him, the consequence just indicated does not arise.[23] Moreover, the counter-position expressed in the proposition, entities originate from entities which are other to them, was in its turn refuted by the Madhyamaka. Thus, the Madhyamaka's acceptance of the alternative position is not at all implied by his refutation of the position advocated by the opponent. This will presently become abundantly clear, when a few of the arguments *ad absurdum* employed by Nāgārjuna are considered.

The statements of the Madhyamaka cannot be thought to impose upon him the acceptance of a position which he does not admit. It is not as though words have the power to deprive their speaker of his liberty. The following analogy may serve to clarify the point at issue. It might so happen that someone employs a stick or rope to control and manipulate creatures. It does not follow that he who holds the stick or rope should himself be controlled by that very stick or rope. Words indeed only possess the power to express the intention of the speaker. They do not possess any intrinsic power of their own.[24]

Indeed, it is evident that Nāgārjuna most frequently resorted to arguments *ad absurdum* when refuting the doctrines of his opponents. He has said, "If form exists disassociated from the cause of form, then it follows that form will exist without a cause. However, nowhere does any object exist without a cause."[25] He has also said, "Before any characterisation of space, space does not exist. If it were to exist before any characterisation, then it would follow that space exists without any characterisation."[26] Again Nāgārjuna has said, "Nirvāṇa is not existence, since, then it would be characterised by decay and death because existence is never found apart from decay and death."[27]

The positive counterparts of the three arguments just cited from the *Mūlamadhyamakakārikā* would be stated as given below. For the sake of simplicity, the hypothetical propositions contained in the first two instances may be legitimately converted into negative propositions.

Thus, the argument found in the first example adduced may be initially restated as follows. Form does not exist disassociated from the cause of form, since it would then follow that form exists without a cause. This, however is untenable, because nowhere does any object exist without a cause. The positive counterpart of this argument will run, form exists associated with the cause of form, since form will then exist with a cause, because everywhere all objects are established with causes.

The argument presented in the second example may be initially restated in the following way. Space does not exist before any characterisation, since it will then follow that space exists without any characterisation. This is, however, unacceptable from the pont of view of the opponent, the Naiyāyika, for whom no entity can exist apart from a characterisation. In this case, the reason proper, i.e., because no entity can exist apart from a characterisation, is left unstated by Nāgārjuna. The positive counterpart of this argument will run, space exists simultaneous with, or subsequent to its characterisation, since space will then exist possessed of a characterisation, because all entities exist endowed with characterisations.

Again, Nāgārjuna has said, "Nirvāṇa is not existence, since then it will be characterised by decay and death, because existence is never found apart from decay and death." If reformulated positively, this argument will run: Nirvāṇa is non-existence, since then it will not be characterised by decay and death, because non-existence is always such as is not characterised by decay and death.

It is quite obvious that none of the positive formulations of Nāgārjuna's arguments just outlined could be approved by the Madhyamaka. The latter neither admits that form ultimately exists associated with a cause, nor that space ultimately exists endowed with a characterisation, nor again that Nirvāṇa is non-existence. Indeed, it is difficult to see how Bhāvaviveka could have in good conscience raised the objection under consideration.

Again, it will be recalled that Bhāvaviveka had asserted that when the statement, "Entities do not originate from themselves, since their origination will then be futile and will go on *ad infinitum*," is reformulated positively, a counter-proposition and a counter-reason will emerge by implication. He has no doubt rightly interpreted the phrase, "Entities do not originate from themselves", to express the proposition. He has, however, chosen to regard the phrase, since their origination will then be futile and will go on *ad infinitum*, as the reason. Thus, he alleged that the following positive counter-argument would emerge by implication, "Entities originate from entities which are other to them, since their origination will then not be futile and will not go on *ad infinitum*."

It has, however, been argued earlier in this chapter that the words, "since their origination will then be futile and will go on *ad infinitum*" contained in Buddhapālita's argument do not, in fact, constitute the reason, but rather the secondary predicates of the major term or proposition. This interpretation is amply supported by the fact that subsequent Prāsaṅgika commentators, from Candrakīrti onward, have invariably maintained that the phrase, "because they exist in their own substantiality," constitutes the reason in Buddhapālita's argument, not the words, "since their origination will then be futile and will go on *ad infinitum*." The latter phrase, indeed, can only be regarded as a reason at all, insofar as it functions as a condition which impels the acceptance of the primary predicate, i.e., the negation of self-origination. The precise relationship obtaining between the primary predicate and the secondary predicates, i.e., purposeless origination and origination *ad infinitum* has already been indicated earlier in this chapter, hence it will not be stated again here.

It will suffice to say that the same analysis, which was applied to the terms of Buddhapālita's argument against self-origination, is also applicable to the arguments cited above from the *Mūlamadhyamakakārikā*. Thus, for example, when Nāgārjuna says that Nirvāṇa is not existence, since it will then be characterised by decay and death, because existence is never found apart from decay and death, the reason is expressed by the words, "because existence is never found apart from decay and death." The primary predicate is expressed in the words, "not existence." The secondary predicate reveals itself in the phrase, "since it will then be characterised by decay and death". The opponent is, thus, compelled either to admit that Nirvāṇa is subject to decay and death, or to admit that Nirvāṇa is not existence. Since the opponent cannot admit that Nirvāṇa is subject to decay and death, he is obliged to relinquish the idea that Nirvāṇa is existence and to accept the conclusion that it is not existence. The secondary predicate, "since it will then be characterised by decay and death" does function as a condition of the acceptance of the proposition qualified by the primary predicate, "Nirvāṇa is not existence." The reason, however, is expressed in the words, "because existence is never found apart from decay and death."

Finally, it may be thought that the utterances of Nāgārjuna suggest a wide variety of interpretations and hence their significance may also be expressed through independent syllogisms. In that case, the Prāsaṅgikas countered, the statements of Buddhapālita may also be thought to contain implicit significance.

Therefore, Bhāvaviveka's accusation that Buddhapālita failed to state a reason and example is inconsistent.

Again, it may be thought that it is the responsibility of those who compose commentaries to produce independent syllogisms in order to explicate the import of the stanzas. However, this is also not necessarily the case. Nāgārjuna indeed composed an autocommentary to the *Vigrahavyāvartanī*, yet he did not in that work produce any independent syllogisms,[28] nor are any to be found in his autocommentary to the *Śūnyatāsaptati*.

References

1. *dBu-ma spyi-ston*, pp. 343-345.
2. Stcherbatsky, Th., *The Conception of Buddhist Nirvāṇa*, pp. 138-178.
3. *Op. cit.* p. 344.
4. *dBu-ma spyi-ston*, p. 345.
5. *Ibid.*
6. *Ibid.*
7. *Ibid.* pp. 345-347.
8. *Ibid.* p. 347.
9. *Ibid.* p. 348.
10. Murti, T.R.V., *The Central Philosophy of Buddhism*, p. 131.
11. *dBu-ma spyi-ston*, p. 351.
12. *Ibid.* p. 352.
13. *Ibid.* p. 353.
14. *Ibid.* pp. 353-354.
15. *Ibid.* p. 354.
16. *Ibid.* p. 355.
17. Kajiyama, Y., *Bhāvaviveka and the Prāsaṅgika School*, pp. 317-318, in Mookerjee, Satkari, (ed.), The Nava-Nalanda-Mahavihara Research Publication.
18. *dBu-ma spyi-ston*, p. 348.
19. *Ibid.* pp. 350-352.
20. *Ibid.* p. 355.
21. *Ibid.* p. 348.
22. *Ibid.* p. 350.
23. *Ibid.* p. 355.
24. *Ibid.*
25. *Mūlamadhyamakakārikā*, IV. 2.
26. *Ibid.* V. 1.
27. *Ibid.* XXV. 4; *dBu-ma spyi-ston*, p. 356.
28. *dBu-ma spyi-ston*, p. 356.

Chapter XIII

BHĀVAVIVEKA'S INDEPENDENT SYLLOGISM CRITICISED

Candrakīrti was not content simply with the refutation of the objections raised by Bhāvaviveka against the arguments employed by Buddhapālita and the Prāsaṅgikas. He also undertook to criticise the independent syllogism advocated by Bhāvaviveka. Thus, he hoped to establish conclusively the exclusive acceptability of the argument *ad absurdum*, on the occasion of the determination of the nature of ultimate reality.

Candrakīrti's criticism of the independent syllogisms proposed by Bhāvaviveka is developed along two general lines. Firstly, he argued that the composition of independent syllogisms is incompatible with the Madhyamaka philosophy. Secondly, he maintained that when an independent syllogism is advanced on the occasion of ascertaining the nature of the ultimate truth, the syllogism itself is subject to irremediable logical errors. Hence, Bhāvaviveka's independent syllogism is not only inconsistent with the Madhyamaka philosophy, but is also invalid from the point of view of formal logic.

It has already been said on numerous occasions that the definitive characteristic of the Madhyamaka philosophy is its rejection of the ultimate existence of all entities or elements. Thus, it is his interpretation of the nature of ultimate reality which distinguishes the Madhyamaka from other philosophers. The arguments advanced by the Madhyamaka are intended to communicate his interpretation of the nature of ultimate reality to his opponent, thereby vindicating the philosophical standpoint of the Madhyamaka.

Candrakīrti and the Prāsaṅgikas argued that on the occasion of determining the nature of ultimate reality, an independent syllogism is inadmissible, because an alternative position is not accepted on that occasion by the Madhyamaka. Thus, when the origination of entities from themselves is to be refuted, the Madhyamaka does not accept the alternative position.[1]

In his case, the doctrine of self-origination, advocated by the

Sāṅkhya, constitutes the initial position accepted by the opponent. Non-origination from self constitutes the alternative position, i.e., the position opposed to the initial position. The alternative position, i.e., non-origination from self is not admitted by the Madhyamaka when he undertakes to refute self-origination. Therefore, the Prāsaṅgikas held that it is incorrect to employ an independent syllogism on the occasion of the refutation of the origination of entities from themselves.

An independent syllogism, they contended, must necessarily contain a logical subject or substratum established by one of the four conventional valid instruments of cognition; perception, inference, testimony and comparison. Moreover, the substratum of an independent syllogism ought to be established commonly for both the proponent and the opponent. Upon the ground of such a commonly admitted substratum, the position accepted by the opponent is refuted and the position advocated by the proponent is vindicated. This constitutes the *modus operandi* of an independent syllogism.[2]

However, on the occasion of the determination of the nature of ultimate reality, a substratum established by virtue of the conventional valid instruments of cognition does not exist for the Madhyamaka. When the nature of the ultimate truth is to be determined, neither the initial position accepted by the opponent, nor the alternative position exist independently for the Madhyamaka. This interpretation may be supported by the following citation adduced from the *Catuḥśataka* of Āryadeva. "Even after prolonged effort," he has said, "objections cannot be raised against one who neither advocates existence, nor non-existence, nor both existence and non-existence."[3] Similarly, Nāgārjuna has said, "If I had a proposition, I could be at fault, but since I have none, I cannot be at fault."[4] These citations, adduced from the works of Āryadeva and Nāgārjuna, the Prāsaṅgikas contended, demonstrate conclusively that when the nature of ultimate reality is to be determined, an independent position is not accepted by the Madhyamaka. Hence, on that occasion, an independent syllogism is invalid.

A valid independent syllogism presupposes the existence of elements which are admitted commonly by both the proponent and the opponent. The Madhyamaka, however, does not admit the ultimate existence of any entity or element. When arguments are advanced by the Madhyamaka against the notion of origination, it is his avowed intention to demonstrate that no entity or element exists in reality. Hence, he cannot on that occasion employ an independent syllogism which by its very nature must contain elements which are commonly accepted to exist without involving himself in contradiction.[5]

Candrakīrti, moreover, accused Bhāvaviveka of wishing only to exhibit his great skill in the science of logic. Thus, it is said, that though Bhāvaviveka accepts the Madhyamaka philosophy, he nonetheless composes independent syllogisms when the ultimate emptiness of elements (dharmaniḥsvabhāva or dharmaśūnyatā) is to be established. As a result, the arguments which he produces, Candrakīrti contended, are subject to manifold errors.[6]

For example, the following independent syllogism has been advanced by Bhāvaviveka. "Ultimately, the subjective poles of consciousness certainly do not originate from themselves, because they exist, like the conscious principle." Candrakīrti contended that this syllogism produced by Bhāvaviveka is subject to a total of six critical errors. One—the special qualification "ultimately" introduced by the author is purposeless; two—the substratum contained in the syllogism—"the subjective poles of consciousness," is unproven; three—the reason adduced, "because they exist," is unproven; four—Bhāvaviveka has himself recognised the logical errors of an unproven substratum and reason; five—the errors contained in Bhāvaviveka's syllogism against self-origination are also to be found in the other independent syllogisms produced by him; six—even from the standpoint of the opponent, the Sāṅkhya, the reason adduced, "because they exist", is uncertain.[7]

First of all, it may be enquired, for what purpose the special qualification, "ultimately", introduced by Bhāvaviveka is added to the syllogism cited above. Is the qualification meant to modify the object refuted, i.e., self-origination, or is it meant to modify the logical subject, the subjective poles of consciousness? If it is intended to qualify the object refuted, then it may again be enquired, for what purpose is it introduced?[8]

It may be replied that if the qualification is not expressed, origination which is admitted phenomenally by the Madhyamaka will also be refuted. Hence, a doctrinal error will occur. So the qualification is introduced in order to avoid this consequence.[9]

It is countered that this justification is inadmissible, because even phenomenally, the origination of entities from themselves is not accepted by the Madhyamaka. No scriptural evidence can be adduced in support of the notion that self-origination is admitted phenomenally by the Madhyamaka. On the contrary, it is said, in the *Śālistambhasūtra*, "A sprout, the cause of which is a seed does not originate from itself, nor from another, nor from both itself and another, nor without cause, nor again from god, time, atoms, nature or own being." Similarly it is said in the *Lalitavistarasūtra*, "Dependent upon the existence of a seed, a sprout originates, however, the sprout is neither identical with the seed nor different from it. Thus, it is neither eternal nor annihilated."[10] Indeed, Nāgārjuna has also said that any entity which exists dependently, is neither identical with nor different from the entity upon which it depends.[11] Hence, it is abundantly clear that even phenomenally self-origination is not accepted.[12]

Again, it may be argued that if the qualification "ultimately" is not introduced, the phenomenal origination of entities from themselves which is admitted by the opponent will be refuted. Therefore, the qualification is expressed in consideration of the opinion held by the opponent.

It is replied that this also is unacceptable since the doctrine advocated by the opponent ought not to be admitted even phenomenally by the Madhyamaka. Indeed, non-Buddhists, like the Sāṅkhyas, do not appreciate the distinction between the two truths. Therefore, it is characteristic of the Madhyamaka philosophy to refute opposing doctrines both ultimately and phenomenally. Hence, if the qualification is introduced in consideration of the opinion held by the opponent, it is likewise unjustified.[13]

Then again, it may be argued that the qualification is introduced in order to avoid the refutation of the origination of entities from themselves which is admitted by ordinary people.

It is replied that this also is unacceptable, since ordinary people do not entertain the notions of self-origination and the like. Without entering into the consideration of the four alternatives, ordinary people simply accept that from a cause an effect originates. Indeed, though Nāgārjuna has rejected the four alternatives, even conventionally, he too has accepted only so much, that in the world an effect originates from a cause.[14]

If on the other hand the qualification "ultimately" is intended to modify the substratum, i.e., the subjective poles of consciousness, since otherwise the origination of the eye and the like, which exist phenomenally, will be refuted, then in that case the independent syllogism advanced by Bhāvaviveka will be subject to the following logical errors. The substratum of the inference will be unproven, inasmuch as Bhāvaviveka himself does not admit that the subjective poles of consciousness such as the eye and the like exist ultimately. Inasmuch as the substratum will then be unproven, the proposition, of which it is an essential component, will also be faulty. Similarly, the reason adduced, i.e., because they exist, will be invalid, since it will appertain to an unproven substratum.

It may be contended that since the phenomenal existence of the subjective poles of consciousness is admitted, the substratum of the syllogism is not unproven. Therefore, the logical errors of a faulty proposition and an invalid reason do not occur.

Then in that case, if after all, the qualification is intended to modify the negation of origination expressed by the Madhyamaka, the argument ought to have been stated in the following way. It ought to have been said that the ultimate origination of the subjective poles of consciousness, like the eye etc., which exist phenomenally is refuted. However, Bhāvaviveka's syllogism was not in fact stated in that way.[15]

The argument as it is formulated in the preceding paragraph undoubtedly expresses Bhāvaviveka's real intention. The question of whether the qualification added to the independent syllogism advanced by him is intended to modify the logical subject or the predicate of the proposition seems to have been raised by Candrakīrti merely as a rhetorical device. The fact that the question could have been raised at all, however, is evidence of a certain imprecision in Bhāvaviveka's choice of expression.

Be that as it may, the difficulties of the independent syllogism proposed by Bhāvaviveka do not arise simply from the imprecise manner in which it is expressed. If that were so, they could be overcome easily enough by merely restating the argument as indicated above. In fact, the independent syllogism advanced by Bhāvaviveka will still be defective even if it is reformulated to express more accurately his real intention.

Indeed, the Sāṅkhya does not admit the Madhyamaka conception of phenomenal existence. For him, all entities exist ultimately. Thus, the substratum of the syllogism is in this case unproven for the opponent since he does not accept that the subjective poles of consciousness exist phenomenally. Therefore, the proposition will still be faulty, inasmuch as it contains an unproven substratum, and the reason adduced will still be invalid, since it appertains to the same unreal subject.[16]

In all this, it must be remembered that in order to be valid, the substratum and major premise of an independent syllogism must be commonly accepted by both parties to a discussion. If the substratum of an inference is unproven, for either the proponent or the opponent, then the argument cannot legitimately be considered a valid independent syllogism.

Thus, if the logical subject, i.e., the subjective poles of consciousness, contained in the syllogism advanced by Bhāvaviveka is thought to exist ultimately, the substratum of the inference will be unproven for the Madhyamaka. If on the other hand, the subjective poles of consciousness are thought to exist phenomenally, the substratum of the inference will then be unproven for the Sāṅkhya. In either case, the argument produced by Bhāvaviveka does not constitute a valid independent syllogism.[17]

At this point, Bhāvaviveka and the Svātantrikas attempted the following defence of their doctrine. They contended, as it will be recalled,[18] that the terms employed in syllogisms ought to be interpreted only generally. Thus, the theories, entertained by rival schools, regarding the ultimate nature of the empirical facts utilised in inferences, ought not to be entered into. Inference, they contended, is properly concerned only with the relationships obtaining between a substratum in general and its properties in general. Otherwise, they argued, inferential argument would become impossible since no two schools are likely to agree in regard to the ultimate nature of any given empirical fact.[19]

The Svātantrikas advanced the following analogy in support of their interpretation. When for instance, they said, it is inferred that sound is impermanent, an unqualified substratum, i.e., sound, is commonly accepted in general, by both the proponent and the opponent. In this case also, if the particular theories entertained by rival schools regarding the ultimate nature of sound were to be taken into consideration, no commonly accepted substratum would exist or be possible.

Thus, if the interpretation advocated by the Buddhist Realist according to which sound is a material element dependent upon the four great elements (earth, water, fire and air) were to be admitted, the substratum would be unproven for the Vaiśeṣika. The latter on the contrary maintains that sound is a quality of space, a theory which is in its turn unacceptable to the Buddhist. Again, the Mīmāṁsaka for his part holds the view that sound is nothing but the individual manifestation of an eternal substance which is once more unacceptable, either to the Buddhist or to the Vaiśeṣika. Therefore, the Svātantrikas contended that when the impermanence of sound is inferred, the substratum is disassociated from the particular interpretations advocated by rival schools and is accepted in general by both parties to a debate.

The same practice, they maintained, ought to be adopted when the Madhyamaka undertakes to refute the notion of origination. Just as an unqualified substratum, in general, is commonly admitted by both the proponent and the opponent when the impermanence of sound is inferred, so also the subjective poles of consciousness in general ought to be admitted as an unqualified substratum when origination is refuted. In the latter case also, the Svātantrikas maintained, the substratum, i.e., the subjective poles of consciousness, ought not to be held to exist either ultimately or phenomenally by the proponent and the opponent. Thus, the subjective poles of consciousness ought to be accepted only in general by both parties to the discussion.[20]

The Prāsaṅgikas maintained that on the occasion of the determination of the nature of ultimate reality, a substratum does not exist for the Madhyamaka even phenomenally. Thus, when the origination of entities is refuted, the subjective poles of consciousness are not to be admitted either ultimately or phenomenally. Moreoever, inasmuch as for the Madhyamaka, all objects of cognition, without exception are included within the limits of the two truths, the subjective poles of consciousness are also not accepted in general.

Thus, Candrakīrti and the Prāsaṅgikas argued that this attempted defence of their doctrine by the Svātantrikas was inadmissible on two grounds. Firstly, they maintained that the interpretation advocated by the Svātantrikas was itself unacceptable. Secondly, they contended that the alleged analogy with the argument establishing the impermanence of sound did not exist.

The Prāsaṅgikas maintained that Bhāvaviveka had himself admitted that when the negation of origination is produced as the predicate of the proposition, the substatntiality or reality of the substratum, i.e., the subjective poles of consciousness, is consequently negated. Therefore, the refutation of origination dependent upon the foundation of an unreal substratum is defective and inconclusive.

Bhāvaviveka had also accepted, the Prāsaṅgikas pointed out, that the negation of origination is an expression of the perfect knowledge of ultimate reality which is altogether free from erroneous notions. As for the subjective poles of consciousness and the like, they are erroneously apprehended by the unenlightened. Hence, when considered in the light of faultless knowledge, they do not exist.[21]

Error and perfect knowledge, the Prāsaṅgikas held, are mutually incompatible. Entities, such as the subjective poles of consciousness and the like, do not then exist in reality. Their existence is mistakenly apprehended, just as hair and the like are perceived by one suffering from a defect of vision. When the nature of ultimate reality is perfectly understood, the existence of entities, which in reality do not exist, is not apprehended, just as hair and the like are not perceived by one endowed with faultless vision. Thus, inasmuch as in the light of perfect knowledge no entity or element whatsoever is apprehended, phenomenal reality is not apprehended from the standpoint of ultimate truth. As Nāgārjuna said in the *Vigrahavyāvartanī*, "If I rejected or approved anything on the basis of perception and the like, I could be blamed, but as I apprehend none of these, I cannot be accused in such a way."[22]

The considerations adduced by Candrakīrti and the Prāsaṅgikas expose the inconsistency of the interpretation advocated by the Svātantrikas. Indeed, when the nature of ultimate reality is to be determined, the Madhyamaka cannot admit even the phenomenal existence of entities. The existence of phenomenal reality is after all only acknowledged by the Madhyamaka as a pragmatic expedient in consideration of the erroneous notions commonly admitted in the world. If considered critically in the light of the perfect knowledge of ultimate truth, phenomenal reality cannot be rationally admitted. The refutation of origination reflects the Madhyamaka interpretation of the nature of ultimate reality according to which all entities which exist phenomenally, do not exist in reality. Therefore, on the occasion of the refutation of origination, the Madhyamaka cannot consistently admit the reality of entities which exist phenomenally.

Y. Kajiyama[23] has suggested that Bhāvaviveka may consistently admit the existence of entities even on the occasion of the refutation of origination. He argues that Bhāvaviveka's intention is simply to reject the notion of origination but not that of the existence of entities. This suggestion is, however, altogether unacceptable, since it has been repeatedly indicated that for the Madhyamaka, the refutation of origination and the assertion that all entities do not exist are identical in import. Indeed, it may be asked, how is it possible to hold that all entities are unoriginated, while at the same time maintaining that they exist? If entities are in fact unoriginated, i.e., if they have not come into existence, then in what manner do they exist?

As for the analogy proposed by Bhāvaviveka and the Svātantrikas, the Prāsaṅgikas contended that it does not exist. No doubt when the impermanence of sound is established, an unqualified substratum may be admitted commonly by both parties to the discussion. On that occasion, a general agreement does exist between the proponent and the opponent regarding the empirical nature of sound. Moreover, when it is inferred that sound is impermanent, the particular interpretations advocated by rival schools regarding the ultimate nature of sound need not be taken into consideration. When however the nature of ultimate reality is to be determined, no such agreement exists between the critical philosopher (niḥsvabhāvavādin) and the realist (svabhāvavādin) regarding the general nature of the subjective poles of consciousness. In this case, it is precisely the ultimate nature of the substratum, i.e., the subjective poles of consciousness, which is under consideration. Therefore, as it was explained above, on the occasion of the refutation of origination, the subjective poles of consciousness are neither admitted phenomenally, nor in general, by the Prāsaṅgikas.[24]

Bhāvaviveka, however, has retained the phenomenal subjective poles of consciousness as the substratum in his syllogism refuting the notion of self-origination. Therefore, the syllogism is still subject to the logical errors of a defective proposition, the substratum of which is unproven, and of an invalid reason which likewise appertains to an unproven substratum. These logical errors still remain, notwithstanding the attempt made by the Svātantrikas to justify the composition of their independent syllogism.

In addition, the Prāsaṅgikas maintained, the same criticism which was applied to the substratum of Bhāvaviveka's syllogism refuting self-origination is likewise applicable to the reason, i.e., because they exist, which he has adduced. Thus, if it is held that the subjective poles of consciousness do not originate from themselves because they exist ultimately, the reason will be unproven for the Madhyamaka. Alternatively, if it is maintained that the subjective poles of consciousness do not originate from themselves because they exist phenomenally, the reason adduced will be unproven for the opponent, the Sāṅkhya. Hence in either case, the argument produced by Bhāvaviveka does not constitute a valid independent syllogism. Again, existence in general is not admitted in the light of faultless knowledge.[25]

Indeed, the Prāsaṅgikas contended that this very line of argument was adopted by Bhāvaviveka himself when he undertook to criticise the following syllogism produced by a Buddhist Realist.[26] The latter has said, "The causes which give rise to the subjective poles of consciousness just exist", i.e., have a real existence, "because this has been taught by the Tathāgata. Whatsoever has been taught by the Tathāgata exists, as for example that Nirvāṇa is peace."

Bhāvaviveka responded to this argument advanced by his opponent in the following way. "What is the intention", he asked, "of the reason adduced by the opponent in this syllogism? If it is meant that the causes which give rise to the subjective poles of consciousness really exist because this was taught phenomenally by the Tathāgata, then the reason adduced is unproven for the opponent himself", i.e., the Buddhist Realist, "since he maintains that whatsoever was taught by the Tathāgata exists ultimately.[27] Alternatively, if it is meant that the causes which give rise to the subjective poles of consciousness really exist, because this was taught ultimately by the Tathāgata, then the reason adduced is unproven for the Madhyamaka."[28] As Nāgārjuna has said, "When an element does not arise from existence, non-existence, or both, how can there be an efficient cause? Thus, such a cause is not admitted."[29]

Thus, Bhāvaviveka has himself explicitly admitted that the

reason adduced in the foregoing syllogism is either inconsistent from the standpoint of the author of the argument or unproven for the opponent against whom it is directed, i.e., the Madhyamaka Bhāvaviveka. Thus, he has accepted the ultimate unreality of every logical ground. Hence, it naturally follows that all attempts to determine the nature of ultimate reality by means of independent syllogisms must necessarily be rejected, because in all such cases reasons are adduced which are ultimately unreal in the opinion of the Madhyamaka.

The foregoing criticism applies equally to all the other cases in which independent syllogisms are produced by Bhāvaviveka, such as when he undertakes to refute the origination of entities from entities which are other to them. In all these cases the substratum and the reason produced by Bhāvaviveka are, if thought to exist ultimately, unproven for the author of the syllogism himself and if thought to exist phenomenally, unproven for the opponent. In general, they are not admitted in the light of faultless knowledge.

The fault which Bhāvaviveka detected in the syllogism cited above, advanced by the Buddhist Realist, applies equally to the independent syllogisms produced by himself. The logical subject and major premise contained in all such syllogisms are not established commonly by valid instruments of cognition for both the proponent and the opponent. Hence, the arguments do not constitute valid independent syllogisms.

For instance, Bhāvaviveka has produced the following argument against the notion of origination from another. Ultimately, the subjective poles of consciousness do not originate from causes which are other to them, because they are other, as for example in the case of a jar, the causes of which, such as clay and the like, are other to the jar. The substratum and the reason produced in this syllogism may be analysed as before. It will thus become apparent that in this case also, the substratum and the reason do not exist commonly for both the proponent and the opponent.[30]

Here again, if the substratum and the reason are thought to exist ultimately, they will be unproven for the author of the syllogism himself. Alternatively, if they are thought to exist phenomenally, they will be unproven for the opponent. In general, they are unacceptable in the light of faultless knowledge.

Finally, the existence of the subjective poles of consciousness was adduced as the reason by Bhāvaviveka in his syllogism refuting self-origination. The reason which was adduced will not necessarily accomplish the negation of the origination from themselves of the objective poles of consciousness, such as a jar and the like. The reason is therefore uncertain (anekāntika) from the standpoint of the opponent, the Sāṅkhya, since it applies equally to dissimilar objects.

The Sāṅkhya system indeed admits two varieties of existence, the changeless existence of the subject, i.e., spirit, and the changing existence of the object, i.e., matter, exemplified by the existence of jars and the like. The subjective poles of consciousness, the substratum of Bhāvaviveka's syllogism against self-origination, possess a double nature for the Sāṅkhya system. They are in themselves material, while at the same time, they reflect the changeless existence of the subject, i.e., spirit. Hence, the reason adduced by Bhāvaviveka, i.e., because the subjective poles of consciousness exist, is uncertain from the standpoint of the opponent against whom the syllogism is directed.[31]

At this point it may be objected that the criticism advanced against the independent syllogism produced by Bhāvaviveka will apply equally to the arguments employed by the Prāsaṅgikas. Thus, as it has been indicated, the substratum and the reason contained in the arguments produced by the Prāsaṅgikas will likewise not exist commonly for both the proponent and the opponent. Hence, inasmuch as the errors described also occur in the arguments produced by the Prāsaṅgika, the criticism levelled against the independent syllogisms advanced by Bhāvaviveka is unjustified.

The Prāsaṅgikas replied that the errors uncovered in the independent syllogisms advanced by Bhāvaviveka do not in fact occur in the case of their own arguments. On the contrary, the above criticisms apply only to those who like Bhāvaviveka, though they accept the Madhyamaka philosophy, nonetheless produce independent syllogisms.

Though it is undoubtedly true, the Prāsaṅgikas contended, that in the case of an independent syllogism the substratum and the reason must necessarily exist commonly for both the proponent and the opponent, the Prāsaṅgikas for their part do not produce independent syllogisms. The critical arguments employed by the Prāsaṅgikas are designed to expose the inconsistency inherent in the position advocated by the opponent through the *reductio ad absurdum*. In the case of an argument *ad absurdum*, it is sufficient if the minor premise and the major premise are accepted by the opponent alone. For example, the opponent holds that the sense of vision perceives external objects. He has also admitted that the sense of vision does not possess the capacity to perceive itself. In addition, he has accepted the invariable concomitance of the capacity to perceive oneself with the capacity to perceive other objects.

In this case it is said, the sense of vision does not perceive external objects, because it does not possess the capacity to perceive itself. Whatsoever does not possess the capacity of self-perception also does not possess the capacity to perceive external objects, as for example a jar.

The minor premise, i.e., the sense of vision does not possess the capacity of self-perception, and the major premise, i.e., whatsoever does not possess the capacity of self-perception also does not possess the capacity to perceive external objects, are accepted by the opponent. Thus, the proposition that the sense of vision perceives external objects advocated by the opponent is refuted through an inference which is acceptable to the opponent alone.[32]

Finally, it may be asked if there exists any effectiveness in an inference which is admitted by only one party. This is a significant question because it had come to be generally accepted by logicians, including Diṅnāga, that an inference which was admitted by only one of the participants in a debate was subject to doubt.[33] They contended that only if an argument is commonly accepted by both parties can it result in a certain conclusion. Moreover, it was argued, that an argument which is accepted by the opponent alone is invalid, inasmuch as it is precisely the opinion of the opponent which the argument is intended to reject.

Candrakīrti and the Prāsaṅgikas replied that it is, after all, the concern of logic to reflect the practices commonly followed in the world. Hence, the imposition of formal criteria of the acceptability of arguments is to no avail. They maintained that, there are indeed, many instances in which an argument accepted by only one party results in a definitive conclusion. It often happens, in common practice, that a judge is appointed to arbitrate a dispute between a plaintiff and a defendant. In such cases, it is the opinion of the arbitrator alone which determines victory and defeat. Then also, it sometimes happens that the statement of only one of the parties to a dispute results in victory and defeat. Again, in the case of disputes concerning scriptural authority, the defeat of the opponent need not be accomplished on the basis of scriptures accepted by both parties. In fact the defeat of the opponent may also be accomplished on the basis of scriptures accepted by him alone. Moreover, in inference for onself (svārthānumāna), it is knowledge acquired by one party alone which prevails. Thus, Candrakīrti and the Prāsaṅgikas concluded, it cannot be categorically maintained that an argument must necessarily be accepted by both parties to a discussion in order to accomplish its objective.[34]

In conclusion, it may be suggested that the question of the nature of the substratum or logical subject constitutes the fundamental issue around which the controversy over the ultimate acceptability of the independent syllogism centred. It is, indeed, upon the substratum that the validity of the reason as well as the proposition depends. Hence, it is not surprising that this question should have been discussed at such length by the Prāsaṅgikas and the Svātantrikas.

Candrakīrti and the Prāsaṅgikas, as it has been seen, maintained that on the occasion of the examination of the nature of ultimate reality, the existence of a substratum is not admitted even phenomenally by the Madhyamaka. Nor, according to the Prāsaṅgikas, can the existence of a substratum be admitted in general when the ultimate truth was in question, because to do so would be incompatible with the faultless knowledge of ultimate reality, which the arguments of the Madhyamaka are intended to communicate.

For their part, Bhāvaviveka and the Svātantrikas contended that the existence of an unqualified substratum ought to be admitted by the Madhyamaka, even on the occasion of the determination of the nature of ultimate reality. They held that the data of ordinary experience is commonly given to all. Hence, a simple substratum ought to be uncritically admitted by the Madhyamaka in conformity with the commonly accepted conceptions regarding the nature of inference.

Be that as it may, it is evident that the validity of independent syllogisms on the occasion of the determination of the nature of ultimate reality is open to serious question. The independent syllogisms advanced by Bhāvaviveka indeed contain terms which reflect mutually opposed orders of reality. The predicate of the syllogisms, i.e., the negation of origination admittedly belongs to the level of ultimate reality, while the substratum and reason belong to the level of empirical reality. The difficulties of establishing a relationship of invariable concomitance, between a reason or probans which reflects empirical reality and a probandum which reflects ultimate reality, appear to be insurmountable.

The Svātantrika system represents an attempt to synthesise the Madhyamaka philosophy with the tenets of formal or objective logic. The school was ontologically critical, but epistemologically realistic. Thus, like most synthetic formulations attempted in philosophy, the Svātantrika doctrine was liable to be considered inconsistent. While the school attempted to satisfy the requisites of both the Madhyamaka philosophy on the one hand and of formal logic on the other, it in fact succeeded in accomplishing neither of these objectives. As a result the Svātantrika system was open to criticism both from the standpoint of the Madhyamka philosophy and from that of formal logic.

References

1. *dBu-ma-spyi-ston*, p. 348.
2. *Ibid.*
3. *Catuḥśataka*, XVI. 24 quoted in the *dBu-ma-spyin-ston*, p. 348 and in the *Madhyamakālaṁkārakārikā*, verse 68.
4. *Vigrahavyāvartanī*, Stanza 29.
5. *dBu-ma spyi-ston*, pp. 348-349.
6. *Ibid.* pp. 356-357.
7. *Ibid.* p. 357.
8. *Ibid.*
9. *Ibid.* p. 358.
10. Stcherbatsky, Th., *The Conception of Buddhist Nirvāṇa*, p. 157.
11. *Mūlamadhyamakakārikā*, XVIII.10.
12. *dBu-ma spyi-ston*, p. 358.
13. *Ibid.*
14. *Ibid.*
15. *Ibid.* pp. 358-359.
16. *Ibid.* p. 359.
17. *Ibid.*

18. See Chapter VI.
19. *Op.cit.*
20. *dBu-ma-spyi-ston*, pp. 359-360.
21. *Ibid.* p. 360.
22. *Vigrahavyāvartanī*, Stanza 30.
23. Kajiyama, Y., *Bhāvaviveka and The Prāsaṅgika School*, p. 316, in Mookerjee, Satkari (ed.), The Nava-Nalanda-Mahavihara Research Publication, Vol. 1.
24. *dBu-ma spyi-ston*, p. 360.
25. *Ibid.*
26. An adherent of the Ābhidharmika philosophy.
27. Professor Stcherbatsky renders the foregoing sentence as follows: "If it is taken in the phenomenal sense, the reason has (*eo ipso*) no ultimate reality for Buddhist himself." *The Conception of Buddhist Nirvāṇa*, p. 167. However bSod-nams-Sen-ge's commentary clearly shows that the reference is here not to Buddha but rather to the opponent.
28. *dBu-ma-spyi-ston*, pp. 360-361.
29. *Mūlamadhyamakakārikā*, I. 7.
30. *Op.cit.* p. 361.
31. *dBu-ma-spyi-ston*, p. 362.
32. *Ibid.* pp. 362-363.
33. See Chapter VI.
34. *dbu-ma-spyi-ston*, p. 363.

Chapter XIV

THE REFUTATION OF THE SECOND ALTERNATIVE

As it was indicated in Chapter XI, the first alternative expresses an uncritical affirmation of the notions of identity, substantiality and permanence. The second alternative, on the contrary, expresses a semicritical philosophical attitude which while it rejects identity, substantiality and permanence, affirms difference, properties (dharmas) and impermanence. For the former, universal identity constitutes reality while for the latter, it is the particular and the discrete which alone is real. The two philosophical attitudes expressed in the two alternatives thus explain reality from mutually opposed standpoints.

As it has already been shown, the philosophical attitude represented by the first alternative found its expression in Indian philosophy in the doctrines of the Sāṅkhya and the Vedānta. The attitude expressed by the second alternative, on the other hand, was elaborately developed within Buddhist philosophy among the schools of the Ābhidharmika. While the Sāṅkhya and the Vedānta sought to explain reality in terms of an exclusive conceptual pattern of identity and permanence, the Buddhist Realists explained it exclusively in terms of difference and impermanence.

It was left to the critical philosopher, the Madhyamaka, to expose through dialectical analysis, the untenability of these attempts to explain reality by means of an exclusive conceptual pattern.

In the area of the interpretation of the nature of the causal relationship, the first alternative, as it has been shown, emphasises the continuity which is felt to exist between cause and effect. Its conclusion is expressed in the affirmation of the ultimate identity of cause and effect. The second alternative on the contrary interprets the cause and effect to represent different entities. It emphasises the emergent character of the effect and asserts the ultimate difference of cause and effect. Thus, while the Sāṅkhya system maintains that the cause and effect are substantially identical, the latter pre-existing in the former, the Buddhist Realists maintain that the cause and effect are different. Thus, the Buddhist Realists advocate the doctrine of origination from another, i.e., that entities originate from entities which are other to them.

The schools of Buddhist Realists including the Vaibhāṣikas, Sautrāntika and Vijñānavāda advocate the doctrine of origination from another (parata utpattiḥ). In addition, the Svātantrika school, while it refuted the ultimate origination of entities from any of the four alternatives in conformity with the Madhyamaka philosophy, accepted conventionally the doctrine of origination from another advocated by the Buddhist Realists.[1] The Prāsaṅgikas, however, refused to admit origination from another even conventionally and so Candrakīrti and his successors also undertook to refute the conventional origination from another accepted by the Svātantrikas.

In refuting the doctrine of origination from another advocated by the Buddhist Realists, Nāgārjuna has referred to four conditions (pratyaya), other to the effect, from which the latter is thought to originate. The four conditions which appear to have been drawn from the Ābhidharmika philosophy are: one—primary or material cause (hetu-pratyaya), two—objective condition (ālambana-pratyaya), three—sequential condition (samanantara-pratyaya) and four—dominant condition (adhipati-pratyaya). The four conditions, just indicated, are in general admitted by all the schools of Buddhist Realists.

The precise signification to be assigned to each of the conditions, however, is difficult to ascertain definitely. The first (hetu-pratyaya) clearly enough corresponds, by and large, to what is normally understood by the term material cause. It is the cause which directly produces the effect (nirvarttaka-hetuḥ) as in the case of the seed which is the material cause of the sprout. The second of the four conditions (ālambana-pratyaya) seems to obtain only in the case of the production of mental events. It is the object which functions as the cause in the production of knowledge. The third condition (samanantara-pratyaya) also appears to pertain primarily to the production of mental events. In this primary sense, it may be taken to refer to the extinction of the immediately preceding moment of consciousness which engenders the succeeding mental state. Alternatively, the sequential condition may refer to the immediately preceding extinction of a cause, like a seed, which allows for the emergence of the sprout, i.e., the effect. The fourth condition (adhipati-pratyaya) refers to the indirect influence which any entity exercises upon all other entities excluding itself. The dominant condition (adhipati-pratyaya) is, thus, the most inclusive of the four conditions mentioned. The Madhyamaka criticism applicable to the four conditions taken individually need not be gone into. They are mentioned here only with a view to familiarize the reader with the particulars of the causal theory advocated by the Buddhist Realists.[2]

A number of other heterogeneous causes asserted by non-Buddhists such as: god, nature, time and the like are not admitted by Buddhists of any school. They are regarded as equivalent to non-causes since they cannot account for the variety determination and regularity of phenomena.[3]

Nāgārjuna has criticised the doctrine of origination from another in the *Mūlamadhyamakakārikā*, as well as in the *Śūnyatāsaptati* and other works. A number of arguments against origination from another, suggested by Nāgārjuna, have already been considered in chapter X. Nāgārjuna's criticism of the doctrine of origination from another proceeds along two general lines. Firstly, he contends that inasmuch as all entities are devoid of self-existence, they do not exist in reality. Therefore, it is inadmissible to hold that entities which do not really exist could function as the causes of other entities. Again, inasmuch as the effect also does not exist in reality, it cannot be maintained that it has originated from conditions. Secondly, Nāgārjuna argues that if the cause and effect are taken to be different entities, as is entailed by the doctrine of origination from another, then inasmuch as the cause and effect are totally disassociated, they cannot be related to each other as cause and effect since relationship presupposes some sort of co-presence. Therefore, causality on this hypothesis is impossible. Moreover, if the effect is thought not to exist in the cause, its emergence from the latter is inconceivable. Oddly enough, subsequent commentators seem to have left the first contention advanced by Nāgārjuna largely unexplicated and have concentrated upon the elucidation of the latter argument.

In the *Mūlamadhyamakakārikā*, Nāgārjuna expresses the first criticism outlined above in the following way. He writes, "In these conditions (i.e. hetu-pratyaya, ālambana-pratyaya, samanantara-pratyaya and adhipati-pratyaya) the self-existence of entities does not exist. Since self-existence does not exist, other existence (parabhava) also does not exist."[4] Here, the term other existence (parabhava) can be taken to refer to the existence of an entity which is thought to exist or to originate dependent upon other entities. Inasmuch as the self-existence, i.e., the real existence, of entities is not admitted, so also the real existence of entities which exist dependent upon other entities, which are equally unreal, is not admitted.[5]

Nāgārjuna has also said in the *Śūnyatāsaptati*, "How can what is not established in its own being produce another? Thus another condition which is not established is not what causes the origination (of another)."[6] The point at issue may be further elucidated by the following passages from the *Śūnyatāsaptati*.

Nāgārjuna, is on this occasion, engaged in the examination of the existential status of form (rūpa) which the Ābhidharmika philosophy believes to originate from the four great elements which are other to form. He writes, "If form were originated from the great elements, form would originate from an imperfect (cause); it is not (originated) from its own actuality, since that is non-existent, it is not (originated) from another. If it is held that form originates from the great elements, (then) if it were so, form would originate from an imperfect (cause). "From an imperfect (cause)" is explained as from an insubstantial (cause). Similarly, form is not (originated) from its own-actuality...So it is, it (form) is not (originated) from its own-actuality, but it is (originated) from another, because the great elements are other than it......"Since that is non-existent, it is not (originated) from another." That form is not (originated) from another... Since it is non-existent, that other is non-existent. Thus, since it is not established in its own actuality, the so called (origination) from another is not justified, because that which is non-existent cannot justly be called (originated) from (that which is) other than it. What is called other than the non-existent is not existent."[7] Thus, inasmuch as no entity is admitted to exist in reality it cannot be maintained that entities originate from entities which are other to them because neither the entity which is thought to originate nor the entity from which it is said to originate exist.

Again, Nāgārjuna has said that conditions cannot legitimately be thought to pertain to non-existence, since if the effect itself does not exist, the notion of causal conditions is not obtained.[8] Conditions cannot exist disassociated from an effect. Again, the effect cannot exist disassociated from conditions.[9] Thus, if cause and effect are thought to be totally different, then in that case, neither cause nor effect are intelligible.

Again, Nāgārjuna has said, "If the effect arises out of an assembly of causes and conditions and does not exist within such an assembly, how does it come about within such an assembly."[10] Thus, if the effect does not exist within the assembly of causes and conditions, its origination through such an assembly is inconceivable. Moreover, if the effect does not exist within the assembly of causes and conditions then the causes and conditions will be equal to non-causes and non-conditions.[11] That is to say, if the effect is not in some way present within the assembly of causes and conditions, the latter cannot be in any way related to the former. Therefore, inasmuch as the causes and conditions will in that case be unrelated to the effect, they will be equal to non-causes.

Again the Ābhidharmika philosophy holds that the effect originates only after the cause is extinguished.[12] In that case however the cause and effect will be temporally disassociated. Nāgārjuna has said that if the cause gives rise to the effect after the cause has been extinguished, then the effect which originates subsequent to the extinction of the cause will originate without a cause.[13] Indeed, if the effect originates subsequent to the extinction of the cause, it follows that the cause will not exist at the time when the effect originates. Therefore, the origination of the effect will take place in the absence of an existent cause.

The notion that the cause and effect represent different entities separated in time entails the denial of any conjunction between the cause and effect. However, Nāgārjuna has said that without existing in conjunction with the cause the effect cannot originate from the former. If the two, i.e., cause and effect, are not conjoined, then it follows that cause and effect will be disassociated—a condition which entails the negation of the causal relationship.[14] Indeed, again if the cause and effect are different, then the cause will be equal to a non-cause.[15]

Nāgārjuna's criticism of causes and conditions absolutely different from the effect is summed up in the following way. He writes that there is no effect created either from an assembly or a non-assembly of causes and conditions. Separated from the effect, where indeed is the assembly of causes and conditions ?[16] Here again, the argument seeks to indicate the unintelligibility of causes and conditions absolutely different from an effect. If cause and effect are indeed different, it follows that no relation is possible between them. This, in turn, renders the concept of causality impossible.

Thereafter, Buddhapālita advanced the following argument against origination from another. He contended that entities do not originate from other entities which are different from them, since in that case everything would originate from anything. Thus, if indeed the cause and effect are absolutely different, any effect could originate from any cause inasmuch as the necessary relationship between cause and effect will then be severed. In that case, determinate causality would be impossible, since difference or otherness obtains equally with respect to all entities without exception. Thus, Buddhapālita's argument lays stress on the fact that the absolute difference of cause and effect advocated by the Buddhist Realists entails the equivalence of causes and non-causes. As it was shown, Nāgārjuna also made this point.[17]

Bhāvaviveka assailed the argument advanced by Buddhapālita on already familiar grounds. He argued that since the argument is a mere *reductio ad absurdum*, it necessarily implies an affirmation to the contrary. Thus, if the positive counterparts of the predicate and the reason adduced are taken into account, it will follow that entities originate from themselves, or from both themselves and others, or without cause, since particular entities have particular causes. This, Bhāvaviveka contended, will contradict the previously established point, i.e., that entities do not originate from themselves. Therefore, he concluded, Buddhapālita's argument fails to establish what is intended and is thus irrelevant.

The Prāsaṅgikas replied that Buddhapālita's argument was not at all irrelevant. It had already been conclusively shown, they contended, that an argument *ad absurdum* does not at all imply any affirmation to the contrary. Therefore, Bhāvaviveka's contention that Buddhapālita's argument against origination from another implicitly contradicts the negation of self-origination, expressed earlier, is out of place. The Prāsaṅgikas did not consider it necessary to reply in detail to this accusation of Bhāvaviveka, inasmuch as its refutation had already been conclusively accomplished, on the occasion of the consideration of the arguments against self-origination.[18]

Bhāvaviveka advanced an independent syllogism of his own against the doctrine of origination from another as it was shown in the foregoing chapter. Inasmuch as it was considered there, it does not seem necessary to deal with it again at this point. It suffices to say that the syllogism does not differ formally from that advanced by Bhāvaviveka against the notion of self-origination. Moreover, as it was indicated, his syllogism refuting origination from another is subject to the same difficulties which afflict the independent syllogism refuting self-origination.

Candrakīrti and the Prāsaṅgikas thereafter turned their attention to the refutation of the doctrine of origination from another both ultimately and conventionally. Their criticism of ultimate origination from another is directed against the schools of Buddhist Realists, while their subsequent criticism of conventional origination from another is directed against the Svātantrika school. The Prāsaṅgikas refuted the ultimate origination of entities from entities other to them through arguments *ad absurdum* and through analysis.

Their refutation of the doctrine of origination from another through arguments *ad absurdum* may be divided into the simple statement of the *reductio ad absurdum* and the refutation of the counter arguments which the opponent may advance in defence of his doctrine.

Thus, it is said that if origination occurs from another, then origination will take place from non-causes as well as from causes, because otherness to the effect is equally present in both. In that case an effect like a sprout will be as likely to originate from fire and coal, as from a seed, since all are equally other to the effect.[19] Again, as Candrakīrti said in the *Madhyamakāvatāra*, if dependent upon another, any other entity originates, then from fire darkness will originate.[20]

The opponent may contend that nonetheless the doctrine of origination from another is acceptable since an effect like a sprout originates only from its own cause, not from what is a non-cause. In that case, it may be asked: what differentiates cause from non-cause inasmuch as both causes and non-causes are equally other to the effect? The opponent maintains that though seed, fire and coal are all equally different from a sprout, the latter originates from a seed but not from fire and coal. He is, therefore, obliged to state the ground of distinction which enables him to differentiate cause from non-cause.

In support of his position, the opponent may put forward the following grounds of distinction. He may contend that a sprout originates from a seed, but not from fire and coal because this is what is attested to in experience. Again, he may hold that the sprout originates from the seed, but not from fire and coal because the one possesses the power to produce the sprout while the latter do not. Again, the opponent may argue that the sprout originates from the one but not from the others because of the nature (dharmatā) of the entities concerned.[21]

All of these grounds are summarily rejected by the Madhyamaka. If it is held that a sprout originates from its cause, i.e., a seed, but not from fire and coal because this is proven through direct perception, it is no real answer. The Madhyamaka replies that though it may appear so to the deluded intellect, and may, therefore, be uncritically accepted, if examined ultimately, direct perception is not admitted. Though entities may appear to originate, their origination is ultimately not established. All that has been said in the *Vigrahavyāvartanī* regarding the ultimate unacceptability of valid instruments of cognition including perception is applicable on this occasion. Moreover, while entities may be believed to exist in reality by the opponent the Madhyamaka holds that if examined critically, they are found to be in no way different from dream and illusion.

Again, the supposed power which entities are said to possess as well as the nature of entities are not admitted by the Madhyamaka to constitute legitimate grounds of distinction between causes and non-causes in which otherness, to the effect, is equally present. When they are examined critically the power which entities are supposed to possess, as well as their individual nature, are rejected. The so called power of entities is refuted, when examined through the three temporal categories. Similarly, the individual nature of entities cannot be ultimately established through any valid logical ground. Therefore, the doctrine of origination from another remains subject to the inconsistency, which was brought out above through the *reductio ad absurdum*, notwithstanding the attempts made by the opponent to vindicate his position.[22]

At this point, the Buddhist Realist may raise the following objection against the negation of origination expressed by the Madhyamaka. He may argue that if indeed origination is to be rejected, then the effects of actions also will fail to originate. In that case, the certainty of the moral law, i.e., the law of Karma which is central to Buddhist religion will be destroyed. This fundamental objection against the standpoint of the Madhyamaka has already been encountered on other occasions such as in the *Vigrahavyāvartanī*. In the *Vigrahavyāvartanī* the opponent raised the objection that the negation of the real existence of entities entailed the denial of actions and their effects. On this occasion, it is contended that the negation of origination from another has similar consequences. Hence, it is argued that according to the view expressed by the Madhyamaka the infallibility of the consequences of virtuous and non-virtuous actions which were taught by the Buddha will be denied.

For the Madhyamaka, however, even that which appears phenomenally is found not to exist when it is examined critically. When they are not examined critically, actions and their effects just appear with regularity to the deluded intellect. Therefore, actions and their effects are taught with certainty by the Madhyamaka from the pre-critical standpoint. The infallibility of the law of karma, therefore, remains uneffected by the critical negation of origination.

Indeed, even phenomenal reality is not critically accepted by the Madhyamaka. Actions and their effects do not exist when they are examined critically. Nonetheless, they are said to exist for the sake of the fruits of spiritual discipline because they are accepted by the world. Therefore, actions and their effects are taught to exist.[23]

According to the Madhyamaka phenomenal reality has no rational justification. Relative to causes, phenomena simply appear to the intellect conditioned by habitual ignorance and delusion. The regular succession of actions and their effects holds good so long as ignorance of the ultimate truth persists. The infallibility of the law of karma is thus guaranteed by the existential condition of the phenomenal world which subsists through common delusion. Karma cannot be justified rationally, nor is it admitted to exist when it is examined critically.

Again, origination from another is refuted analytically by the Madhyamaka. Thus, it is said that if an effect originates from a cause which is other to it, it can do so either from an extinguished cause, or from an unextinguished cause. If it is held that an effect originates from an extinguished cause, i.e., the position of the Buddhist Realists, then the effect will come into existence without a cause, since on the occasion of the origination of the effect, the cause will not exist. If on the other hand it is held that the effect originates from an unextinguished cause, then the cause and effect will exist simultaneously. The latter position, in fact, belongs properly to the doctrine of self-origination and is mentioned here only for the sake of analytical completeness.[24]

The Buddhist Realists, in fact, hold that in order for the effect to originate, the cause must first cease to exist. Thus according to their doctrine, the cause and effect belong to different moments of time. The cause and effect are, therefore, unrelated, since relationship necessarily pre-supposes the co-presence of the related entities which is in this case absent.

The Buddhist Realist may attempt to overcome the problem posed by the disassociation of the cause and effect by postulating an activity (kriyā) which is initiated by the cause and which in turn gives rise to the origination of the effect. This postulated activity, however, is unintelligible, because it cannot be admitted to belong either to the cause or to the effect. The postulated activity is unintelligible unless it can be shown to pertain to an entity or agent.[25]

The activity cannot belong to the effect, for in that case it would be altogether superfluous inasmuch as the effect already exists independent of the activity. Neither can the activity be thought to belong to the cause, since according to the opponent, the cause is supposed to cease to exist before the origination of the effect. Nor can the activity be thought to exist at the moment when the effect originates, i.e., in the process of the origination of the effect, because apart from the preceding and succeeding moments, no intermediate moment is admitted.

The postulation of an entity which is in the process of origination involves the assertion of mutually contradictory predicates of a single entity. Thus, Nāgārjuna wrote in the *Śūnyatāsaptati*,

"The originated is not the (entity) which is to be originated; the non-originated is also not the (entity) which is to be originated; the (entity) which is in the process of origination is also not the (entity) which is to be originated, since it would (then) be originated and not originated."[26] Thus, the notion of an intermediate moment, when the entity which is the effect might be said to originate or to be in the process of origination, is rejected because no entity can be thought to be at once partly originated and partly unoriginated. Therefore, the activity postulated by the Buddhist Realist far from overcoming the difficulties entailed by origination from another, only serves to complicate them.

Again, if the effect is thought to originate from a cause which is other to it, it may be asked if the effect originates through conjunction with the cause or without conjunction with it. If it is held that the effect originates through conjunction with the cause, then the cause and effect will exist together. Alternatively, if the effect is believed to originate without conjunction with the cause, then the effect will come into existence without any relation to the cause. In this case also, the first alternative presented is rightly applicable only to the doctrine of self-origination. The second alternative expresses a situation compatible with the position maintained by the Buddhist Realists. If however, it is to be admitted that the effect originates without conjunction with the cause, causality is once more unintelligible.[27]

Moreover, if the effect does not exist in the cause, as the Buddhist Realists maintain, its origination from the latter is unintelligible. A non-existent entity, indeed, cannot originate, since it, inasmuch as it does not exist, is devoid of activity and devoid of efficiency. No conceivable combination of causes and conditions can bring about the existence of an entity which by its very nature does not exist.[28]

The doctrine of origination from another advocated by the Buddhist Realists is therefore as untenable as the doctrine of self-origination advocated by the Sāṅkhya. If on the first alternative, causality is impossible, it is equally impossible if the cause and effect are thought to be absolutely different. According to the position favoured by the Buddhist Realists, the cause and effect are never obtained together. The effect does not exist on the occasion of the cause, nor does the cause exist on the occasion of the effect. The former cease to exist before the latter originates. Therefore, cause and effect remain ultimately disassociated, hence the former cannot be the cause of the latter. If on the first alternative, the notion of the identity of cause and effect leads to the vacuity of the relative concepts of cause and effect, so also on the second alternative, the notion of their ultimate difference, similarly results in the vacuity of the concepts involved.

Finally, as it was mentioned earlier in this chapter, the Svātantrika school accepted the notion of origination from another conventionally. The Prāsaṅgikas, on the contrary, did not accept origination from another even conventionally. They held that conventionally, only origination is admissible. According to the Prāsaṅgikas none of the four alternatives is to be accepted either ultimately or conventionally. They held that any attempt to describe the relation between cause and effect even conventionally as one of identity or difference was unjustified. Conventionally, the Prāsaṅgikas argued, it can only be said that from a cause, an effect originates. This distinction, according to bSod-nams Sen-ge, constitutes the primary ontological difference between the Prāsaṅgika and the Svātantrika schools.

The Prāsaṅgikas contended that even ordinary people do not accept origination from another. Ordinary people, they argued, admit only that an effect originates from a cause. They do not in the least understand the cause and effect to be different objects. Thus, common people plant the seed of a son, and thereafter, when they observe the birth of the son, they conclude that the son has been produced by them. In the same way they plant the seed of a tree, and thereafter, when they observe the growth of the tree, they maintain that it was planted by them.

It may be objected that if this interpretation is to be accepted, self-origination will be approved by common convention. However, this conclusion does not follow. If ordinary people are asked whether the seed previously planted by them is identical with the effect; i.e., the tree, they will reply that it is not. They will maintain that previously they planted the seed of a tree and that as a result of it the tree which exists at present has sprung up. Common people assert only so much. Therefore, the Prāsaṅgikas concluded, even conventionally, cause and effect cannot be said to be either identical or different.[29]

REFERENCES

1. *dBu-ma-spyi-ston*, p. 363.
2. Murti T. R. V., *The Central Philosophy of Buddhism*, pp. 170-172.
3. *Ibid.* p. 172.
4. *Mūlamadhyamakakārikā*, I.2.
5. *Ibid.* I.13, XX.23.
6. *Śūnyatāsaptati*, Stanza 12.
7. *Ibid.* Stanza 45 and commentary; see also *Mūlamadhyamakakārikā*, I. 11.
8. *Mūlamadhyamakakārikā*, I.6.
9. *Ibid.* I.11.
10. *Ibid.* XX.2.
11. *Ibid.* XX.4.
12. *Ibid.* I.9.
13. *Ibid.* XX.6.
14. *Ibid.* XX.15.
15. *Ibid.* XX.20.
16. *Ibid.* XX.24.
17. *dBu-ma spyi-ston*, p. 371.
18. *Ibid.* p. 372.
19. *Ibid.* p. 364.
20. *Ibid.* p. 367.
21. *Ibid.* p. 365.
22. *Ibid.* pp. 365-366.
23. *Ibid.* p. 366.
24. *Ibid.* p. 368.
25. *Ibid.* p. 368.
26. *Śūnyatāsaptati*, Stanza 5 and commentary.
27. *dBu-ma spyi-ston*, p. 368.
28. *Ibid.*
29. *Ibid.* p. 369.

CHAPTER XV

THE REFUTATION OF THE THIRD ALTERNATIVE

As it has been shown, the first and second alternatives present one sided interpretations of reality in general and of causality. The third alternative represents an attempt at a synthetic interpretation. It reflects a certain awareness of the inadequacy of the explanations offered by the first and second alternatives. The third alternative seeks to overcome the difficulties of interpreting reality in terms of a single conceptual pattern through admitting, at the same time, both of the primary alternatives.

However, as it has already been pointed out in another place, synthetic formulations in philosophy are liable to be considered contradictory. In addition, the simple conjunctive affirmation of the two primary alternatives expressed by the third alternative does not succeed in avoiding the objections which were reaised by the Madhyamaka against the two primary alternatives taken separately. Therefore, the synthetic alternative, like the two primary alternatives, fails to provide a coherent explanation of reality.

In Indian philosophy, the Jaina system constitutes the clearest example of the synthetic philosophical attitude. The Jaina system, indeed, applied a synthetic solution to virtually all the problems of philosophy. It stands midway between the philosophical attitudes expressed in the doctrines of the Brahmanical schools, particularly the Vedānta and that embodied in the doctrines of the Ābhidharmika schools within the Buddhist tradition. Not surprisingly, the Jaina philosophy, which attempted a synthesis of the mutually opposed attitudes developed in these two conflicting traditions, found favour with neither the Brahmins nor the Buddhists.

With regard to the interpretation of causality, the third alternative seeks to escape the exclusiveness of the notions that cause and effect must be either identical or different, through affirming that cause and effect are both identical and different. This synthetic position was in fact advocated by the Jaina philosophy, and it is with reference to the Jaina doctrine that the third alternative, isolated through the dialectical analysis of the Madhyamaka, is usually interpreted.

The Jaina system supported their contention that cause and effect are both identical and different, i.e., that entities originate both from themselves and others, through examples like the following one. They argued that for instance in the case of the production of a gold ring, cause and effect are both identical and different. Inasmuch as the gold ring is produced from gold, it is produced from itself, i.e., cause and effect are identical. Nonetheless, they maintained, inasmuch as causes like an artisan and heat are also required for the production of the effect, i.e., the gold ring, it is produced from another, i.e., cause and effect are different. Therefore, just as in the example just cited, the causal relation is one of both identity and difference.[1]

While the Jaina philosopher is most commonly thought to be the opponent against whom the Madhyamaka refutation of the third alternative is directed, bSod-names Sen-ge's account indicates that there may well have been another system against which the arguments of the later Madhyamakas at least also could have been directed. He says that those who uphold the reality of primordial matter (pradhāna) as well as that of God (Īśvara) advocate the doctrine that cause and effect are both identical and different. They maintain, he says, that inasmuch as entities originate from primordial matter, they originate from themselves, i.e., cause and effect are identical. However, inasmuch as entities are created by God, they originate from another, i.e., cause and effect are different. Therefore, they maintain that the refutation of self-origination and that of origination from another does not affect their position, since origination from self alone and origination from another alone are not admitted by them.[2]

The question of precisely who those who uphold the reality of primordial matter as well as that of God might have been is an interesting one. While almost all the Brahmanical systems accept God (Īśvara) in one form or other, the doctrine of primordial matter (pradhāna) is particularly associated with the Sāṅkhya system. The Sāṅkhya, however, at least in its classical formulation, did not on any occasion admit origination from both self and another. Indeed, as it has been shown, the doctrine, of the identity of cause and effect belongs unquestionably to the Sāṅkhya system.

The only plausible solution to the problem which immediately suggests itself is that bSod-nams Sen-ge's reference to those who uphold the reality of primordial matter as well as that of God is an allusion to a theistic phase of the Sāṅkhya. This would explain the school's advocacy of the reality of primordial matter and self-origination while at the same time allow for the importance accorded to God in the area of causality and the acceptance of origination from another.

Inasmuch as the detailed investigation of this question lies outside the scope of this present study, no attempt has been made to identify the school to which bSod-nams Sen-ge has referred definitively or to explore its origins and development. Nonetheless, the inclusion of the school in the account given by bSod-nams Sen-ge seems to indicate that the school achieved sufficient importance to receive individual consideration by the later exponents of the Madhyamaka system.

Many of the stanzas of Nāgārjuna's *Mūlamadhyamakakārikā* which deal with the problem of causality contain references to the third alternative. Indeed, the third alternative is often mentioned even when the fourth alternative is omitted. The following examples may be cited.

Nāgārjuna has said, "When an element does not arise from existence, non-existence nor both, how can there be an efficient cause. Thus such a cause is not admitted."[3] Again he said, "Origination relative to either existence or non-existence cannot be justified. Nor is it possible in the case of existence and non-existence at once."[4] He has also said, "Existence neither arises from itself, nor from another, it does not arise from both, how then does it arise?"[5]

While these references to the notion of combined causality are clear, Nāgārjuna does not in the *Mūlamadhyamakakārikā* seem to suggest any arguments against the third alternative. This is perhaps because the refutation of the third alternative which expresses the simple conjunctive affirmation of the two primary alternatives does not really require the introduction of any new arguments not already employed on the occasions of the refutation of self-origination and origination from another. For the same reason, this chapter is the shortest contained in the present study.

The supposition that cause and effect are both identical and different, i.e., that entities originate from both themselves and others entails the admission that the effect both exists and does not exist in the cause. Thus, the notion of combined causality is open to the charge of being contradictory, since it implies that an entity, i.e., the effect possesses mutually contradictory characteristics, i.e., those of existence and non-existence in the cause. This, as it has been shown on a previous occasion, is not admitted by the Madhyamaka because, according to the latter, a single entity cannot possess mutually opposed predicates.

This objection advanced by the Madhyamaka against the doctrine of combined causality may be further amplified through the following citations adduced from the *Śūnyatāsaptati*. In that work, Nāgārjuna has said, "The (both) existent and non-existent also does not (originate) since these, properties are dissimilar...Since (the properties) are dissimilar, i.e., mutually contradictory. Since the both existent and non-existent is heterogeneous—having mutually contradictory properties, how does the (both) existent and non-existent originate?"[6]

The Madhyamaka does not admit the reality of an entity which both exists and does not exist. As Nāgārjuna has said, "An entity and a non-entity are not identical...An entity and a non-entity cannot be existent at one time (and in one place)."[7] Thus, inasmuch as the possibility of an entity which simultaneously both exists and does not exist is denied, the notion that an entity, i.e., the effect which both exists and does not exist in the cause originates, is rejected. Hence, the doctrine of combined causality is contradictory.

Moreover, as it has been suggested the doctrine of combined causality may be effectively refuted through the arguments advanced against self-origination and origination from another. Thus, insofar as the cause and effect are held to be identical, the objections raised against the notion of self-origination will be applicable. Similarly, insofar as the cause and effect are thought to be different, the arguments against origination from another will apply. Therefore, the doctrine of combined causality offers no solution to the problem of origination.

Finally, if the doctrines of self-origination and origination from another were individually capable of providing a cogent explanation of causality, then origination through a combination of the two might be justified. However, as it has been demonstrated, neither self-origination, nor origination from another are possible, if considered separately. Therefore, origination from both self and another is likewise impossible.

If entities do not individually possess a given property, no combination or multiplication of those entities can be thought to give rise to the desired property. Grains of sand, for instance, do not individually possess the property of yielding oil when squeezed in a press. No matter how many grains of sand are combined together, the property of yield oil will not appear in the collection of grains of sand, inasmuch as individually the grains of sand do not possess this property.[8] Similarly, an assembly of blind men, no matter how numerous, will not possess the faculty of vision, since this faculty is absent in the individual members. Therefore, since neither self-origination nor origination from another are justified individually, so also origination from both self and another is untenable.

In the final analysis then, the conjunctive affirmation of self-origination and origination from another is unacceptable. The mere combination of two alternatives, each of which is subject to insurmountable difficulties does not make for a satisfactory solution to the problem of causality. While the synthetic solution expressed by the third alternative may at first appear to be more plausible and moderate than those offered by the first two alternatives, it, upon examination, turns out to be just as unacceptable as the interpretations expressed by the two former alternatives.

References

1. Kajiyama, Y., *Bhāvaviveka and the Prāsaṅgika school*, p. 328 in Mookerjee, Satkari, *The Nava Nalanda-Maha-vihara Research Publication* Vol. 1. Nalanda, 1957.
2. *dBu-ma-spyi-ston*, p. 373.
3. *Mūlamadhyamakakārikā*, I.7.
4. *Ibid.* VII.20.
5. *Ibid.* XXI.13.
6. *Śūnyatāsaptati*, Stanza 4 and commentary.
7. *Ibid.* Stanza 19 and commentary.
8. *dBu-ma-spyi-ston*, p. 373.

CHAPTER XVI

THE REFUTATION OF THE LAST ALTERNATIVE

The fourth alternative has already been described as representing the sceptic attitude in philosophy. In the case of the interpretation of causality, the fundamental problem in Indian philosophy, the last alternative is somewhat unlike the preceding three. The fourth alternative appears to be invariably associated with nihilism for the Madhyamaka.

The formal statement of the fourth alternative as a disjunctive denial has from time to time tended to mislead opponents of the Madhyamaka, as well as modern scholars. Some have in fact suggested that the fourth alternative represents the position of the Madhyamaka. Indeed, as it is expressed formally, the last alternative could well be confused with the standpoint of the Madhyamaka. Madhyamakas like Nāgārjuna and Candrakīrti however have consistently interpreted the last alternative to express nihilism, materialism and scepticism. Therefore, it is clear, as it will be shown shortly, that the Madhyamaka never regarded the fourth alternative as expressive of his view.

Considered as expressing nihilism, the fourth alternative can be regarded as representing the doctrine of annihilation or interruption (ucchedavāda) which comprises one of the two primary dialectic alternatives of eternalism and nihilism. In this sense the fourth alternative may be considered as logically one of the two primary alternatives of the tetralemma.

Though it has been said that the first two alternatives of the tetralemma constitute the primary alternatives while the latter two are secondary, it must be mentioned that this can be true only insofar as their order of polemic importance and scholastic attention. Indeed there is evidence to support the contention that the fourth alternative of the tetralemma, as employed by the Madhyamaka, was at times taken as one of two primary alternatives by the Buddha.[1]

It may be hazarded that the doctrine advocated by the Buddhist Realists, i.e., the Ābhidharmika schools, came to occupy the place of the second alternative in the Madhyamaka tetralemma because of two possible factors. It has already been mentioned that Nāgārjuna, by and large, established the Madhyamaka system through a critique of the earlier phase of Buddhism. That the consideration of the views of the Ābhidharmika philosophy should be given a primary place, in the structure of Nāgārjuna's dialectical analysis is therefore not surprising. It has also been pointed out that the Ābhidharmika schools represent a semi-critical philosophical attitude. The outstanding doctrines of the Ābhidharmika philosophy, such as those of impermanence and the theory of elements (dhātu) are arrived at through a negative method. Moreover, if the ontology implied by the theory of the discrete particular and the like is to be pushed to its logical conclusions, it will clearly result in the standpoint expressed by the fourth alternative. Hence, it is apparent that the second and fourth alternatives do, in any case, exhibit a certain similarity in their approach to philosophical questions.

In the light of these considerations, it is natural enough that the Ābhidharmika school should be taken by the Madhyamaka as representative of the second alternative, while the strictly nihilist or materialist position should be treated under the fourth alternative.

Thus, the four alternatives, isolated through the Madhyamaka dialectic, may be logically co-ordinated as follows. The first and fourth alternatives may be taken as analytically primary, as bSod-nams Sen-ge does.[2] The third alternative is formally secondary to and associated with the first alternative inasmuch as they both take the form of an assertion and reflect the affirmative attitude in philosophy. The second alternative is formally secondary to and associated with the fourth inasmuch as they both take the form of a denial and reflect the negative attitude in philosophy.

As for the apparent similarity between the standpoint expressed by the fourth alternative and that of the Madhyamaka, it must be admitted that on the surface the formal statement of the fourth alternative does bear some similarity to some of the statements of the Madhyamaka. The disjunctive denial which takes the form, neither existence nor non-existence and the like, does indeed, seem to reflect an intention similar to that of the Madhyamaka. The apparent similarity between some of the statements of the Madhyamaka, and those which reflect the fourth alternative in philosophy, i.e., the sceptic attitude, may be one of the reason why the Madhyamaka was charged with nihilism and scepticism by some of its opponents. The Madhyamaka refutation of the fourth alternative is therefore particularly interesting because it brings into relief the difference which exists between the Madhyamaka and the nihilist. In short, as it will be seen, the attitude of the nihilist is philosophically dogmatic and ethically injurious, while the Madhyamaka standpoint is philosophically critical and ethically salutary.

The Madhyamaka, indeed, explicitly rejects the fourth alternative expressed as neither existence nor non-existence. The Madhyamaka's refutation of the notion of neither existence nor non-existence clearly exhibits the critical attitude of the Madhyamaka. Nāgārjuna says that if it were possible to comprehend either existence or non-existence, it might be possible to maintain that Nirvāṇa is neither existence nor non-existence.[3]

The conditioned or relative nature of the notion of neither existence nor non-existence is immediately pointed out by the Madhyamaka. Indeed the concept of neither existence nor non-existence is possible only in relation to the notions of existence and non-existence. Candrakīrti comments that the judgement that Nirvāṇa is not existence would be possible if it were known what real existence is. In that case, Nirvāṇa could be defined by the negation of existence. Similarly, if there were any real non-existence, then the statement that Nirvāṇa is not non-existence could be comprehended. However, since existence and non-existence are not apprehended their negation is altogether incomprehensible.[4] The fourth alternative which disjunctively denies both existence and non-existence is thus clearly ultimately untenable from the critical standpoint of the Madhyamaka.

It is evident that the Madhyamaka refuses to characterise the ultimate even in terms of neither existence nor non-existence. Candrakīrti indicates that the doctrine of neither existence nor non-existence cannot be comprehended through ultimate knowledge, because such ultimate knowledge is the knowledge of emptiness (śūnyatā). The knowledge of the ultimate is inexpressible. How could one then comprehend the statement that Nirvāṇa is neither existence nor non-existence.[5] The notion of neither existence nor non-existence is thus clearly rejected by the Madhyamaka as a description of the ultimate, since the ultimate is beyond thought and expression.

Moreover, the attitude expressed by the last alternative is also untenable from the phenomenal or conventional standpoint. This is clearly shown through an examination of the position expressed by the fourth alternative in the area of causality. The opposition from the standpoint of the Madhyamaka to that expressed by the fourth alternative is evident in the Madhyamaka's criticism of the last alternative, as it is applied to empirical causality. Through it also the relation between the formal statement of the last alternative and, what may be termed, its philosophical content is revealed. This, in itself, should help to clear up the confusion which has existed of the standpoint of the nihilist with that of the Madhyamaka.

The association of the last alternative with materialism or scepticism in the area of the interpretation of causality is already evident in the opening stanza of the *Mūlamadhyamakakārikā*. It is important to note that, formally the fourth alternative presented in the stanza ought to have been stated neither from themselves nor from others, in the form of the disjunctive denial which is supposed to constitute the last alternative. However, both the Sanskrit original and the Tibetan translation render the fourth alternative presented in the stanza as without cause (ahetu). Thus, it is clear that the fourth alternative solution to the problem of causality was specifically associated with materialism or scepticism for Nāgārjuna.

The schools which seem to have been the principal representatives of the attitude expressed by the last alternative were the Materialists (Cārvaka) and the Sceptics (Svabhāvavādin). It is quite possible that the Svabhāvavādins may also be classified philosophically as Materialists, however their denial of empirical causality appears to merit terming them Sceptics.

It must be remembered that the Madhyamaka criticism of the last alternative is undertaken essentially from the phenomenal or conventional standpoint. This indicates the difference between the critical attitude of the Madhyamaka and the dogmatic attitude of the Materialist or Sceptic. The latter makes his assertion without having penetrated the nature of phenomena through critical examination. The doctrine of the Materialist or Sceptic is therefore in conflict with conventional reality while at the same time it affords no way of attaining to the ultimate and unconditioned.

The Madhyamaka on the contrary relies upon the distinction between the two truths, conventional and ultimate. The Madhyamaka therefore is in complete agreement with the ordinary pragmatic interpretation of causality current in the world from the conventional or it may be said precritical standpoint. It is ultimately, i.e., from the post critical standpoint, that the Madhyamaka rejects causality. The philosophical disparity between the attitude of the Materialist or Sceptic and the Madhyamaka is thus indicated.

In addition, Nāgārjuna, as well as subsequent Madhyamaka scholars, clearly regarded the doctrine advocated by the nihilists as ethically detrimental or morally objectionable. In this connection, it is apparent that the nihilist's denial of causality destroys the value of religious discipline. Thus, the Madhyamaka affirms the conventional reality of origination, relative to causes against the dogmatic denial of causality expressed by the nihilist. The conception of origination relative to causes is central to the law of karma. This principle of origination, relative to a combination of causes and conditions, constitutes the very foundation of the Madhyamaka philosophy. The principle of phenomenal interdependent origination and the reality of karma are taught conventionally by the Madhyamaka. The materialists and sceptics on the contrary rejected origination relative to causes and the law of karma.

Again, at this point the doctrines advocated by the schools which exemplify the fourth alternative may be considered briefly before proceeding with their refutation. The position of the Materialists is summarised by Candrakīrti as follows. "Some accept only the four elements, i.e., earth, fire, water, air. They maintain that just as the combination of boiled rice, water and yeast produces, after maturation, an intoxicating beverage, so also, in the womb, the co-mingling of the paternal element with the maternal gives rise to consciousness. Pre-existence, subsequent existence and liberation are denied. There is no fruit which results from good and evil actions performed. ...Disparaging all these, striving to attain the sublime fruits of heaven and liberation is relinquished. Continuously performing only non-virtuous actions, one is always liable to fall into the great precipice of hell and the like."[6]

bSod-nams Sen-ge gives a somewhat more specific description of the doctrine advocated by the Materialists in the dBu-ma-spyi-ston. His presentation is in keeping with that of Candrakīrti, however, the implications of the doctrine advocated by the Materialists for the concepts of rebirth and Karma are explicitly drawn.

According to bSod-nams Sen-ge, the Materialists hold that the present consciousness, i.e., the consciousness which appertains to this life, as well as the happiness and suffering experienced in this life, do not originate from the consciousness appertaining to the former life and good and evil actions performed in the past. The Materialists, he says, do not admit that consciousness, happiness and suffering originate from causes which appertain to a previous life. Consciousness and so on, the Materialists hold, originate from the compounded elements of this world through a combination of fortuitous conditions. Thus, bSod-nams Sen-ge concludes that the Materialists are those who deny unperceived causes.[7]

It becomes apparent from these two assessments of the doctrine of the Materialists offered by Candrakīrti and bSod-nams Sen-ge, that the former denied rebirth and karma. Nāgārjuna's references to the nihilist alternative by and large agree with this characterisation.

The fact that bSod-nams Sen-ge refers to the Materialists as those who deny unperceived causes would seem to suggest that the Materialists did perhaps accept some form of empirical causality, i.e., causality as it functions in practical matters of everyday life. How this could have been reconciled with their insistence upon only a single valid instrument of cognition, i.e., perception, is an open question.

By contrast, the Svabhāvavādins seem to have advocated an extreme form of scepticism which rejected the idea of any connection between cause and effect even empirically. bSod-nams Sen-ge gives the following summary of the position of the Sceptics. He comments that, according to the Svabhāvavādins, all phenomena like the rising of the sun, the descending of water, the cylindrical bean, the pointed thorn, the colour and shape of the peacock and so on; all originate from nothing. All phenomena originate, according to the Svabhàvavādins, from their own spontaneity. Hence, bSod-nams Sen-ge concludes, the Sceptics are those who deny even perceived causes.[8]

The position advocated by the Sceptics is clearly an extreme one which could not have enjoyed much widespread acceptance. This is perhaps why the Madhyamaka devoted comparatively less attention to the refutation of this Sceptic standpoint of the Svabhāvavādins.

While the fourth alternative is sometimes presented in the treatment of the notion of causality in the *Mūlamadhyamaka-kārikā*,[9] the refutation of the nihilist solution of the problem of causality, i.e., that entities originate without cause, is largely left unattended to by Nāgārjuna. The same may be said of Nāgārjuna's examination of causality found in the *Śūnyatāsaptati*. Notwithstanding the neglect of the topic in the above two works, Nāgārjuna has undertaken to refute the standpoint of the nihilists in the *Ratnāvalī*.

This fact may be explained by the consideration that the *Mūla-madhyamakakārikā* and *Śūnyatāsaptati* are principally concerned with the exposition of the Madhyamaka interpretation of the nature of ultimate reality, while, as it has been suggested the refutation of the nihilist interpretation is undertaken from the conventional standpoint by the Madhyamaka.

At this point, before proceeding with the consideration of the refutation of the last alternative advanced by the Madhyamaka scholars who followed Nāgārjuna, we may do well to consider some of the master's statements about the last alternative found in the *Ratnāvalī*.

In that work Nāgārjuna has said, "In brief, the view of nihilism is that actions have no result; it is without merit, and leading to a bad state. It is regarded as the wrong view." Again the master has said, "Seeing origination as caused, one passes beyond non-existence."[10] Nāgārjuna has also said, "When this exist that arises, like short when there is long. When this is produced, so is that, like light from a flame. When there is long there must be short; they exist not through their own nature just as without a flame light too does not arise. Thus having seen that effects arise from causes, one asserts what appears in the conventions of the world and does not accept nihilism."[11] Moreover he has said in the *Ratnāvalī* that those who adhere to nihilism suffer miserable rebirths, while happy rebirths accrue to those who adhere to eternalism.[12]

Nāgārjuna also rejects the misconception that the Madhyamaka philosophy represents nihilism in the following way. He writes, "Those who rely on enlightenment have no nihilistic proposition, behaviour or thought, how can they be seen as nihilists."[13]

In the *Śūnyatāsaptati* also Nāgārjuna affirms that the conventional truth according to which dependent upon that this originates, ought not to be rejected.[14]

Two important points, which have already been touched upon, emerge from a consideration of the foregoing citations. In the first place, it is clear that the Madhyamaka refutation of the position of the nihilist is undertaken from the phenomenal standpoint. Secondly, the ethically injurious consequences of the doctrine advocated by the nihilist, which denies that actions bear any fruit, are stressed by Nāgārjuna, in his criticism of nihilism.

Thereafter, Buddhapālita assailed the last alternative, characteristically, through an argument *ad absurdum* which exposes the inconsistency between the position advocated by the nihilist and the situation as it appears in the world. At this point also the connection between the second and the fourth alternatives is evident in the similarity of the arguments produced by Buddhapālita. The same undesirable consequence of indiscriminate causality was suggested by him in his argument against the notion of cause and effect as comprising different entities. Indeed, the notion that cause and effect represent different entities ultimately does, if examined, entail the consequence of origination without cause as it was shown in chapter XIV.

Buddhapālita argues that entities do not originate without causes, since in that case everything would originate at any time and at any place.[15] In this argument of Buddhapālita, stated as were the previous arguments advanced by him in the form of a *reductio ad absurdum*, the undesirable consequence of the position advocated by the opponent, i.e., indiscriminate causality or promiscuous origination, is clearly indicated. Inasmuch as it is evident that phenomena do not originate indiscriminately at any place and at any time, the nihilist is compelled to admit that his doctrine is in conflict with the ordinary perception of reality.

Bhāvaviveka has also assailed the argument *ad absurdum* advanced by Buddhapālita against the last alternative. He asserted that in as much as this argument also was a mere *reductio ad absurdum*, its real intention could be disclosed by a positive argument employing the counterparts of the proposition and reason. In that case, Bhāvaviveka argued, it would be stated that entities originate from causes, since entities originate at a particular time and at a particular place. This argument constitutes the positive counterpart of Buddhapālita's argument *ad absurdum* negating the doctrine that entities originate without causes. However, if the latter is what Buddhapālita really intended, says Bhāvaviveka, the argument will contradict the conclusions previously established by the Madhyamaka. Bhāvaviveka expressed this criticism of the argument advanced by Buddhapālita against the last alternative.[16]

It is immediately apparent that this censure voiced by Bhāvaviveka does not differ in any significant way from that which he advanced on the occasions of the consideration of the preceding alternatives.

In his turn, Bhāvaviveka advanced the following independent syllogism against the notion of origination without cause. It is interesting to note that the special qualification, i.e., ultimately, which distinguished Bhāvaviveka's other independent syllogisms is not added to his argument refuting the last alternative. This is in agreement with the practice adopted by the Madhyamaka of refuting the last alternative from the conventional standpoint.

Bhāvaviveka advanced the following argument. Proposition—the subjective poles of consciousness do not originate without causes. Reason—because they possess universal (sāmānya) and specific (viśeṣa) properties. Example—as in the case of a sprout. The determinate perception of a sprout is endowed with generic and specific properties, i.e., it is non-eternal and green etc.[17]

In addition, Bhāvaviveka seems to have assailed the Sceptics who maintained that everything originates spontaneously in the following way. If the Sceptic adduces no reason in support of the proposition he advocates, his position remains altogether unsupported. Thus, it is an instance of a mere dogmatic assertion which is unlikely to receive serious consideration from rational people. Alternatively, if the Sceptic attempts to defend his doctrine through producing a reason, he is guilty of inconsistency, because though he denies co-ordinated causes, he at the same time would vindicate his position through the presentation of a logical ground.[18] This difficulty with the doctrine advocated by the nihilist or Sceptic has also been noted by Professor Murti.[19]

The Prāsaṅgikas did not consider it necessary to defend their standpoint again against the criticism advanced by Bhāvaviveka. Candrakīrti confines himself to observing that an objection has been raised by Bhāvaviveka with regard to this point and repeating that from his point of view the criticism is inadmissible.[20] He comments that the refutation of the objections advanced by Bhāvaviveka have already been refuted. bSod-nams Sen-ge also remarks that the appropriate replies to the objections raised by Bhāvaviveka were given on previous occasions. Hence, the matter was not thought to require any further comment from the Prāsaṅgikas.[21]

Candrakīrti's refutation of the solution to the problem of causality offered by the last alternative contains three principal components. The first, like the argument produced by Buddhapālita elicits the undesirable consequence of the notion of origination without cause, i.e., indiscriminate origination. The second element evident in Candrakīrti's criticism relies upon the pragmatic standpoint which governs action in the world. Finally Candrakīrti contends that the notion of origination without causes logically results in a universe totally devoid of properties which would not be apprehended by consciousness.

The first and last of Candrakīrti's arguments against the last alternative seem to be directed against the attitude of nihilism in general. The second argument advanced by him appears to assail the position of the Sceptics, though it may have also been extended to the doctrine of the Materialists as well. As is evident from the passage cited earlier from the *Prasannapadā*, Candrakīrti was not unaware of the ethical consequences of nihilism in general and of the doctrine advocated by the Materialists.

Candrakīrti argued that if entities originate without causes, then their origination will not be conditioned by time, place and the like. This would follow, as a logical consequence, of the unconditioned character of origination.[22] It is immediately apparent that this argument advanced by Candrakīrti is virtually identical with that produced by Buddhapālita.

Again, Candrakīrti argued that if entities originate without causes, then actions performed for the sake of an effect, would be futile. Thus, if entities originate without causes, the harvest of grain will originate without causes. Consequently, the labour expanded for the sake of obtaining the harvest would be futile and superfluous. This consequence is however untenable, according to Candrakīrti, because causal efficiency appears to direct perception. Therefore, he concludes, that entities originate from causes.[23]

Finally, Candrakīrti contended that if entities originate without causes they would be similar to a sky lotus inasmuch as they would be devoid of colour, shape, scent and the like. In that case, nothing at all would appear as an object before consciousness. On the contrary, however, phenomena are most apparent, and are objects of consciousness.[24]

This argument like the others is a variety of *reductio ad absurdum*. Candrakīrti concludes that the world originates dependent upon causes as does the individual consciousness.[25] This statement again contains a clear reference to the position of the Materialist who rejects the antecedent existence of consciousness.

The Madhyamaka refutation of the last alternative may be described as having three principal elements. They can be said to be the logical, the practical and the ethical. This does not mean to imply that all three types of arguments are not logical. Rather the terms are meant to take into account the standpoint from which the arguments are advanced. Buddhapālita's argument against the last alternative as well as the first and third arguments employed by Candrakīrti are examples of arguments of a specifically rational character. They expose the contradiction which exists between the position advocated by the opponent and immediately evident phenomena which are cognised in ordinary experience.

An example of a pragmatic argument employed by Candrakīrti is that regarding the utility of farm labour cited above. This argument relies upon the commonly accepted belief in the utility of efficient causality. Finally, there is the third element in the Madhyamaka criticism of the last alternative which was termed the ethical. It is not given much attention by Candrakīrti and bSod-nams Sen-ge but both explicitly acknowledge it. Moreover, it is an important element in Nāgārjuna's treatment of the fourth alternative as has been seen. In this case, the Madhyamaka affirms the reality of the conceptions of rebirth and karma which are morally salutary and relatively prudent from the conventional standpoint. As a result, he differs sharply from the Materialist who dogmatically rejects the possibility of another world. As it is seen from the statements of Nāgārjuna, the view advocated by the nihilist, i.e., that actions bear no fruit, was rejected as leading to misery. Candrakīrti also agrees with this assessment.

In conclusion, it may be said that the objections which may be brought against the doctrines of Materialism and Scepticism are of two kinds. In the first place, the position advocated by the Materialists and Sceptics is incapable of supplying a coherent interpretation of phenomena, which agrees with the evidence of ordinary experience. The doctrine is therefore faulty from the phenomenal or conventional point of view since it does not yield relative benefits in this world or in the next.

In the second place, the doctrine advocated by the Materialists and Sceptics certainly cannot stand as a description of ultimate reality. The assertion of the nihilist is a dogmatic one. It purports to supply a definitive characterisation of the ultimate in the form of a judgement. However, the ultimate transcends thought and expression. Thus, the doctrines advocated by the Materialists and Sceptics in as much as they are not critical afford no means of comprehending the ultimate nature of phenomena and reaching the unconditioned.

References

1. *Brahmajāla Sutta* of the *Dīgha Nikāya*.
2. See Chapter V.
3. *Mūlamadhyamakakārikā*. XXV.15.
4. Stcherbatsky, Th. *The Conception of Buddhist Nirvāna*, p. 311.
5. *Ibid.* p. 314.
6. *Prasannapadā* commentary to *Mūlamadhyamakakārikā*, XVIII, 6.
7. *dBu-ma-spyi-ston*, pp. 373-374.
8. *Ibid.* p. 374.
9. *Mūlamadhyamakākārika*, I.1; XII.1.
10. *Ratnāvalī*, I. 43 and 46.
11. *Ibid.* 48-50.
12. *Ibid.* 57.
13. *Ibid.* 60

14. *Śūnyatāsaptati*, Stanza 71.
15. *dBu-ma-spyi-ston*, p. 375.
16. *Ibid.*
17. Kajiyama, Y., *Bhābaviveka and the Prāsaṅgika School.* Mookerjee, Satkari (ed.), *The Nava-Nalanda-Mahavihara Research Publication.* Vol. I. p. 322.
18. *Ibid.* pp. 321-322.
19. Murti, T. R. V., *The Central Philosophy of Buddhism*, p. 135.
20. Stcherbatsky, Th., *The Conception of Buddhist Nirvāṇa*, p. 182.
21. *dBu-ma-spyi-ston*. p. 375.
22. *Ibid.* p. 374.
23. *Ibid.*
24. *Ibid.* p. 375.
25. *Ibid.*

CHAPTER XVII

A FINAL LOOK AT THE DIFFERENCES BETWEEN THE PRĀSAṄGIKA AND SVĀTANTRIKA SCHOOLS

As we suggested at the outset of our detailed discussion, the origin of the division between the Prāsaṅgika and Svātantrika schools may be traced to the interpretation of the opening stanza of the *Mūlamadhyamakakārikā*. It has been our contention that the principal difference between the Prāsaṅgika and Svātantrika schools may be ascertained by means of a consideration of the arguments offered by Prāsaṅgika and Svātantrika commentators in support of the proposition set forth in the first stanza.

Inasmuch as according to our view, the interpretation of the first stanza serves as a paradigm for understanding the primary difference between the two schools, it has been dealt with in detail. The four alternative solutions to the problem of causality presented in the stanza, have been considered formally and historically, as well as the arguments refuting them advanced by the principal exponents of the two Madhyamaka schools, i.e., Buddhapālita, Bhāvaviveka and Candrakīrti. An attempt has been made to preface this in each case by a close examination of the statements of Nāgārjuna. Thus, the characteristic difference between the method of argument favoured by the Prāsaṅgikas and Svātantrikas was revealed, as well as the relation of the arguments presented with the utterances of Nāgārjuna.

It is our contention that, just as the Prāsaṅgika and Svātantrika schools differ in the arguments they employed on the occasion of the refutation of the four alternative theories of origination, so also they differed in the interpretations which they offered of the whole contents of the *Mūlamadhyamakakārikā*. Just as on the occasion of the refutation of origination the Prāsaṅgikas resorted to arguments *ad absurdum* while Svātantrikas advanced independent syllogisms so also the very same difference may be ascertained throughout the whole of the text. This is true in the case of the interpretations given by the two schools of the eight properties (dharmas) cited in the 'maṅgalācaraṇa', i.e., unextinguished and the rest. Indeed, the difference in the arguments advanced by the exponents of the two schools evident on the occasion of the refutation of origination is found in every chapter, from the one on conditions, through motion and concluding with the one on view.[1]

Thus, the examination of the respective arguments advanced by Prāsaṅgika and Svātantrika scholars on the occasion of the refutation of origination supplies ample evidence of the ground of distinction between the two schools, which also obtains uniformly in their interpretations of the whole of Nāgārjuna's authoritative work. In their attempt to convince their opponents of the truth of the Madhyamaka philosophy, the Prāsaṅgikas consistently employed varieties of arguments *ad absurdum*. The Svātantrikas resorted to a peculiar form of independent syllogism. This is apparent in the following examples cited by bSod-nams Sen-ge, the first of which has already been considered in Chapters IV and XIII. The sense of vision, indeed, does not perceive itself. If it cannot perceive itself, how can it perceive external objects?[2] The argument *ad absurdum* exposes the inconsistency between the opponent's acceptance of the absence of the capacity of introspection in the sense of vision and his initial position according to which the sense of vision perceives external objects. Since the opponent also accepts the relation of invariable concomitance between the capacity of introspection and the capacity to perceive other objects, his position is impossible.

The proposition advocated by the opponent is also refuted by the Svātantrikas by means of a five-membered syllogism like the following one. Proposition—ultimately the operating sense of vision does not perceive form, reason—because it is the sense of vision, example—like the non-operating sense of vision, major premise—whatsoever is a sense of vision certainly does not perceive form. Alternatively, this independent syllogism might be produced. Proposition—ultimately the sense of vision does not perceive form, reason—because it is originated from the elements, i.e., it is material, example—just like form itself, major premise—whatsoever is material does not perceive form. Thus, independent reasons and examples like the foregoing were stated by Svātantrika scholars in order to explicate the intention of Nāgārjuna's treatise.[3]

The arguments advanced by the Prāsaṅgikas were constructed from the point of view of the opponent and were not admitted to be valid by the Prāsaṅgika himself. This characterisation is consistently true of the arguments advanced by the Prāsaṅgikas, whether they take the form of a simple *reductio ad absurdum* or that of an inference familiar to the opponent. The Svātantrikas for their part constructed syllogisms whose elements they admitted to be established by virtue of valid instruments of cognition. This, indeed, constitutes the principal difference between the doctrines of the Prāsaṅgika and Svātantrika schools.

In addition to what has been termed the primary difference between the Prāsaṅgika and Svātantrika schools, i.e., the difference in the arguments which they advanced in support of the Madhyamaka's interpretation of the nature of ultimate reality, the schools also differed with regard to their interpretations of the nature of conventional reality. This aspect was already touched upon briefly in chapter VI. bSod-nams Sen-ge regards these differences in the two schools' respective descriptions of conventional reality as minor. At the very outset it may be said that the Prāsaṅgikas employ a wider number of conventions than do the Svātantrikas.

Conventionally, the Prāsaṅgikas admit and employ the four valid instruments of cognition well known in the world (lokaprasiddha pramāṇa), i.e., perception, inference, testimony and comparison. By contrast, the Svātantrikas, as it has been indicated, tended to recognise only two valid instruments of cognition, i.e., perception and inference. Nonetheless, when the existence of a real element, i.e., the principal object of refutation for the Madhyamaka, is to be refuted, the Prāsaṅgikas do not accept an independent reason and proposition. bSod-nams Sen-ge says that the Prāsaṅgikas accept whatsoever was taught in the holy discourses of the Buddha, such as: the aggregates (skandha), elements (dhātu), sense spheres (āyatana), the store house consciousness (ālaya-vijñāna), the three natures (parikalpita, paratantra and pariniṣpanna) as well as the inherent potential Buddhahood (tathāgatagarbha).[4]

With regard to phenomenal truth (saṁvṛtisatya), a distinction is sometimes made between the so-called true phenomenal (tathyasaṁvṛti) and the false phenomenal (mithyāsaṁvṛti). The Prāsaṅgikas for the most part do not admit this distinction within the compass of their own philosophical system, nonetheless, they admit the distinction acknowledged in the conventions of the world. The Svātantrikas on the other hand consistently divided the phenomenal truth into the true and the false. Indeed, the Svātantrikas seem to have set forth a twofold division of the phenomenal truth into the true phenomenal and the false phenomenal, as acknowledged in the conventions of the world and a true phenomenal and a false as accepted by the Svātantrikas themselves.

The characteristics of the true phenomenal according to the Svātantrika conception are: one—not truly established, two—relationally dependent, three—not imputed and four—efficacious. The characteristics of the false phenomenal, according to the Svātantrika view, are the opposite of these. The Svātantrika's description of the true phenomenal, as acknowledged, in the conventions of the world is as follows. Its characteristics are: one—efficacious, two—dependently originated, three—common ly given and four—not imputed to be truly established and the like. The opposite of these, the Svātantrikas say, are the characteristics of the false phenomenal as it exists in the conventions of the world. An example cited by the Svātantrika's to illustrate the distinction between the true phenomenal and the false, insofar as they are efficacious or not, is that of the moon in the sky and its reflection in water. The former is supposed to be efficacious while the latter is not so. Be that as it may, the distinction between efficacious and non-efficacious is difficult to maintain absolutely since hallucinations and other forms of common and uncommon perception normally termed false are also sometimes seen to be efficacious.

Among Prāsaṅgikas there are those who hold that the phenomenal truth need not be divided into a true phenomenal and a false phenomenal inasmuch as both are determined by the conventions of the world. A representative of this point of view is bSod-nams Sen-ge.[5] Others hold that the phenomenal truth ought to be divided into a true and a false insofar as the former is efficacious and the latter is not so. Still others, like Mi-pham, hold that what appears before unimpaired senses constitutes the true phenomenal while what appears before impaired senses like hairs and so on is the false phenomenal.[6] Candrakīrti also seems to have suggested this. Moreover, the Prāsaṅgikas also do not accept themselves the distinction which is commonly made with regard to the subject and the object of cognitions into the true and the false.[7]

Much has been made by some scholars[8] of the distinction of two types of ultimate suggested by Bhāvaviveka and other Svātantrikas.[9] Svātantrikas divide the ultimate into the describable ultimate (paryāya-paramārtha) and the indescribable (aparyāya-paramārtha). The Prāsaṅgikas however also seem to accept this division, so it cannot be thought to be an exclusive tenet of the Svātantrikas. In any case the describable ultimate is, properly speaking, really only conventional truth, since ultimate truth does not conform to concepts.

Conventionally the Prāsaṅgikas do not accept origination from another. The Prāsaṅgika polemic against the Svātantrika's conventional acceptance of origination from another has already been considered in chapter XIV. Hence, it will not be taken up again at this point. The Prāsaṅgikas for their part admit only origination conventionally, but reject the four alternatives. Svātantrikas, however, hold that their doctrine of conventional origination from another represents something quite different from the second alternative.

The Prāsaṅgikas maintain that though both Mahāyānist and Hīnayānist saints comprehend the two kinds of insubstantiality (pudgalanairātmya and dharma nairātmya), a difference may be found in that which they accept as the view which is free from thought constructions (prapañca). bSod-nams Sen-ge holds that when the saint belonging to the Hīnayāna achieves one-pointed meditation, he does not apprehend origination, extinction, impermanence and the rest. Nonetheless, a distinction may be made in the Hīnayānist's comprehension of the insubstantiality of the person (pudgalanairātmya).[10]

Indeed, a minor controversy had arisen between Bhāvaviveka and Candrakīrti over whether Śrāvakas and Pratyekabuddhas comprehend the insubstantiality of elements. Bhāvaviveka had held that they do not while Candrakīrti had taken the opposite view. Candrakīrti's comments on this point may be found briefly in the *Prasannapadā* and in detail in the *Madhyamakāvatāra*.[11]

As we indicated almost at the very beginning of our discussion of the division between the Prāsaṅgika and Svātantrika schools, the question of the nature and relevance of the valid instruments of cognition was central to the controversy throughout its history. For this reason, it will perhaps be worthwhile to take a final look at the interpretations of valid instruments of cognition offered by the Prāsaṅgikas.

The Prāsaṅgikas, in constructing their theory of valid instruments of cognition, took as their starting point the treatment accorded to the question by the Master Nāgārjuna in the *Vigrahavyāvartanī* and its autocommentary. There, perception etc. the four valid instruments of cognition are spoken of. The great Prāsaṅgika Candrakīrti also held that in the world objects of knowledge ought to be cognised through the four valid instruments of cognition.

bSod-nams Sen-ge, taking the statements of Nāgārjuna on the question of valid instruments of cognition together with those of Candrakīrti, gives the following interpretation from the Prāsaṅgika point of view of perception and the rest. Thus, he delineates the Prāsaṅgika conception of valid instruments of cognition based upon the authority of Nāgārjuna and Candrakīrti.

bSod-nams Sen-ge says that there are two sets of four valid instruments of cognition, i.e., four appertaining to the phenomenal and four appertaining to the ultimate. The four valid instruments appertaining to the phenomenal are termed conventional valid instruments of cognition. These instruments of cognition are only produced or employed when the nature of the phenomenal is to be determined. They are the conventional valid instruments of cognition which are familiar to the world. They are termed conventional valid instruments of cognition just because they are believed to be so in the conventions of the world. The Madhyamaka does not admit the validity of the conventional valid instruments of cognition from his own standpoint.

According to bSod-nams Sen-ge, it is contradictory to suppose that a false object could correspond to a true subject. That is to say if the conventional valid instruments of cognition, i.e., the subjects, are thought to be true then their objects ought also to be thought to be true. However, this cannot be admitted.

bSod-nams nen-ge goes on to say that valid instruments of cognition, to be valid, ought to be right cognition and right vision. However on the contrary the conventional valid instruments of cognition are false cognition and false vision.[12]

bSod-nams Sen-ge gives the following description of the four valid instruments of cognition appertaining to the ultimate, from the Prāsaṅgika standpoint. His interpretation is particularly illuminating with respect to the Madhyamaka conception of the first and second ultimate valid instruments of cognition.

First, the ultimate valid instrument of cognition of perception is described as follows. When the Saints (āryans), belonging to the three vehicles (yānas) attain one-pointed meditation beyond duality, they perceive the ultimate, i.e., ultimate reality. They perceive it through their supernatural faculty of perception (yaugika-pratyakṣa). This description of the ultimate valid instrument of cognition of perception through which the ultimate is known is particularly interesting because it shows the stress laid upon the direct and altogether non-conceptual knowledge of the ultimate attained in meditation.[13]

Indeed, apprehension of the ultimate for the Madhyamaka is said to be of two kinds. The former is obtained by the Saints through their supernatural perception. It is right and perfect perception and is actual. The latter kind of cognition of the ultimate is an intellectual cognition which approximates the aforesaid. This kind of cognition of the ultimate is not obtained by oneself but is conditioned by another, i.e., is indicated by another. The three latter valid instruments of cognition, i.e., inference, testimony and comparison, all share this characteristic of supplying mediate intellectual cognitions of the ultimate. The latter three are also termed ultimate valid instruments of cognition because they are associated with the methodology appertaining to the ultimate.

The valid instrument of cognition of inference has reference to what cannot be cognised through perception. An object of cognition, which is not cognised through perception is cognised by the epistemological subject by means of the reason or logical ground (hetu). It is accepted that the reason does not lead the cognition astray, i.e., does not stray from that which it intends to prove, i.e., the probandum. The cognition which is conditioned by a reason which does not stray from the object intended is termed the valid instrument of cognition of inference.[14]

bSod-nams Sen-ge stresses that inference is also applied on the occasion of establishing emptiness. He says that it is taught in the *Prasannapadā* where various types of logic (yukti) and argument are presented. He then supplies the following fourfold classification of Prāsaṅgika arguments.

The first type of argument is the *reductio ad absurdum* which exposes inconsistency. It is followed by the inference familiar to the opponent, the equality of the reason, and the final class which covers situations when the probans, similar to the probandum, is unproven.

If the opponent is induced to relinquish his initial misconception, when a *reductio ad absurdum* is produced by the Madhyamaka, then it may be termed a case of a *reductio ad absurdum* which exposes the inconsistency. It has already been noted that a *reductio ad absurdum* ought to possess three characteristics—fallacious proposition, major premise and minor premise. Such an argument, possessing the three characteristics, is termed a perfect *reductio ad absurdum* (prasaṅga).[15]

The matter may be clarified as follows. If when the *reductio ad absurdum* is produced, the opponent is unable to avoid defeat in any of four ways, then it may be termed a perfect *reductio ad absurdum*. Suppose a hypothetical opponent accepts the fallacious proposition that a hill possesses smoke because it does not possess fire. The position advocated by the opponent may be refuted through an argument *ad absurdum*, i.e., that hill does not possess smoke because it does not possess fire. The minor premise, i.e., the hill does not possess fire, is accepted by the opponent. The major premise may be stated, wheresoever there is no fire, there is no smoke. Its positive formulation (anvaya) takes the form wherever there is smoke, there is fire and is accepted to be proven by valid instruments of cognition. Thus, the proposition advocated by the opponent is fallacious, i.e., that hill possesses smoke because it does not possess fire. The minor premise—that hill does not possess fire, is accepted by the opponent, and the positive formulation of the major premise—wherever there is smoke, there is fire, is proven by valid instruments of cognition. Therefore, the three characteristics of a perfect *reductio ad absurdum* are present on this occasion. Alternatively, the second constituent of a perfect *reductio ad absurdum* may simply be termed the reason or logical ground (hetu), in this case expressed in the phrase, does not possess fire.

When, as in this case, the argument produced is a perfect *reductio ad absurdum*, the four possible avenues open to the opponent by means of which he might salvage his position are closed to him. In the first place, the opponent cannot admit the argument advanced by the Madhyamaka because to do so would entail the surrender of his proposition. The opponent also cannot assail the *reductio ad absurdum* in any of the following three ways either. He cannot assert that the minor premise or the reason is unproven because he himself has accepted them. Again, inasmuch as the positive concomitance of the major premise is proven by valid instruments of cognition, the opponent cannot argue either that the invariable concomitance is uncertain or that the reason adduced is contradictory, i.e., that the reason is contrary to the probandum. Thus, in this case, the *reductio ad absurdum* endowed with the three characteristics results in the refutation of the position advocated by the opponent, since the latter can make no cogent reply to the argument. The simplicity of the example, used to illustrate the *modus operandi* of the *reductio ad absurdum*, may be excused, since here the purpose intended is to indicate the formal operation of the argument.

In addition, as it has been seen, the simple *reductio ad absurdum* may also be stated in the form of a five-membered inference familiar to the opponent.[16] Inasmuch as the five-membered inference familiar to the opponent was discussed in detail in chapters XI, XII and XIII, it will not be taken up again here.

The third type of argument employed by the Prāsaṅgikas, termed the equality of the reason, is somewhat different from the *reductio ad absurdum* and the five-membered inference familiar to the opponent. While it too may be termed an argument *ad absurdum*, it lacks the simplicity of the *reductio ad absurdum* (prasaṅga). With respect to the argument termed the equality of the reason there is no mention of the three properties which characterise a perfect *reductio ad absurdum*. Nonetheless, the argument, known as the equality of the reason, exposes undesirable consequences for the opponent.[17]

The most easily accessible example of the use of the argument is found on the occasion of the refutation of the second alternative solution to the problem of causality. In that case, the predicate, other, is produced by the opponent in the proposition, entities originate from another. Here otherness is taken to be invariably concomitant with origination. However, the property otherness applies as equally to fire and coal as it does to the genuine cause of a sprout. Thus, the property, otherness, which is taken to be invariably concomitant with origination, is too wide in extent because it includes both causes and non-causes. Considered in the form of a statement of invariable concomitance, it may be said that the probandum, i.e., origination, fails to pervade the probans, i.e., otherness. The probans is faulty since it is greater in extent than the probandum. Therefore, the relation of invariable concomitance expressed in the proposition is uncertain. In this way, the assertion that entities originate from another is refuted, since it is shown to be uncertain.

The following considerations may account for the difference evident between the *reductio ad absurdum* and the five-membered inference familiar to the opponent employed on the occasion of the refutation of the first alternative and the argument *ad absurdum* employed against the notion of origination from another. In the former case, the proposition advocated by the opponent is contradictory, i.e., inconsistent, while in the latter case, it is only uncertain. It is for this reason that the argument against origination from another does not take the form of a simple *reductio ad absurdum* and does not possess the three characteristics of the former.

The fourth type of argument employed by the Prāsaṅgika which bSod-nams Seṅ-ge terms the similarity of the probans to the probandum, i.e., the probans like the probandum is unproven, has already been encountered briefly in chapter XII. This type of argument represents a simple rejection of the position advocated by the opponent. Inasmuch as it only serves a negative function, one does not see how it could have been of much use in convincing opponents of the correctness of the Madhyamaka philosophy. Perhaps, this is why it does not seem to have been used much by Madhyamaka scholars.

A case of the probans being, like the probandum, unproven is as follows. An opponent adduces a logical ground in support of the predicate, i.e., probandum which he desires to establish. If he adduces as the probans any entity which is conceived to exist in reality, i.e., exist ultimately, then in that case, the minor premise of his argument is unproven. If alternatively, the opponent adduces as the probans any entity which appears, i.e., is phenomenal, then in that case, the argument will lack a valid major premise.[18]

Something along these lines has already been suggested in chapter XIII. If the opponent adduces as the probans any term which is conceived to exist ultimately as part of a syllogism directed against the Madhyamaka, then inasmuch as the Madhyamaka does not admit that any entity exists ultimately, the minor premise will be unproven for the Madhyamaka. Alternatively, if an entity which appears is adduced as the probans of a syllogism, then, since no relation of invariable concomitance can be established between what merely appears and what exists in truth, i.e., ultimately, the argument advanced by the opponent will be devoid of a valid major premise.

The following two hypothetical arguments may be cited by way of illustration. For instance, it may be said, fire exists truly, i.e., exists ultimately, because smoke exists ultimately. In this case, the reason or minor premise is unproven for the Madhyamaka, since he does not admit that smoke exists ultimately. Alternatively, it may be said, fire exists ultimately because it is endowed with colour. In this case, the reason adduced is an apparent fact. Nonetheless, the argument is faulty because though fire does indeed possess colour, the relation of invariable concomitance between possessing colour and existing ultimately cannot be established. In both the cases just cited, the probans is, like the probandum, unproven.

bSod-nams Sen-ge goes on to describe the valid instrument of cognition of testimony. His interpretation makes use of the division of texts into those of direct meaning (nītārtha) and those of expedient meaning (neyārtha) and outlines the Madhyamaka view on the matter. He says that the scriptures which demonstrate emptiness constitute those of direct meaning (nītārtha). In passing, it may be noted that the Vijñānavāda contrary to the Madhyamaka, holds that the scriptures which demonstrate the ultimate reality of consciousness are those of direct meaning, while those which demonstrate emptiness are those of expedient meaning (neyārtha).[19]

Finally, there is the valid instrument of cognition of comparison which bSod-nams Sen-ge describes as follows. He says that in order to produce an understanding that all entities, though they appear, do not exist in reality, they are likened to an illusion and a mirage. An argument constructed by Nāgārjuna in conformity with this valid instrument of cognition of testimony has been presented in chapter X.

With respect to valid instruments of cognition dKon-mchog 'jigs-me dbang-po comments that objects of knowledge may be divided into the visible and invisible and again into ultimate and conventional. Perception has reference to the former, i.e., any sensory object, such as sound. He writes further that what can only be cognised dependent upon a reason has the characteristic of being inferred. An example of the latter is the cognition that sound is impermanent. Thus, the valid instruments of cognition of perception and inference correspond according to dKon-mchog 'jigs-me dbang-po to the two types of objects of cognition, i.e., the visible and the invisible. He too notes that the visible and the invisible are mutually contradictory, thus suggesting that the same object cannot be cognised by both valid instruments of cognition.

Again, for dKon-mchog 'jigs-me dbang-po, the ordinary perception of a jar constitutes an example of the conventionally real, while the knowledge that the jar does not exist in reality constitutes an instance of the ultimate truth.

Indeed, oddly enough, dKon-mchog 'jigs-me dbang-po does not recognise the valid instruments of cognition of testimony and comparison, but accepts only perception and inference.[20]

Lama Mi-pham in his summary of philosophical systems mentions the following five arguments used by the Prāsaṅgika to establish that an entity does not exist ultimately. The five are also recognised by other Tibetan scholars. Four are negations, while one takes the form of a positive argument.

They are listed as follows: one—free from one and many, two—not originated from the four alternatives, three—whatsoever is not an entity is devoid of origination. This argument relies upon the dialectic categories of existence and non-existence inasmuch as origination is equally imposisble with respect to both existence and non-existence. Four—the knowable is not efficient, since a mere moment cannot be efficient, nor can a series of moments. Five—because relationally dependent, entities do not exist in their own being.[21]

At this point we may again take a brief look at the question of the so-called objective valid instruments of cognition. The matter has already been mentioned in chapters VII and VIII. It may also be recalled that the Tibetan Prāsaṅgika rMa-bya had condemned independent syllogisms on the ground that they were constituted by the objective valid instruments of cognition. It was said on that occasion that the objective valid instruments of cognition are perception and inference inasmuch as they are conceived to correspond to an object (vastu). Indeed, all the schools of Realists advocate objective valid instruments of cognition, though their descriptions of them vary in accord with their ontological presuppositions.

rMa-bya's criticism was, however, out of place because although it may be said that the independent syllogism is constituted by the objective valid instruments of cognition, it is not the fact of their being objective, i.e., being conceived to correspond to an object which renders independent syllogisms unacceptable to the Madhyamaka on the occasion of determining the nature of the ultimate. The Prāsaṅgikas hold that a syllogism constituted by the objective valid instruments of cognition may be employed by the Madhyamaka with the specific provision that the ultimate existence of the object to which the instruments correspond is not admitted. Therefore, according to the view expressed by later Tibetan Prāsaṅgikas like bSod-nams Sen-ge, a syllogism constituted by the objective valid instruments of cognition possesses functional utility, though the object with which the syllogism is concerned is itself illusion like. With this condition the Prāsaṅgikas find no difficulty in employing arguments constituted by the objective valid instruments of cognition conventionally and ultimately.

Independent syllogisms of the type employed by the Svātantrika school on the occasion of the determination of the nature of ultimate reality, though they be objective, are more importantly held to be constituted by valid instruments of cognition as such. It is the fact that independent syllogisms are held by the Svātantrikas themselves to be constituted by valid instruments of cognition that renders such syllogisms inconsistent from the Prāsaṅgika point of view. This is true because the notion that a syllogism is constituted by virtue of valid instruments of cognition entails the admission that its elements including the substratum are accepted by both parties to a debate. The Prāsaṅgika will not accept the existence of a substratum and so on, on the occasion of the examination of the ultimate truth, hence he contends that independent syllogisms constituted by valid instruments of cognition are not possible, when the nature of ultimate reality is to be determined. For his part the Prāsaṅgika does not assert that his own arguments are constituted by valid instruments of cognition.

Thus, it may be said that whether the arguments which are employed, on the occasion of demonstrating emptiness, are said to be constituted by valid instruments of cognition or not distinguishes the Prāsaṅgika Madhyamaka from the Svātantrika Madhyamaka. As it has been said, the arguments employed by the Svātantrikas are, according to them, constituted by valid instruments of cognition. Specifically what this means is that their elements, most significantly the substratum and reason, exist commonly for both the proponent and the opponent.

So far as conventional reality is concerned, even the Prāsaṅgikas accept independent syllogisms. Therefore, the question of the legitimacy of independent syllogisms ought properly to be limited to their application at the time of examining the nature of ultimate reality. Nonetheless, the question is a crucial one because it is with the examination of ultimate truth that the Madhyamaka is most concerned. This will be evident if the Madhyamaka's universe of discourse is recalled. Indeed, it was the Madhyamaka philosophy which introduced the distinction between conventional and ultimate reality into Indian philosophy. The schools which preceded the Madhyamaka, both historically and logically, invariably presumed that their respective descriptions of reality were ultimately valid. Thus, when the opponent asserts, for instance, that entities originate from any of the four alternatives, he takes it for granted that his statement constitutes a description of ultimate reality. Therefore, inasmuch as the proposition advanced by the opponent is concerned with the nature of ultimate reality, its elements do not then exist for the Madhyamaka, according to the Prāsaṅgika interpretation.

Thus, on the occasion of the determination of the nature of ultimate reality, the substratum does not exist for the Madhyamaka. It follows that an independent syllogism is impossible, on that occasion, just because its elements, i.e., the substratum etc., do not exist commonly for both parties to the discussion.

Again, it must be remembered that conventionally an unqualified substratum is also accepted by the Prāsaṅgikas. Thus, independent syllogisms like the one establishing fire from the existence of smoke are quite legitimate for the Prāsaṅgikas since the arguments are only concerned with determining the nature of conventional reality. In such a situation, the existence of a substratum like the hill is accepted even by the Prāsaṅgikas.

An important element of the polemic advanced by the Svātantrikas against the Prāsaṅgika's rejection of a common substratum on the occasion of the determination of the nature of the ultimate, is the contention that if nothing whatsoever exists commonly, the Madhyamaka will not then advance any proposition or argument. If, indeed, nothing whatsoever exists for the Madhyamaka, when the ultimate is in question whence comes his assertion of the ultimate emptiness of all entities and whence his arguments in support of this standpoint.

Now, as it has been mentioned, the existence of a substratum is accepted conventionally by the Prāsaṅgikas. bSod-nams Sen-ge supplies the following extremely interesting description of the method of the Prāsaṅgika. His description makes use of a division into three stages, the first two of which successfully resolve the apparent inconsistency between the Madhyamaka's propositions and arguments and his non-acceptance of the existence of any entity on the occasion of the examination of the nature of ultimate reality. His interpretation is based upon a critically important stanza authored by Nāgārjuna which occurs both in the *Mūlamadhyamakakārikā* and in the *Vigrahavyāvartanī*. The stanza in question is the tenth of the twenty-fourth chapter of the *Mūlamadhyamakakārikā* and reads as follows. "Without relying upon the conventional, the ultimate is not taught. Without reaching the ultimate, Nirvāṇa is not attained." The same stanza is also cited by Nāgārjuna in the *Vigrahavyāvartanī* where it is used to explain the origin of the Madhyamaka's refutation of the ultimate existence of all entities.

For convenience sake we may term the three stages, outlined by bSod-nams Sen-ge, the precritical, critical and postcritical. He says that on the occasion of the examination of any entity, through logic appropriate to the determination of the ultimate truth, the substratum and the example are unproven for the Madhyamaka. Therefore, an independent reason (hetu) is not then produced by the Prāsaṅgika.

Nonetheless, even on that occasion, the substratum which represents the object of examination, i.e., any entity such as a sprout and the like is apprehended by means of one of the four conventional valid instruments of cognition. This occurs on the precritical stage before any argument is produced. This is the meaning, says bSod-nams Sen-ge, of the statement made by the Master cited above, i.e., "Without relying upon the conventional the ultimate is not taught."

On the second stage, which we have termed the critical stage, when the ultimate examination of the object has commenced, the Madhyamaka takes up his characteristic standpoint. Then, the existence of the object is not admitted by the Madhyamaka. Therefore, on the critical stage when the ultimate examination of an entity is in progress, an independent syllogism is impossible, according to bSod-nams Sen-ge, because the substratum and reason do not exist for the Madhyamaka. The opponent, on the contrary, continues to admit the reality of the object or entity even on the second critical stage.

Finally, on the third and last stage, when the argument produced by the Madhyamaka has exercised its function and the opponent has been brought to an understanding of emptiness, he also will abandon his notion that anything exists in reality. On the final stage then, no difference is apprehended between the standpoint of the Madhyamaka and that of the opponent.[22]

While no doubt, the third stage set forth by bSod-nams Sen-ge, may not have always been realized in actual fact, it must still be admitted that the interpretation, which he gives constitutes a highly intelligible schema for understanding the soteriological transition from the conditioned to the unconditioned and ultimate expressed in the concepts of logic and philosophy. Thus, the purity of the critical philosophy of the Madhyamaka's is preserved while at the same time the pragmatic concerns of soteriology are satisfied. In conclusion it may simply be noted that this interpretation of the Madhyamaka method is in complete agreement with the opinions expressed by Nāgārjuna and Candrakīrti.

REFERENCES

1. *dBu-ma-spyi-ston*, p. 376.
2. *Mūlamadhyamakakārika*, III. 2.
3. *Op.cit.* pp. 376-377.
4. *dBu-ma-spyi-ston*, p. 377.
5. *Ibid.* p. 378; dKon-mchog 'jigs med dbang-po, holds that to be conventional is to be false. Guenther, H. V., *Buddhist Philosophy in Theory and Practice*, p. 144.
6. Guenther, H. V., *Buddhist Philosophty in Theory and Practice*, p. 153.
7. *dBu-ma-spyi-ston*, p. 377.
8. Kajiyama, Y., *Bhāvaviveka and the Prāsaṅgika School*, Mookerjee, Satkari (ed.). *The Nava-Nalanda-Mahavihar Research Publication*. Vol. 1, pp. 291-331. Nalanda. 1957; Iida Shotaro, The nature of samvṛti and the relationship of paramārtha to it in Svātantrika-Madhyamaka. Sprung. M, (ed.), *Two truths in Buddhism and Vedanta*. pp. 64-77, Holland, 1973.
9. Bhāvaviveka's *Madhyamakārtha Saṁgraha* was restored into Sanskrit by Pt. Aiyāswami Sāstri; JOR (Madras) Vol. V, pp. 44 ff. Murti, T. R. V., *The General Philosophy of Buddhism*, p. 98.
10. *dBu-ma-spyi-ston, B.* 378.
11. *Prasannapadā* commentary to *Mūlamadhyamakakārikā*, XVIII and *Madhyamakāvatāra*, VI.
12. *Op. cit.* p. 379.
13. *dBu-ma-spyi-ston*, p. 380.
14. *Ibid.*
15. *Ibid.* p. 381.
16. *Ibid.* p. 382.
17. *Ibid.*
18. *Ibid.* p. 384.
19. *Ibid.*
20. Guenther, H. V., *Buddhist Philosophy in Theory and Practice*, pp. 144-145.
21. *Ibid.* pp. 150-151.
22. *dBu-ma-spyi-ston*, p. 385.

CONCLUSION

As has been stressed, the Madhyamaka is a philosophy of a qualitatively different order. The Madhyamaka seeks to dismantle the phenomenal universe which is constructed by imagination through sustained dialectical analysis. In this way, the Madhyamaka attempts to reveal the unconditioned and non-differentiated nature of the ultimately real.

The Madhyamaka philosophy expresses the quintessence of the teaching of the Buddha Śākyamuni. In the Madhyamaka the full extent of the Buddha's characteristic philosophical attitude is disclosed and elaborated. Thus the Madhyamaka constitutes a complete and systematic critical philosophy.

Through the expedients of concepts and language, the Madhyamaka attempts to indicate the actual nature of ultimate reality, which transcends thought and expression. The conception of the ultimately real offered by the Madhyamaka is a revolutionary one. It is for this reason that the advent of the Madhyamaka system represented a significant turning point in the development of Indian philosophy. Indeed, it may be said without fear of contradiction that nearly all the major philosophical systems of India were profoundly affected by the appearance of the Madhyamaka.

The fundamental characteristics of the Madhyamaka account, in large part, for the influence which the system had upon Indian philosophy as a whole. The Madhyamaka was, in the first place, acutely aware of the subjective character of thought which, according to the Madhyamaka conception, fabricates the universe of appearance. This awareness led, more or less directly, to a conception of ultimate reality as a state in which appearance is dispelled through the extinction of subjective imagination. Thus, it may be said that the cessation of subjective imagination results in the dissolution of the universe of appearance which obscures the non-differentiated and non-dual nature of the ultimately real.

The revolutionary character of these conceptions will be appreciated if it is recalled that no philosophy prior to the Madhyamaka realised the universality of the activity of subjective imagination or conceived of reality as an ineffable and unconditioned state altogether free from duality. Hence, the Madhyamaka clearly represents the first systematic formulation of a philosophy of absolute non-duality in India.

It is, however, important to remember that the implications of these conceptions elaborated in the Madhyamaka extend beyond the limits of what may be termed scholastic philosophy. The Madhyamaka, as it has been emphasised, is above all a soteriological philosophy. It is intended to produce an existential transformation in the individual. Philosophy, therefore, for the Madhyamaka is more than simply an intellectual exercise. On the contrary, philosophy supplies a means of achieving an actual transition from a condition of ignorance and bondage to one of knowledge and freedom. It is the critical awareness of the subjective origin of the universe of appearance which enables one to remove the subjective illusion which obscures the actual nature of the ultimately real.

It is a primary concern with any soteriological philosophy that it be successfully communicated to others. The extraordinary knowledge which has, in the case of the philosopher, engendered the desired existential transformation must be communicated to those who are ignorant of it. This communication must necessarily be accomplished through concepts and language, even when the extraordinary knowledge which is to be communicated ultimately transcends thought and expression. In this context, it is clear that the process of communication is an especially difficult one for the Madhyamaka, because, as it has been noted, the Madhyamaka is a philosophy of a radically different order.

The approach of the Madhyamaka to the problem of communicating the extraordinary knowledge achieved through philosophy to the uninitiated tends to be rational or analytical, rather than symbolic or suggestive. Thus, it is that the Madhyamaka philosopher employs various arguments which conform, to a greater or lesser degree, to the conventionally accepted patterns of logical discourse. Through these arguments, the Madhyamaka seeks to lead the uninitiated, gradually to a comprehension of the existential import of the Madhyamaka philosophy.

In the process of communicating the extraordinary knowledge

initially available only to the philosopher, ordinary facts must necessarily be employed. Only then can the extraordinary knowledge achieved by the philosopher be successfully communicated to the uninitiated. The arguments employed by the Prāsaṅgika and Svātantrika schools of the Madhyamaka system, therefore, represent attempts to communicate the extraordinary knowledge embodied in the Madhyamaka philosophy to the uninitiated through concepts and language.

Yet when the philosopher attempts to express extraordinary knowledge through concepts and language, amenable to the understanding of the uninitiated, he must take great care to preserve the essential purity of the extraordinary philosophical knowledge which he is anxious to communicate. Otherwise, the clarity and precision of his extraordinary philosophical vision will become obscured and distorted in the process of communication. If this occurs, the extraordinary knowledge, embodied in the Madhyamaka philosophy will be only imperfectly communicated. Perhaps even more importantly, there exists the danger that the philosopher himself may unconsciously forsake, in some degree, the perfection of the extraordinary knowledge which it was his intention to communicate. The controversy between the Prāsaṅgika and Svātantrika schools must, in the final analysis, be seen in the light of this fundamental problem. The exponents of both schools clearly desired to communicate the extraordinary knowledge embodied in the Madhyamaka philosophy to the uninitiated. In their attempt to do so, they resorted to divergent modes of argument. The success or failure of their respective approaches to the problem of communication must be measured within the twofold context suggested earlier. It must be judged to what degree the arguments employed by the two schools succeed in communicating effectively the extraordinary knowledge embodied in the Madhyamaka philosophy, while, at the same time, preserving the purity and perfection of that very extraordinary knowledge.

The verdict delivered by the history of the development of the Madhyamaka philosophy eventually favoured the Prāsaṅgikas. Over the course of centuries, the approach adopted by the Prāsaṅgikas emerged as the predominantly accepted one. The Svātantrika interpretation, on the other hand, steadily lost ground after the collapse of Buddhism in India until, at present, only vestiges of it are preserved in the living Buddhist traditions of Tibet and Mongolia.

Though the controversy with which this study has been largely concerned may have been decided by the history of philosophy, the central problem which has been indicated in these concluding pages continues even today to be a very relevant one. Indeed, all those who are at present engaged in the communication of the knowledge contained in the ancient and now, for the most part, fragmented philosophical traditions of India to modern men cannot afford to ignore the central problem which divided the two Madhyamaka schools. Thus it is that all attempts to communicate the essential import of ancient Indian philosophical systems through concepts and language amenable to the comprehension of modern men must be judged within the twofold context which has been suggested. All such attempts must seek to accomplish satisfactorily two indispensable objectives. They must seek to communicate effectively the knowledge embodied in ancient Indian philosophy in contemporary concepts and language, while at the same time preserving the purity of the ancient philosophical vision. Only then will it be possible to ensure the vitality, purity and continuity of the philosophical wisdom of ancient India.

APPENDIX A

An Abridged Biography of bSod-nams Sen-ge

(Based upon the Tibetan biography entitled, *The Marvellous Jewel Garland—Ño-mtshar-Rin-po-che'i Phren-ba*).[1]

The teacher, bSod-nams Seṅ-ge, was born in 'Bom-la-stan-' 'bom-luṅ-mdah.[2] His father was Ru-tsha Shan-skyabs. His mother was rgyal-ba-sman. He was born in the Tibetan earth-bird year, i.e., 1429.

As a child, bSod-nams Seṅ-ge was precocious. He mastered reading effortlessly.

When he attained the age of ten, bSod-nams Seṅ-ge reflected that all living beings who dwell in the world are afflicted by many various kinds of sufferings. Hence, he resolved to renounce the world and begged his parents' permission to do so.

When his parents had given him their consent, he was given the vows of a novice monk by the abbot Byan-chub-sems-pa Kun-dgah-'bum. It was then that he was given the name, bSod-nams Seṅ-ge.

Then bSod-nams Seṅ-ge began formally to study Buddhist philosophy under the abbot Kun-dgah-'bum. He was introduced to logic and began to commit texts to memory. He was remarkably diligent and soon excelled among the students of Kun dgah-'bum.

By the time bSod-nams Seṅ-ge had attained the age of nineteen, he had mastered a wide variety of texts, including the texts of logic and Pāramitā. It was then that an overwhelming desire took hold of him to go to central Tibet in search of further instruction in the holy Dharma. Thus, he set about gathering together travelling companions and provision for the journey.

At the beginning of the following year, he left his native land together with many young students. Travelling via the Koṅ-lam they eventually reached bSam-yas, then bSaṅ phu, and finally Lhasa. At all the holy places along their route, bSod-nams Seṅ-ge offered prayers.

In the summer of the same year, bSod-nams Seṅ-ge came to the monastery of Na-lindra,[3] where the renowned scholar Roṅ-ston was teaching. He was received by the master and was greatly pleased. At that time, a great number of students had assembled to hear discourses from the great Roṅ-ston. bSod-nams Seṅ-ge developed a firm faith in the master and decided to remain at Na-lindra, where he pursued his studies throughout the summer. He made rapid progress and, even at Na-lindra equalled the most gifted students in intellectual ability.

In the autumn, bSod-nams Seṅ-ge proceeded to Lhasa, where he met the scholar, gLiṅ-sman Paṇḍita Śe-rab dPal-ldan-pa from whom he received the āgama of the Manjuśrī-nāmasaṅgiti. Śe-rab dPal-ldan-pa also taught him the biographies of a number of great teachers, including that of Roṅ-ston.

bSod-nams Seṅ-ge could not study further with the great Roṅ-ston, because the master, unfortunately, passed away that very year. Then, hearing of an excellent scholar called Saṅs-rgyas-'phel who was teaching at the institute of Bras-yul, bSod-nams Seṅ-ge decided to go there to pursue his studies of the doctrine. At the institute of 'Bras-yul, he studied advanced philosophy under the scholar Saṅs-rgyas-'phel. There too, all were amazed by his extraordinary intelligence.

After bSod-nams Seṅ-ge had been at the institute of 'Bras-yul, he conceived the idea of going to the great monastery of Ae-wam chos-sde to study Tantra under the famous master rDo-rje-' chaṅ Kun-dgah-bzaṅ-po.[4]

At Ae-wam chos-sde, he was ordained by the master Kun-dgaḥ-bzaṅ-po at the age of twenty six.

There bSod-nams Seṅ-ge studied Tantra under Kun-dgaḥ-bzaṅ-po and his successor dKon-mchog rGyal-mtshan. In addition, he studied ethics at Ae-wam chos-sde. It is said that he not only mastered all the instructions which he received, but also practised them.

In the iorn-dragon year, i.e., 1461, when bSod-nams Seṅ-ge was thirty two years old, he left Ae-wam chos-sde, in the company of his elder half brother, with the intention of returning to Khams to visit his parents and practise meditation. On their way to Khams they stopped at the institute of 'Bras-yul where bSod-nams Seṅ-ge had studied philosophy under Saṅs-rgyas-'phel.

bSod-nams Sen-ge distinguished himself as the foremost among all the learned scholars there in philosophical debate. His skill in debate amazed all who were present, particularly because he had for many years devoted himself primarily to the study of Tantra. As a result of his success, the head of the institute, Saṅs-rgyas-'phel asked bSod-nams Seṅ-ge to remain there to study and teach. Though he was unwilling to remain, he was eventually pursuaded to do so through the intervention of dKon-mchog rGyal-mtshan. bSod-nams Seṅ-ge then remained at the institute of 'Bras-yul, while his half brother proceeded alone to Khams.

Not long after two of the senior instructors at the institute left to pursue their studies in different parts of Tibet. bSod-nams Seṅ-ge then assumed the role of assistant teacher at the institute.

When the Head of the institute, Saṅs-rgyas-'phel, left to receive additional Tāntric instructions from dKon-mchog-rGyal-mtshan, he asked bSod-nams Seṅ-ge to act as the Head of the institute in his absence. After Saṅs-rgyas- 'phel's departure, bSod-nams Seṅ-ge taught the texts of Pāramitā, logic, Vinaya and Abhidharma at the institute. The knowledge of the students at the institute increased markedly during the course of his teaching. As a result, his fame spread throughout the dBus-gTsaṅ[5] region. It was then, that he composed, among other works, a commentary on the sDom-gsum Rab-dbye of Sa-skya Paṇḍita and a summary of Pāramitā.

When Saṅs-rgyas-'phel returned to the institute, bSod-nams Seṅ-ge went to Ae-wam Chos-sde at the request of dKon-mchog rGyal-mtshan. There he continued his studies under dKon-mchog rGyal-mtshan, meditated, taught and composed a number of biographies and works on Tantra. He became acquainted with bSod-nams Chos-kyi-kun-dgaḥ bKra-śis-rgyal-mtshan dPal-bzaṅ-po who suggested that bSod-nams Seṅ-ge found a monastic institute of his own. bSod-nams Seṅ-ge accepted bSod-nams Chos-kyi-kun-dgah bKra-śis-rgyal-mtshan dPal bzaṅpo's suggestion and together they resolved to found an institute in the near future. Shortly thereafter, bSod-nams Seṅ-ge first founded a small monastic institute at rTa-nag gSer-gliṅ in upper gTsaṅ.

bSod-nams Seṅ-ge founded his institute at rTa-nag gSergliṅ with the objective of furthering the study of Buddhist religion and philosophy in Tibet. The method of instruction pursued at the institute conformed to the tradition which had been established by Roṅ-ston and other masters of the Sa-skya doctrine.

Eventually a permanent location was found for the institute at rTa-nag Rin-che-rtse and in 1474, bSod-nams Seṅ-ge took up his residence there. He named the monastery Thub-bstan rNam-rgyal. At Thub-bstan rNam-rgyal, bSod-nams Seṅ-ge taught logic and Pāramitā with detailed explanations. He also taught Vinaya and composed works on Sūtra and Tantra.

Among others, he taught the following texts: the *Abhisamayālaṅkāra*, with its commentary composed by Haribhadra, the *Abhidharmakośa* of Vasubandhu, the *Abhidharmasamuccaya* of Asaṅga, the five principal texts of the Madhyamaka system composed by Nāgārjuna, the *Catuḥśataka* of Āryadeva, the *Madhyamakāvatāra* of Candrakīrti, the *Bodhicaryāvatāra* of Śāntideva, the *Pramāṇavārttika* of Dharmakīrti, the *sDòm-gsum Rab-dbye* and the *Tshad-ma Rig-gter* of Sa-skya Pandita. bSod-nams Seṅ-ge taught all these texts from memory, along with detailed explanations. In addition, he taught numerous Tāntric texts, including the three Hevajra Tantras, the *Cakrasaṁbharatantra* and the *Guhyasamājatantra* with its commentary composed by Candrakīrti, the *Pradīpa-uddyotana*.

bSod--nams Seṅ-ge wrote numerous works, including several texts on Pāramitā, a commentary on the *Pramāṇavārttika*, a commentary on the *Tshad-ma Rigs-gter* of Sa-skya Pandita, a commentary on the *Mūlamadhyamakakārikā*, a commentary on the *Madhyamakāvatāra*, an exposition of the Madhyamaka system entitled the *dBu-ma spyi-ston*, a summary of the six treatises of Nāgārjuna and the like. In addition, he composed many works on Tantra.

bSod-nams Seṅ-ge was, moreover, a skilled debator who vanquished many opponents in philosophical disputations. Thus he performed the three activities of a scholar, i.e., instruction, composition and philosophical disputation.

bSod-nams Seṅ-ge also later assumed the post of abbot of the great monastery of Ae-wam Chos-sde. He held the post for four years. There he delivered many Tāntric teachings, most notably that of the Lam 'Bras. Throughout the years during which he held the post of abbot of the Ae-wam chos-sde monastery, he continued to look after his own monastery of Thub-bstan rNam-rgyal, dividing his time between the two institutions. After his retirement from the post of abbot of Ae-wam chos-sde monastery, bSod-nams Seṅ-ge devoted himself to the further improvement of the standard of study at Thub-bstan rNam-rgyal.

bSod-nams Seṅ-ge also visited many places throughout central Tibet to teach on the invitations extended by various persons. In particular, he often taught at mDo-mkhar Khro-phu and 'Bo-sdoms. He twice visited Sa-skya where he taught, prayed and received numerous offerings. During the later portion of his life, he was acclaimed throughout Tibet as a genuine Buddha.

In 1490, while returning to Thub-bstan rNam-rgyal from his second visit to Sa-skya, bSod-nams Seṅ-ge passed away. His cremated remains were enshrined at Thub-bstan rNam-rgyal.

References

1. *The biography of bSod-nams Seṅ-ge* composed by W. Konston, a direct disciple of the former, was edited and published by T. G. Dhongthog. Delhi. 1973.
2. In the province of Khams.
3. The monastery of Na-lindra in Tibet was founded by the great Ron-ston.
4. rDo-rje-'chan Kun-dgah-bzaṅ-po was the founder of the Nor-pa subsect of the Sa-sKya order.
5. dBu-Tsaṅ refers to Central Tibet.

APPENDIX B

English-Sanskrit-Tibetan Glossary of Technical Terms

1. Accepted = Svīkāra, aṅgīkāra = ཁས་བླངས་པ།
2. Action = Karma = ལས།
3. Agent = Kartṛ བྱེད་པ་པོ།
4. Aggregate = Skandha = ཕུང་པོ།
5. Analysis = Vicāra = རྣམ་པར་དཔྱོད་པ།
6. Application = Upanaya = ཉེ་བར་སྦྱོར་བ།
7. Argument *ad absurdum*, reductio *ad absurdum* = Prasaṅga-Vākya, = Prasaṅga = ཐལ་བར་འགྱུར་བའི་ཚིག། ཐལ་འགྱུར།
8. Cause = Hetu = རྒྱུ།
9. Characteristic = Lakṣaṇa = མཚན་ཉིད།
10. Commonly established substratum = Samāna-pratibhāsa-siddha-dharmin = ཆོས་ཅན་མཐུན་སྣང་དུ་གྲུབ།པ།
11. Commonly given = Samāna-pratibhāsa = མཐུན་པར་སྣང་བ།
12. Comparison = Upamāna = དཔེ་ཉེར་འཇལ་གྱི་ཚད་མ།
13. Conclusion = Nigamana = མཇུག་བསྡུ་བ།
14. Condition = Pratyaya = རྐྱེན།
15. Consciousness = Vijñāna = རྣམ་པར་ཤེས་པ།
16. Conscious Principle = Caitanya = བདག་ཤེས་རིག་གི་སྐྱེས་བུ།
17. Constructions of thought = Prapañca = སྤྲོས་པ།
18. Contradiction = Viruddha, Virodha = འགལ་བ།
19. Contradictory reason = Viruddha-hetu = འགལ་རྟགས
20. Convention, Conventional truth = Vyavahāra, Saṁvyavahāra, = Vyavahāra-satya = ཐ་སྙད། ཐ་སྙད་བདེན་པ།
21. Conventional valid instruments of Cognition = Loka-prasiddha-pramāṇa = འཇིག་རྟེན་ན་གྲགས་པའི་ཚད་མ།
22. Delusion = Bhrānti, Bhrānta = འཁྲུལ་པ།

23. Effect = Phala = འབྲས་བུ།
24. Efficacious = Arthakriyākāri = དོན་བྱེད་པ།
25. Element = Dharma = ཆོས།
26. Emptiness = Śūnyatā = སྟོང་པ་ཉིད།
27. Entity = Bhāva, vastu = དངོས་པོ།
28. Error = Viparyāsa = ཕྱིན་ཅི་ལོག།
29. Established = Siddha = གྲུབ་པ།
30. Established by valid instruments of cognition = Pramāṇa-siddha = ཚད་མས་གྲུབ་པ།
31. Examination = Parīkṣā = རྣམ་པར་བརྟག་པ།
32. Example = Dṛṣṭānta, udāharaṇa, upamā = དཔེ།, ཉེ་བར་བསྟན་པ།
33. Fallacious = Nirākṛta = སེལ་བ།
34. False = Mithyā = བརྫུན།
35. Five-membered inference = Pañcāvayavī-hetu = ཡན་ལག་ལྔ་པའི་རྗེས་དཔག།
36. Four alternatives = Catuṣkoṭi = མུ་བཞི།, མཐའ་བཞི།
37. Given or apparent fact = Pratibhāsa-dharma = སྣང་བའི་ཆོས།
38. Ground of distinction = Viśeṣa-hetu = རྒྱུ་མཚན་གྱི་ཁྱད་ཆོས།
39. Illusion = Māyā = སྒྱུ་མ།
40. Imagination = Vikalpa = རྣམ་པར་རྟོག་པ།
41. Imputed = Parikalpita = ཀུན་བརྟགས་
42. Independent proposition = Svatantra-pratijñā = རང་རྒྱུད་ཀྱི་དམ་བཅའ།
43. Independent syllogism = Svatantra-anumāna = རང་རྒྱུད་ཀྱི་རྟགས།
44. Inference = Anumāna = རྗེས་དཔག།
45. Inference familiar to the opponent = Para-prasiddha-anumāna = གཞན་ལ་གྲགས་པའི་རྗེས་དཔག།
46. Infinite regress, *ad infinitum* = Anavasthā = མཐའ་མེད།
47. Insubstantiality = Niḥsvabhāvatā = རང་བཞིན་མེད་པ།
48. Intellect = Buddhi = བློ།
49. Interdependent origination = Pratītya-samutpāda = རྟེན་ཅིང་འབྲེལ་བར་འབྱུང་བ།
50. Knowledge = Jñāna = ཡེ་ཤེས།

51. Knowledge of the right vision = Śuddha-dṛṣṭi-jñāna = གཟིགས་པ་དག་པའི་ཡེ་ཤེས།
52. Logic = Yukti, nyāya = རིགས་པ།
53. Logical subject, minor term = Dharmin = ཆོས་ཅན།
54. Major term = Sādhya = བསྒྲུབ་བྱ།
55. Major premise, invariable concomitance = Vyâpti = ཁྱབ་པ།
56. Manifested = Vyakta = གསལ་བ།
57. Method = Upāya = ཐབས།
58. Minor premise = Pakṣa-dharma = ཕྱོགས་ཆོས།
59. Nature = Dharmatā-paristhiti = ཆོས་ཉིད།, གནས་ལུགས།
60. Negative concomitance = Vyatireka = ལྡོག་ཁྱབ།
61. Non-Buddhist = Tīrthika = མུ་སྟེགས་པ།
62. Object = Artha, Vastu = དོན། དངོས་པོ།
63. Object of cognition = Jñeya = ཤེས་བྱ།
64. Object of refutation = Pratiṣedhya = དགག་བྱ།
65. Objective valid instruments of cognition = Vastuvala-pravṛtta-pramāṇa = དངོས་པོ་སྟོབས་ཞུགས་ཀྱི་མཚན་མ།
66. Only in general = Sāmānya-mātra = སྤྱི་ཙམ།
67. Opponent = Prativādī = ཕྱིར་རྒོལ།
68. Ordinary people = Pṛthagjana = སོ་སོའི་སྐྱེ་བོ།
69. Origination = Utpatti = སྐྱེ་བ།
70. Origination from another = Parata-utpatti = གཞན་སྐྱེས།
71. Own being, self-existence = Svabhāva = རང་བཞིན།
72. Own substantiality = Svātmatā, Svātmā = རང་གི་བདག་ཉིད།
73. Perception = Pratyakṣa = མངོན་སུམ།
74. Phenomenal, Phenomenal truth = Saṁvṛti, Saṁvṛti-satya = ཀུན་རྫོབ། ཀུན་རྫོབ་བདེན་པ།
75. Position = Pakṣa = ཕྱོགས།
76. Positive concomitance = Anvaya = རྗེས་ཁྱབ།
77. Preferred proposition = Abhīṣṭapratijñā = ཞེ་འདོད་ཀྱི་དམ་བཅའ།
78. Primordial matter = Pradhāna = གཙོ་བོ།

79. Probandum = Vyāpaka = ཁྱབ་བྱེད།
80. Probans = Vyāpya = ཁྱབ་བྱ།
81. Property = Dharma = ཆོས།
82. Property or predicate of the proposition = Sādhya-dharma- བསྒྲུབ་བྱའི་ཆོས།
83. Proponent = Vādī = སྨྲ་བ།
84. Proposition = Pratijñā = དམ་བཅའ།
85. Proposition of a truly established element = Satya-siddha-dharma-pratijñā = བདེན་གྲུབ་ཀྱི་ཆོས་ཀྱི་དམ་བཅའ།
86. Proving what is already proved = Siddha-sādhana = གྲུབ་པ་ལ་བསྒྲུབ་པ།
87. Realist = Vastuvādin = དངོས་པོར་སྨྲ་བ།
88. Reason = Hetu = རྟགས།
89. Reason of causality = Kārya-hetu = འབྲས་རྟགས།
90. Reason of identity = Svabhāva-hetu = རང་བཞིན་གྱི་རྟགས།
91. Refutation = Pratiṣedha, niṣedha = དགག་པ།
92. Self-origination = Sva-utpatti = བདག་སྐྱེས།
93. Store house consciousness = Ālaya-vijñāna = ཀུན་གཞི་རྣམ་ཤེས།
94. Subjective poles of consciousness = Ādhyātmikāyatana = ནང་གི་སྐྱེ་མཆེད།
95. Substratum = Āśraya = གཞི།
96. Testimony = Āgama = ལུང་།
97. Three-membered syllogism = Trirūpa-anumāna = ཚུལ་གསུམ་གྱི་རྟགས།
98. True – Satya – བདེན་པ།
99. Truly established = Satya-siddha = བདེན་གྲུབ།
100. Two truths = Satyadvaya = བདེན་པ་གཉིས།
101. Ultimate truth, reality = Paramārtha-satya = དོན་དམ་བདེན་པ།
102. Uncertain reason = Anaikāntika-hetu = མཐའ་མ་ངེས་པ།
103. Unproven invariable concomitance = Asiddha-vyāpti = ཁྱབ་པ་མ་གྲུབ་པ།
104. Unproven substratum = Asiddhāśraya = གཞི་མ་གྲུབ་པ།
105. Valid instruments of Cognition = Pramāṇa = ཚད་མ།
106. View = Dṛṣṭi, darśana = ལྟ་བ།
107. Without cause = Ahetu = རྒྱུ་མེད། རྒྱུ་མེད་པ།

BIBLIOGRAPHY

(a) *Original Texts*

Bodhicaryāvatāra of Śāntideva. Edited by P. L. Vaidya. Buddhist Sanskrit Text No. 12. Published by The Mithila Institute. Darbhaṅga. 1960.

dBu-ma spyi-ston by bSod-nams Sen-ge. Published by Sakya Institute of Tibetan Buddhist Philosophy, Dehradun. 1975.

Mūlamadhyamakakārikā of Nāgārjuna. Edited by P. L. Vaidya in *Madhyamakaśāstram.* Buddhist Sanskrit Text No. 10. Published by The Mithila Institute. Darbhaṅga. 1960.

No-mtshar-Rin-po-che'i-phen-ba (The Biography of bSod-nams Senge) by W. Kon-ston. Edited and published by T. G. Dhongthog. Delhi, 1973.

Prasannapadā of Candrakīrti. Edited by P. L. Vaidya in *Madhyamakaśāstram.* Buddhist Sanskrit Text No. 10. Published by The Mithila Institute. Darbhaṅga, 1960.

Sakya-mchog-ldan-gsun-'bum (The complete works of Sakya-mchog-ldan). Published by Kunzang Tobgey. Delhi, 1975.

Śūnyatāsaptati of Nāgārjuna. bsTan-'gyur, mDo. XVII. 4.

Vigrahavyāvartanī of Nāgārjuna. Edited by P. L. Vaidya in *Madhyamakaśāstram.* Buddhist Sanskrit Text No. 10. Published by The Mithila Institute. Darbhanga, 1960.

(b) *Translations and Modern Works*

Conze, Edward, *The Perfection of Wisdom in Eight Thousand Lines and its Verse Summary.* Four Seasons Foundation, Berkeley, California, 1975.

Guenther, H. V., *Buddhist Philosophy in Theory and Practice.* Shambala Publications. London, 1976.

Hopkins, Jeffrey and Lati Rimpoche, *The Precious Garland* (Ratnāvalī) *and The Song of the Four Mindfulness.* The Wisdom of Tibet series—2. George Allen and Unwin. London, 1975.

Iida, Shotaro, *The Nature of Saṁvṛti and the Relationship of Paramārtha to it in Svatantra-Mādhyamika.* '*Two Truths in Buddhism and Vedānta*'. Edited by M. Sprung. Dordrecht, Holland. 1973.

Inada, Kenneth K., Nagarjuna: *A Translation of his Mūlamādhyamikakārikā with an Introductory Essay*. Hokuseid Press, Tokyo, 1970.

Jamspal, L. and Della Santina, Peter, *The Heart of Inter-dependent Origination* (Pratītyasamutpādahṛdayakārikā of Nāgārjuna). *The Journal of the Department of Buddhist Studies*, University of Delhi, 1974.

Kajiyama, Y., Bhāvaviveka and the Prāsaṅgika School. '*The Nava-Nalanda-Mahavihara Research Publication*'. Vol. I. Edited by Satkari Mookerjee. Nalanda., 1957.

Lama Chimpa and Chattopadhyaya, A., *Tāranātha's History of Buddhism in India*. Indian Institute of Advanced Study, Simla, 1970.

Mookerjee, Satkari, *The Absolutist's Standpoint in Logic. The Nava-Nalanda-Mahavihara Research Publication*. Vol. I. Edited by the Author. Nalanda, 1957.

Mookerjee, Satkari and Nagasaki, Hojun, *The Pramāṇavārttikam* of Dharmakīrti '*The Nava-Nalanda-Mahavihara Research Publication*. Vol. IV. Nalanda, 1964.

Murti, T. R. V., *The Central Philosophy of Buddhism*. George Allen and Unwin. London, 1960.

Obermiller, E., Bu-ston's *History of Buddhism*. Suzuki Research Foundation Reprint Series—5. Heidelberg., 1931.

Ramanan, K. V., *Nagarjuna's Philosophy*. Bharatiya Vidya Prakashan. Varanasi—1, 1971.

Robinson, Richard H., *Early Mādhyamika in India and China*. Motilal Banarsidass, Delhi.

Roerich, G. N., *The Blue Annals* (Parts I and II). Motilal Banarsidass. Delhi, 1976.

Stcherbatsky. Th. *The Conception of Buddhist Nirvāṇa*. Motilal Banarsidass, Delhi.

Vidyabhusana, M. M. Satis Chandra, *A History of Indian Logic*. Motilal Banarsidass, Delhi, 1971.

INDEX

Bu-ston 21, 25, 27,
on Candrakīrti 24
Byan-chub-sems-pa Kum-dgah-'bum 223

Cakrasaṁbharatantra 226
Candragupta 21
Candrakīrti 14, 20, 23, 24, 25, 26, 27, 28, 35, 36, 37, 40, 53, 56, 57, 59, 60, 61, 62, 64, 67, 69, 78, 79, 81, 94, 100, 105, 110, 111, 121, 128, 133, 134, 135, 136, 137, 140, 141, 146, 153, 155, 157, 159, 161, 167, 168, 172, 177, 189, 191, 193, 194, 198, 199, 200, 202, 205, 206, 217
, miraculous powers of 24
, notions cited by 36
Candrakīrti's contributions to philosophical literature of Madhyamaka system 24
Cārvākas 63, 192
Catuḥśataka 21, 24, 40, 156, 226
Catuḥstava 19
Causality 36, 43, 101, 130
, combined notion of 187
, combined refutation of 186, 187
, critique of 43
, empirical 194
, function of 38
, interpretation of 131, 184
, law of 37, 38, 39
, nihilist denial of 193
, notion of 195
, problem of 43, 186, 198, 202, 210
Cause, primary or material (hetu-pratyaya) 172
Cause and effect 43, 63, 121 ff, 126f, 133 f, 180, 184 ff, 171 ff, 176, 180 f, 186, 196
, analysis of 123
, existential status of 125
, relationship between 43
Cause and conditions 105, 106, 118
Cause and non-cause 176, 177, 178, 211
Cintāmaṇicakra 27
Cognition 61, 67, 78, 69, 74, 80, 113
, conventional valid instruments of 156, 207
, four conventional valid instruments of 217
, four valid instruments of 74, 204, 207, 208
, instruments of 69, 70, 90, 100, 113, 114
, objective valid instruments of 213
, objects of (prameya) 113, 114, 208
, problem of valid instruments of 105
, self- 82
, three later valid instruments of 208
, two types of objects of 213
, valid instruments of 109, 110, 111, 112, 113, 114, 125, 148, 165, 204, 206, 207, 208, 209, 210, 212, 213, 214, 215
, ultimate valid instruments of 208
Comparison 100, 109, 110, 125, 204
Concomitance
, invariable (vyāpti) 49, 50, 51, 52, 56
, negative (vyatireka) 52, 53, 149
, positive (anvaya) 52, 53, 146, 147
Condition (pratyaya) 121, 122
, dominant (adhipati-pratyaya) 172, 173, 174, 175
Conditions, examination of (pratyaya-parīkṣā) 120
, four 172, 173, 174
, Madhyamaka criticism of 173
, objective (ālambaṇa-pratyaya) 172
, sequential (samanantara-pratyaya) 172
Consciousness (citta) 35, 89,
, eye (cakṣu-āyatana) 81
, subjective poles of (ādhyātmikāyatana) 61, 64
Constructions, thought (prapañca) 206

Dantapuri monastery 22
Daśabhūmivibhāṣāśāstra 19
dBu-ma-spyi-ston 141, 194, 226
dBus-g Tsaṅ 225
deeds (karma) 109
Devadatta 117
Dharmakīrti 24, 48, 52, 53, 67, 104, 137
, Buddhist formal ligic of 51
Dīgha Nikāya 4
Diṅnāga 24, 25, 48, 51, 52, 53, 57, 64, 67, 70, 137, 167
, logic of 51, 57, 104
, reformed syllogism of 51
Discourses, holy (sūtra) 80
dKon-mchog-'Jigs-med-dbang-po 74, 213
dKon-mchog rGyal-mtshan 224, 225
Doctrine of elements (dharma) 7, 9
of non-differentiation 10
Durdharṣakāla 20

Effect 172
, origination of 180
, pre-existence of 106
Elements (dharma) 83, 180
, insubstantiality of (dharmanairātmya) 74